Your

HERITAGE

Will Still
Remain

Your

HERITAGE

Will Still
Remain

—·—

Racial Identity and
Mississippi's Lost Cause

MICHAEL J. GOLEMAN

www.upress.state.ms.us

The University Press of Mississippi is a member of
the Association of American University Presses.

First printing 2017

∞

Library of Congress Cataloging-in-Publication Data available

ISBN 978-1-4968-1204-9 (hardback)
ISBN 978-1-4968-1205-6 (ebook)

British Library Cataloging-in-Publication Data available

Contents

Acknowledgments

I would like to thank my colleague Jason Phillips for his patience and encouragement. He allowed me to tread my own path and was always there to redirect me when I reached dead ends. He always supported me, and I am extremely grateful for his mentoring. I also learned how to be a better historian under the tutelage of Peter Messer. Anne Marshall and Michael Williams gave important advice and insights in the early stages of this project. Other faculty at Mississippi State University played a role in helping me know my potential as a historian: Richard Damms, Mary Barbier, Jim Giesen, and Matthew Hale. The staff members of the Special Collection departments at Mississippi State University and the University of Mississippi provided significant help in locating and suggesting material that helped in the research of this project. The staff at the Mississippi Department of Archives and History was also extremely gracious in helping me navigate their facility and find what sources I needed. I am greatly appreciative to Lynn Shearer and Lisa Williams, who spent their summer reading through the manuscript with a keen eye and making comments and suggestions. Craig Gill and staff at the University Press of Mississippi have been easy to work with and made the process of publication as painless as possible. The press's peer reviewers gave valuable insights, comments, and suggestions to improve the manuscript. I would like to thank my family: my children, Jonathan, Andrew, Anabel, and Stanley. And, of course, Lynda; you are my all and everything.

Your

HERITAGE

*Will Still
Remain*

Introduction

In December 2009 a groundbreaking ceremony at Jefferson Davis's retirement home, Beauvoir, signaled the beginning of an expansive project to build the Jefferson Davis Presidential Library. "Every American president, as you know, has their presidential library," the director of Beauvoir stated in an interview. "So we thought that Jefferson Davis is an American president, and he deserved his library. That was the idea, to have a library that had the history of him and his family and the confederate soldier to tell their story and that period in history." In addition to attracting more visitors to Beauvoir, the director hoped the new library and museum would help educate the public that Davis's legacy "shouldn't be limited to a fight to preserve slavery." The library, which opened in the summer of 2013, even features a machine in the gift shop that will re-press Lincoln's image on the penny into Davis's image.[1]

In an opinion piece for the *LA Times*, reporter Craig Fehrman noted the absurdity of referring to the Davis library as a "presidential" library. Fehrman reminded readers that Davis "was not exactly an American president." He also noted that the library "will offer an impressive rallying point for the 'Lost Cause,'" since the Sons of Confederate Veterans provided most of the project's funding. Beauvoir's chairman of the board, and member of the Sons of Confederate Veterans, explained to Fehrman that the rest of the nation treated the South unfairly. He believed the library would help to "tell the side of the story that never gets told." Despite the ending of hostilities nearly 150 years ago, some white southerners still desired to "rectify" their image of the South and embrace the Lost Cause legend.[2]

This book seeks to understand how white Mississippians constructed a harmonizing American and Confederate social identity, and how that identity continues to shape the state. Tracing the evolution of Mississippians' social identity beginning in 1850 explains why Mississippians felt the need to create the Lost Cause legend and shaped the way they constructed it. Prior to the bitter debates over the compromise measures in

1850, Mississippians held fast to a social identity based on their American heritage. Even in the midst of secession, their American identity held firm and easily transformed into a Confederate identity that still venerated their American heritage. Following the war, Reconstruction made the readoption of an American identity difficult, but Mississippians managed to construct an identity that celebrated their American and Confederate heritage as compatible and not mutually exclusive. White Mississippians sought to preserve that identity for their posterity, which resulted in Lost Cause writings that tended to produce a historical narrative that vindicated the actions of southerners as patriotic rather than treasonous.[3]

Social identity refers to how a group perceives itself and its standing within a larger social context. The social identity studied in this book focuses primarily on how Mississippians thought of their place within a national context, whether as Americans, Confederates, or both. According to social theorists, individuals and groups desire to maintain a positive group concept through the incorporation of symbols, labels, ideologies, and shared histories. They usually rely on an out-group to juxtapose their identity against. Oftentimes that juxtaposition results in negatively labeling a group, institution, or people as "the other." The sectional conflict, Civil War, and Reconstruction produced several out-groups that Mississippians formed their social identity against. Sometimes these out-groups resided in the state, such as Union soldiers or carpetbaggers, while at other times the out-groups were distant and even abstract, such as generalizations made about northerners or the federal government. Social interaction helped solidify social identity by offering an immediate need to defend or assume a specific identity in opposition to another.[4]

Mississippi provides fertile ground for studying the creation of the Lost Cause legend. Mississippi played a leading role in the sectional conflict, secession, the Civil War, Reconstruction, and the formation of the Lost Cause. During the sectional conflict, Mississippi offered some of the leading voices espousing secession and opposition to any attempts to restrict slavery. When Abraham Lincoln won the election of 1860, secession was all but inevitable with fire-eater governor John Pettus at the helm. Several crucial battles occurred in Mississippi during the war, including the siege of Vicksburg. Mississippi also supplied the Confederate States of America with its only president. Reconstruction witnessed a defiant Mississippi that sought to return to the status quo antebellum. Mississippi also boasted a sizable black population, who, for a brief period, managed to forge their own national identity and steer the state on a path of hoped-for change.

Redeemers in the state offered a solution to Republican rule: they used intimidation and violence to disfranchise the black population, eventually establishing Jim Crow laws. Mississippians also led the crusade of the Lost Cause legend and historical writing, which included Jefferson Davis's influential two-volume history of the Confederacy.

Understanding social identity formation requires looking at how Mississippians thought, spoke, and acted toward various out-groups, or those labeled as "the other." The sources used in this study include personal letters, diaries and journals, newspaper editorials, travelers' accounts, memoirs, reminiscences, and personal histories. Within these sources individuals tended to speak more candidly about their opinions concerning themselves and others, and their biases are often evident and easy to spot. Of course finding a voice for the masses, including African Americans, remains difficult for any historian, but this study seeks to include their perspectives as well. Remnants of the Lost Cause legend across the twentieth and twenty-first centuries are a peculiar fixture in southern history. How and why a group of people would cling so stubbornly to a historical narrative that offers a slanted view of the Old South, the Civil War, and Reconstruction fascinates many southern scholars. This book seeks to add a little bit to our understanding of the phenomenon by tracing the evolution of a positive group identity through the decades of upheaval that transformed southern society. This work is greatly indebted to the historians who have come before to enlighten and increase our understanding of southern history.

"THE SOUTHERN PHALANX"

——— • ———

Then, brothers, to the rescue!
Redeem your country's wrongs.
She has fallen on evil days, indeed—
'On evil days and tongues,'
Let every heart be a holy fane,
Ten thousand stand as one;
And your heritage will still remain
And a shout go up from every plain:
'The Union—it is won!'[1]

Greene Callier Chandler moved to Marion, Mississippi, after completing his education to pursue his career as a lawyer. Before turning twenty-six in 1855, Chandler had edited the *Lauderdale Republican* for fourteen months and served in the state legislature as a Democrat. Writing in his memoirs, Chandler tried to explain the heated passions caused by the sectional conflict. He recounted the settlement of Mississippi to outline the characteristics of the people within the state. "The history of Mississippi from its formation as a State to the beginning of the Civil War was one of progressive development and romance," Chandler wrote, "influenced largely by the people who flocked here from the northeastern and southeastern States, but principally from Virginia, North Carolina, Georgia, Tennessee, and Kentucky." According to Chandler, those who settled on the Mississippi frontier carried with them a "pioneer spirit." He stated that in addition to "those sturdy men and brave women came many educated people with cultural backgrounds, and with the germ of feudalism still lurking in their veins." Chandler declared that these early pioneers sought the "opportunity to build landed estates, and be independent of government or outside influence." The sectional hostilities, initially perpetrated by the introduction of the Wilmot

Proviso following the Mexican cession, caused Mississippians, already "jeal-
ous of their rights" and "contemptuous of those who disagree with them," to
fight back against perceived aggression on the part of the northern states.
Although Chandler adhered to a strict states' rights ideology, he still firmly
believed the Constitution protected southern rights and initially sought
redress through the federalist structure and observance of constitutional
principles.[2]

The sectional conflict of the 1850s produced a series of crises that threatened Mississippians' national identity and place within the Union. Yet,
throughout the decade, Mississippians still cleaved to their American identity in how they viewed themselves and wanted others to view them. While
adherents of southern nationalism increased over the decade, a majority
of southerners still outwardly maintained and declared their primary allegiance to the United States of America. Understanding why Mississippians championed the banner of constitutionalism rather than fully adopt
the doctrine of secession and southern nationalism requires exploring how
white Mississippians constructed their national identity prior to the crisis and how they maneuvered through it as events appeared to spiral out
of control. Mississippians developed particular notions and perceptions of
their station regionally and nationally, and they had specific ideas related to
the characteristics of their unique, burgeoning, agriculturally based society
and culture. The political wrangling and debates over slavery and its expansion westward led many in the state to reevaluate their place within the
nation, its history, and future. As attacks increased against the institution
of slavery, southerners increasingly grew distant toward the North. They
started labeling northerners with undesirable characteristics and perceived
the North as full of rabid abolitionists and radicals who trampled the Constitution. Although radicals and fire-eaters existed in Mississippi, their doctrines did not penetrate and gain substantial converts among the masses
during the 1850s. In Mississippi many called for sectional unity on issues
that involved the expansion and maintenance of slavery, but not necessarily
for the separation of the region from the rest of the country. In the poem
"The Southern Phalanx," the author pled with southerners to stand "hand to
hand, and heart to heart [. . .] until the storm is quelled" and concluded that,
if united, the South could save the Union. The sectional conflict fostered the
idea among southerners that they were the true defenders of the Constitution and the Founders' legacy.[3]

Understanding how Mississippians conceived of their place and identity as part of the Union necessitates a brief analysis of their regional

peculiarities and social structure. As historians have demonstrated, southern distinctiveness existed prior to the Civil War, but in many instances southerners and northerners were more alike than different. Mississippians shaped their national identity in relation to the influences of regionalism and their identity as southerners. However, regional distinctions did not diminish Mississippians' identification as Americans or what it meant to be an American. In many respects, Mississippians maintained a proud heritage centered on the nation's founding and believed they continued to live and foster the revolutionary principles that shaped the nation. As the sectional conflict drove a regional wedge across the country, Mississippians started to reassess their connection to the Union but only because they no longer viewed the North as acting in line with the Constitution. Proud of their station as southerners, Mississippians remained equally proud of their national identity as Americans.[4]

Writing for the Tupelo *Journal* forty years after the close of the Civil War, Washington Clayton explained to his readers that "the South was settled by the chevaliers of England and their descendants, a proud and loyal people." While an example of Lost Cause historical writing, the claim that southerners had descended from aristocratic English cavaliers persisted in the early nineteenth century around the time of the nullification controversy. The Constitutional Convention in 1787 revealed a startling regional divide in the fledgling republic as the issue of slavery stirred passions along sectional lines. While slavery was somewhat of a stumbling block in the composition and passage of the Constitution, those northerners who predicted its natural demise could not have foreseen the dramatic influence the invention of the cotton gin would have on the nation's economic fabric. As southern planters cleared fields to grow cotton, northeastern factory production in cloth manufacturing exploded. Content to ship their cotton northward or to England, southerners preferred planting to manufacturing, since they had a ready supply of slaves to draw upon as well as productive soil. Not only that, but southerners embraced an agriculturally based lifestyle that prominent men such as Thomas Jefferson advocated. Southern planters believed that their economic system represented progress, as they commercialized their agricultural production, retained a steady labor force, and tamed the environment around them. As the nation began to diverge along two separate socioeconomic ideologies (one based on agricultural production and slave labor and the other on manufacturing, modernization, and free labor), northerners and southerners explained why the divide occurred. Southerners viewed and labeled the North as a homogeneous whole, something antithetical to that which was southern. A pseudo-ethnic explanation proved effective that designated the Puritan Roundheads (opponents of the king during the English Civil War) as the founders of the North, by nature industrious and hardworking. The persistent myth stated that the Cavaliers (aristocrats and loyalists) settled the South and preferred a slow-paced, highly cultured lifestyle. While some early Virginians did have Cavalier blood, most southerners could not trace their origins to English aristocracy (quite the opposite), yet the idea that southerners were natural aristocrats became an important fixture of their regional identity and how they viewed themselves in comparison with northerners.[5]

White Mississippians derived much of their social identity through their interaction with slaves. Concepts of honor, patriarchy, and paternalism rested largely on how masters maintained their plantations and cared for their dependents. The demonstrative ability to manage a large estate, serve as the patriarch and father figure, and act according to a strict code of honor determined the planter's place and acceptance within affluent society. For the yeomanry and non-slaveholders, the creation of racial slavery and the supposed fluidity of social and economic mobility kept the majority of whites under the impression that they could one day ascend the ladder and enter into genteel society. While the yeomanry did not maintain large plantations, they could function under the similar social and gender roles as the planter class through their interaction with their dependents, whether slave or family. Non-slaveholders reinforced their superior social status over the slaves by participating in slave patrols, a nightly rendezvous between neighbors who scoured the countryside in search for runaway or wandering slaves. Slavery functioned as more than just an economic labor system, it helped fashion the construction of southern society and white social identity.[6]

Slaves first arrived in Mississippi sometime in the early eighteenth century when the French settled near Natchez. As the region changed hands over the course of the century, British settlers retained permanent residency in Natchez just as the War for Independence commenced. By 1795 the Spanish gave up claims to the area, attracting settlers from the southern states who desired to secure their own land and invest in the cotton boom. Mississippi formally entered the United States in 1817 and interested more settlers in the 1830s with the removal of native Choctaw and Chickasaw Indians in the northern portion of the state following the signing of several treaties. The influx of white settlers increased the demand for slaves: between 1830 and 1840 the slave population increased by nearly 200 percent, followed by the white population, which increased by 150 percent. By 1850 the slave population reached just over 300,000, constituting 51 percent of the state's population. The concentration of slaves followed the path of the Mississippi River, and several of the counties along the river's banks boasted slave populations over 65 percent. The slave population diminished in the state's interior, with a very low concentration in the central and southeastern regions, where the soil and environmental conditions made cotton planting less profitable.[7]

Slaves underwent significant changes during the eighteenth and nineteenth centuries in their conceptualization of themselves and social structure within their communities. Slave social identity would transform from an ethnically based identity to one founded on race and the master–slave relationship. Arriving to the New World from divergent cultural groupings originating in Senegambia, Sierra Leone, the Gold Coast, the Bight of Biafra, and West Central Africa, African slaves maintained their ethnic identities while adapting to their new surroundings and status as chattel. Some areas allowed for slaves to retain their ethnic identities over a prolonged period of time, but by the nineteenth century, slave social identity moved away from an ethnically based identity to one based on race. One causative factor in slave identity transformation occurred due to the decrease in the number of native Africans in America. As the number of native Africans decreased substantially by the early nineteenth century, so too did the stark ethnic divisions in some slave communities. American slaves overlooked African ethnicity (without rejecting the culture) and founded an identity based on commonality of status and experience as chattel. An example of this new social identity came from the standardization of the "capture narrative," which detailed the travails of their African ancestors through capture, transaction, and shipment during the Atlantic slave trade. These narratives related the trickery Europeans used to lure unsuspecting Africans into unfair trade practices that resulted in enslavement, and they strongly contrasted Africans and Europeans in an antagonistic relationship. Rarely did these narratives mention African complicity in the Atlantic slave trade. Some external elements fostered a racial identity among American slaves, as masters tended to give "privileged" assignments to American-born slaves with lighter skin. While labor divisions may have caused stratification within the slave community, it may not have made a profound impact on the social relations within the community, since slaves generally had little control over how the master divided his laborers.[8]

Various other characteristics composed slave social identity and the image they tried to project. In a subservient role, slaves wanted to demonstrate some form of superiority over their masters and often did so through trickster tales or in bragging about instances of "one-upping" their master. Trickster tales that often featured a smaller animal outsmarting a predator through speed, cunning, or wits made the rounds in slave communities throughout the South. Slaves frequently boasted of their encounters with whites and wore it as a badge of honor and respect when they could demonstrate their ability to transcend the usual master–slave relationship through deception or trickery. In his autobiography Henry Bibb of Kentucky said that he could slip off his master's property without much molestation as long as he carried a bridle with him. When questioned by a white passerby "You are a runaway?" he could respond, "No, sir, I am looking for our old mare." Anna Baker of Aberdeen commented that her master asked her as a child to spy on the other slaves and tell him about any plans to run away or cause mischief. Baker said she would "stay 'roun' de old folks an' make lak I was a-playin'. All de time I'd be a-listenin'. Den I'd go an' tell Marster what I hear'd. But all de time I mus' a-had a right smart mind, 'cause I'd play 'roun' de white folks an' hear what dey'd say an' den go tell de Niggers.—Don't guess de marster ever thought 'bout me doin' dat."[9]

In addition, slaves mastered the art of a double identity: one they shared in the presence of their master and one they kept personal and showed only when out of sight of whites. Slaves frequently feigned ignorance, humility, and docility in the company of their masters or other whites for various reasons, whether to avoid punishment or to influence their masters. Such convincing behavior led many masters to believe their slaves found contentment in their enslavement and bolstered arguments in favor of white racial superiority. The stereotype of slaves as docile remained a prominent fixture with whites throughout the nineteenth and twentieth centuries, as minstrelsies that portrayed blacks as buffoons, incompetent, ignorant, and dim-witted gained popularity. Many whites did not witness the other personae that slaves kept private and guarded, available only when in close quarters with the other servants. Times away from the master or overseer, at nights or on the weekends, allowed slaves the ability to worship how they pleased, speak freely within their community, and express their desire for freedom.[10]

Slaves did incorporate their observations of white society into their own social structuring that would eventually lead them to believe they would have the ability, once freed, to assimilate into white society. More conclusive evidence for this comes from how slaves viewed white society and their place within it. Many plantation slaves considered themselves somehow socially superior to the "poor white trash" and believed that the wealth of their master elevated them to a higher-class stratum. Prince Johnson of Coahoma County boasted that "my folks was sho' quality. Marster bought all de little places 'roun' us so he wouldn' have no po' white trash neighbors. Yes sir! He owned 'bout thirty-five hund'ed acres an' at leas' a hund'ed an' fifty slaves." Slaves frequently commented on the low-standing status of overseers hired to scrutinize the daily operations on the plantation. Although forced to obey the commands of one of his former overseers, Jim Allen of West Point deprecatingly said, "I knowed the oberseer was nothin' but po' white trash, jes a tramp." Almost with disgust and regret, Calline Brown of Coahoma County recounted that her owners "warn't nothing but poor white trash what had never had nothing in their lives."[11]

The slave system grew more ingrained in the southern states during the first half of the nineteenth century and, at the same time, came under increased attacks. What southerners had once conceded as a necessary evil transformed into a positive good that helped both the master and the slave. Overwhelmingly, northerners and southerners shared similar racial views and supported the ideas of white supremacy. The emergence of the Cotton Kingdom convinced southerners that they possessed an indispensable place within the Union. Southern cotton helped transform manufacturing in the northern states and provided a valuable asset in foreign trade. In addition to their economic contribution, southerners played prominent roles in the founding of the nation, having supplied eight of the first fifteen presidents who served nearly twelve of a possible eighteen terms. Despite this, southerners found northerners hostile to the institution of slavery, and increasingly so as the century advanced. Abolitionist societies urged southerners to emancipate their slaves immediately and shamed slaveholders with moral infidelity. In 1819 northern politicians tried to block the admittance of Missouri into the Union because it would disrupt the balance between the free and slave states. The "Tariff of Abominations" of 1828 resulted in a constitutional crisis that pitted the agricultural South against the industrial North over the issues of federal authority, states' rights, and even secession. Through it all, though, southerners managed to weave through the tumult as they adhered to the constitutional system of the federal government.[12]

The compromise measures of 1850 ushered in a period of uncertainty in the South that lingered throughout the decade. The Mexican cession, following the Mexican-American War, forced the slave issue out in the open as political leaders in Washington, D.C., debated the expansion of slavery into the newly acquired areas. The issue drove a wedge in traditional party lines and reignited sectional feelings in the nation. The slave issue had hovered over the nation since its inception, but in 1850 southerners aggressively sought to defend and protect what they considered their constitutional right to own and transport property. Some southerners threatened secession as a recourse to invasions on their perceived constitutional liberties and watered the germ of southern nationalism.

In Mississippi the crisis presented an internal struggle over the best means of addressing southern rights within or without the Union. While radicals and fire-eaters passionately promoted southern nationalism, Mississippians overwhelmingly chose to seek redress within the United States and rely on the Constitution as their shield against northern perfidy. As Mississippians championed constitutionalism, they reinforced their national identity as inheritors of the Founders' legacy that they perceived of as southern-conceived in its creation and in the time since its inception. As a result, Mississippians labeled northerners as a fallen people and purveyors of a radical federalism intent on destroying the basic liberties protected by the Constitution.

The internal struggle in the state starting in 1850 centered on the question of states' rights versus federalism. These two factions initially fell along party lines, with Democrats in support of more radical measures and the Whigs advocating for compromise and unionism. Mississippi party tradition was quite often fluid, and the state lacked an established partisan culture. Instead, much of the political exchange occurred "around networks of friends and neighbors, a set of community bonds driven by face-to-face relationships." Many of the political attitudes Mississippians expressed focused primarily on concepts of honor, character, and reputation within communities and among elite families. When confronted with the specter of northern attacks against the state's character and honor (tied very strongly into the institution of slavery), Mississippians responded largely in a nonpartisan manner, demanding redress in a unified effort to combat the threat. To a large degree, Mississippians initially chose unionism, solidifying their national identity and place within the Union. In holding to this national identity, Mississippians branded disunionists and northerners as antipatriotic and harbingers of destruction.[13]

As Congress debated the compromise measures, fear swept throughout the state, prompting Mississippians to prepare for whatever decisions came out of Washington, D.C. In the autumn of 1850, prominent citizens called for assemblage at Union Meetings wherein the citizenry could devise unanimous solutions on dealing with the impending crisis and act in concert. In the lead-up to these meetings, two factions emerged: one promoting a states' rights solution with secession as a last resort, and unionism, as the other, with the focus on compromise and finding answers within the confines of the federal system. Vying for the support of the state, these two factions labeled each other and tried to define the goals and objects of the other. The process of creating a positive self-concept through defining another reveals the construction of a social identity. The "disunionists" and "submissionists" fought for political control and also to define Mississippi's relationship with the Union. Desiring to maintain a positive self-concept at home, regionally, and nationally, Mississippians defined themselves as Americans and inheritors of the Founders' vision for the country.[14]

When speaking of unionists, states' rights proponents often used the derisive label of "submissionist." In nineteenth-century gendered terms, this relegated unionists to the feminine sphere and implied indecisiveness, subservience, and weakness. Slaves submitted to the will of their masters; thus, the term implied that "submissionists" would eventually bring the South into bondage, with northerners as the masters. F. C. Jones, editor of the *Vicksburg Sentinel*, criticized the "abject submissionists," who, if they had their way, would place Mississippi in a state of servility. Jones charged that future generations would hold unionists responsible for acting "like a gang of ninnies when by an overwhelming majority [our legislature] declared that the State would not tolerate or submit to acts which an Abolition Congress has had the temerity to crowd upon us." In another scathing editorial, Jones took aim at "Southern submissionists" who "adopted a 'sliding scale' of ultimatums" in an effort to muscle the northern brass. He explained that with unionists, "the very next provocation [was] always to be their resistance line," and that ultimately "they won't fight." Jones continued by saying that "men who now 'acquiesce,' submit quietly to, and even laud, what has been done, will never reach a point where they think forbearance no longer a virtue." Another paper blatantly labeled unionists with "pitiable weakness" and "ignorance."[15]

In a speech delivered in Lowndes County, Jefferson Davis criticized the "submissionist" sentiment and alluded to the unionists as weak. "Our Union was not formed by men who suppliant bent the knee to power," Davis declared, "and loved a government only as it was powerful and glorious; nor did they leav [sic] us institutions which would be practicable in the hands of men forgetful or careless of the principles on which they were founded." He claimed that only "true friends of the Union" would "resist by all means every invasion on the Constitution." As a moderate states' rights advocate, Davis believed that only a concerted southern effort, one aimed at directly and boldly confronting the North, would "enable us to preserve the principles on which our federal Union was based." Davis believed that the Founders would approve of the states'-rights approach to deal with the sectional conflict, since the issues trampled on basic Constitutional rights. He asserted that unionists did not truly understand the Constitution, and that their submission to northern tyranny would result in southern "territorial subserviency."[16]

Just as the states'-rights contingent labeled unionists as un-American and willing to cede their constitutionally guaranteed rights, unionists placed the same definition on their opponents and slandered them when they called them "disunionists." States'-rights advocates took objection to the term "disunionist" and continually tried to defend their position as patriotic. John Holt, editor of the *Woodville Republican*, responded to the label of "disunionist" by stating "we abhor (and retort) the term Disunionists, for in it are contained many elements of evil." Holt explained that the supposed "disunionists" were those "of the South who have taken a just and bold stand in defence and protection, by every means, of the honor of our States." Like Jefferson Davis, Holt argued that unionists wrongfully assumed that states' rights meant a desire to "sever the bond of union" and "to break our compact solemnly entered into." Rather, those who promoted the course of states' rights did not want "to bring desolation or any confusion, over our country, for the purpose of gratifying any base, selfish end," but to avoid submitting "for peace's sake, to the demands of insatiable passions" in the North. In his counterattack, Holt blamed unionists, "those tender-hearted gentlemen who have kissed Peace until their lips drop distilled sweetness," for being the "co-workers in the foul work of Disunion."[17]

The unionists in Mississippi had much of the momentum in 1850 and sustained attacks on those who promoted disunion. Thomas Palmer changed the name of his paper from the *Southron* to the *Flag of the Union* in late 1850. He repeatedly took aim at the sensitivities of "disunionists." "Our opponents say they are not disunionists," Holt wrote in one editorial, "it is a great offence to call them so, and they will not submit to it; it is a personal insult." "Why is this?" Palmer asked, "Is there any thing odious in the mere name? Does it of itself import crime? Not at all. A mere name cannot of itself be offensive, but it is the thing it represents, or the idea it conveys to the mind, which makes it so." According to Palmer, the reason disunionists took "aversion to the name is plain enough; it represents a thing which is wrong under the circumstances." Acknowledging that the Founders took pride in calling themselves "rebels," Palmer insisted that the Founders stood for a noble cause. On the other hand, states' rights advocates desired personal gain and glory that would lead the state and the South into ruin.[18]

Although Mississippians desired to address the compromise measures in unity, the battle between "submissionists" and "disunionists" spilled into the public sphere. Rather than focus on internal divisions, many Mississippians worked for unity by setting aside traditional party divisions. One paper called for "every good and true patriot, to merge all party distinctions, and to obliterate all party lines." In an editorial an unnamed farmer explained, "I have been a partisan, unflinching, uncompromising, and am yet upon the old issues; but I am like you, gentlemen, in these trying times. . . . [I] willingly lay aside the partisan." In an advertisement for a Union Meeting, one paper "desire[d] to see no exhibition of party feeling," believing the "occasion [was] above party." The *Woodville Republican* hoped that "nothing but Southern feeling should prevail" at the Union Meeting because "there is no aspect in which the whig or democratic party, as such, is concerned."[19]

Mississippians also referred frequently to the Founders and their national heritage in an attempt to build a strong coalition against their northern opponents. By comparing their present dilemma with that of the Revolutionary generation, Mississippians hoped to bridge the chasm of discord within the state and build harmony based on a shared social identity as Americans and inheritors of the Founders' legacy. When advertising for an upcoming Union Meeting, the editor of a unionist paper in Hinds County urged that "all lovers of the Constitution and the Union should unhesitatingly demand of their public servants immediate measures to stop the embarrassing and fatal discontents and destructive discords which now jeopardize and threaten to dash asunder the sacred ties that make us a powerful and harmonious people." The paper explained that the Founders had worked through their problems in the past to create the greatest nation on earth, not by rash action or impulsive behavior, but by "stern, [resolute], and patriotic action, [. . .] mutual concession, generous forbearance, and consummate wisdom."[20]

United States senator Henry Foote championed the unionist cause within the state and Congress. The Washington National Monument Society asked Foote to deliver the main address at the Washington Monument on July 4, 1850. Foote narrated the founding of the Union and focused most of his remarks on the character of George Washington. Near the end of his oration, Foote quoted warnings from Washington's "Farewell Address" that urged Americans to avoid sectional and party differences. Foote closed with an impassioned plea: "I urge you, and all of you—I entreat you, I beseech you, at this moment of awful peril to the Republic—that ye do your duty, and nothing but your duty, to the Constitution, to the Union, and to the sacred cause of Liberty itself!" Foote, like fellow unionists, rallied around an identity based on a shared historical narrative.[21]

In 1851 unionist Samuel Boyd delivered a patriotic discourse at a union festival where he emphatically embraced American patriotism. Boyd celebrated the United States as the "only government under which genuine liberty—liberty regulated by law—is enjoyed." He even sought to dispel the sectional conflict and blamed America's rival and traditional enemy, Great Britain, for inciting the discord. Boyd charged Great Britain with sending their "emissaries" to the United States in an attempt to incite "the work of abolitionism here." He said that jealousies of American prosperity and "the integrity of the Union" motivated the British to seek America's destruction, and that "nothing but an adherence to our Constitution and Union can save us; because it is by our Constitution alone that these designs can be prevented." Boyd's assertions served to remind Mississippians of their past conflicts with Great Britain and tried to draw a parallel between the current disturbances with that of the past.[22]

States' rights adherents also resorted to drawing parallels with the country's revolutionary history. A states' rights planter wrote to a Natchez paper to persuade his fellow planters that submission would not solve the South's problems. He insisted that the South needed to act boldly, with secession as a possible solution, but explicitly declared his American patriotism. "We are proud of our past history," he wrote, "of our long and glorious connexion with the people of the North." The planter explained that their forefathers had fought for a common cause and "died by each others side; and when the aggression of the Mother County stimulated a common defence they united as a band of brothers through nine years of suffering and succeeded in elevating themselves to the dignity of an independent nation." He charged northerners with the work of disunion by "uniting in their exertions to undermine [southern] institutions." Both unionists and states' righters sought uniformity in state sentiment and appealed to a shared history rooted within the union.[23]

Congressman Albert G. Brown shared similar convictions concerning Mississippi's role in the Union despite his fiery rhetoric and staunch states' rights ideology. In a January 1850 message to Congress, Brown, largely speaking to northerners, made clear that "at the first moment after you consummate your first act of aggression upon slave property, I would declare the Union dissolved." Within the same speech, however, Brown argued that "we of the South have ever been the fast friends of the Union." He explained that southerners "have been so from an earnest attachment to its founders, and from a feeling of elevated patriotism, a patriotism which rises above all groveling thoughts, and entwines itself about our country, and our whole country." He claimed that southerners had made greater sacrifices for the Union than any other people within the country, and that southerners remained "devoted to the Constitution" and held "in sacred remembrance the names, the deeds, and the glories of our common and illustrious ancestry."[24]

Once Congress passed the compromise measures later in the year, Brown remained firm in his position concerning the South's place in the Union. Addressing a crowd at Port Gibson, Brown affirmed his desire to stay in the Union as long as the South maintained equal rights with the nation. He criticized the compromise bills and urged Mississippians to show resistance to their implementation, but he stated that he was "more concerned about the means of preserving the Union than [he was] about the means to destroying it." Although the "adjustment bills" denied justice for the South, he said that "we are not to infer that the fault was either in the Union or in the Constitution." He stated that the "Union is strength" and would "secure us that justice and that domestic tranquility which is our birthright." Brown concluded, "The Constitution is our shield and our buckler and needs only to be fairly administered to dispense and exact justice to all parts of this great Confederacy."[25]

As politicians and elite Mississippians championed measures and resolutions to confront the crisis, a majority within the state shared the sentiment of Elijah Walker, a medical student. He commented in his diary about the major issues facing the state during the debates over the compromise bills. Walker attended a speech in Oxford delivered by Senator Foote, which left an indelible impression on him. He commented that "no unprejudiced person could listen to his arguments and then cry disunion while there is no more cause for complaint than now exists." He briefly described the bills under consideration in Congress and declared that each had favorable outcomes in the South. Walker sarcastically opined that there was "a party of the south who are dissatisfied with these bills (and would be with Jesus Christ were he on earth) giving for a reason that they give all the advantage to the north." He further chastised the disunionists: "What fanatics, what misguided creatures, How much better off think they we, the southern division, would be with the bond of union severed, with the dust of Washington divided, and two independent sovereign nations formed?" Walker imagined a world overtaken with the disunionist impulse: "In the event of war which is inevitable in case of disunion, where is our security at home in the heart of the south?" Walker asked, "Where would be the virtue, would be the persons of our beloved and chaste daughters; where the safety of our bosom companions, where the lives of our aged mothers?" His answer to this dystopian fantasy: "All would be in the hands of the rough black buck negroes of our country, lured on by a worse than savage fanatical hosier of the north whose very looks would curdle the blood of our fond loving tender virgins." For Walker and many Mississippians, the moment did not call for radical action to resolve the political impasse in Congress.[26]

In the summer of 1850 southerners sought to combine together to offer a rebuttal to northern proposals concerning the Mexican Cession. Southern states sent delegates to Nashville, Tennessee, to adopt resolutions making the South's position clear. Poorly attended, the convention still yielded influence in presenting possible compromise solutions. The convention elected as president Mississippi judge William Sharkey, who had strongly supported the states' rights position during the nullification controversy decades earlier. Despite the efforts of some southern firebrands, moderation won out in the Nashville Convention, and Sharkey defended its actions. Speaking at a Union Meeting in October, Sharkey explained that the convention "did not meditate anything but preventative measures, except upon the contingency that we should be forced to take an extreme measure." He later declared that "we did not wish to endanger the Union." The convention resolutions did not threaten any resistance or offer any whiff of secessionist impulses. Sharkey claimed that resistance would lead to disunion and felt as though the North had yet to propose anything that warranted resistance. He carefully straddled the line between the disunionists and submissionists and claimed that if the North persevered in its insistence on banning slavery in the territories, the South would have justification "to dissolve the Union in the anticipation of a good cause." At the time, however, Sharkey thought that moment "may never come."[27]

The unionist and states' rights divide defined the statewide elections held in 1851. In 1850 Governor John Quitman, a staunch states' rights supporter, called for elections in September 1851 to seat delegates in a convention for the purpose of responding to the compromise measures Congress passed. Radical southern nationalists in the state hoped to secure a victory and perhaps lead the state to resist the federal bills. Elections for statewide office would follow a few months later in November, headed by Quitman, who sought reelection. Henry Foote secured the gubernatorial nomination from the newly christened Union Party; Quitman and his supporters referred to themselves as States' Rights Democrats. The two sides squared off in a political fight that had simmered for several months.[28]

The election pitted two charismatic and controversial figures against each other. Investigators had recently acquitted Quitman of charges stemming from alleged financial support he gave to filibusterer Narciso Lopez's expedition into Cuba. Foote also faced scrutiny from many newspapers that lambasted him for his support of the compromise bills while he served in the United States Senate. The state legislature censured him for not appropriately representing his constituents at home. From the start, States' Rights Democrats worried that Foote might have enough support to win the fall election. They asked Jefferson Davis, because of his moderate position, to resign his U.S. Senate seat, give it to Quitman, and then run for governor. Davis agreed to the plan, but Quitman initially refused to relent. In September, when the convention delegate returns heavily favored unionists, Quitman stepped aside. Entering the campaign late, Davis struggled for any momentum. The Union Party labeled Davis as a disunionist and secessionist. The Union Party prevailed in the election, and Foote won the governor's chair.[29]

The special convention Governor Quitman called met in Jackson on November 10 and also included Henry Foote as well as many others from the Union Party. Foote made a motion early in the convention, proposing that since the "sovereign people of the State of Mississippi" had made clear their "loyalty and devotion to the Union of their fathers," the convention should dispatch two individuals to South Carolina immediately to express "the wish and desire of the State of Mississippi, that South Carolina should acquiesce in the recent compromise or adjustment measures, and remain as she has heretofore, and now is, a member of this Union." The convention approved Foote's motion with a two-thirds majority and declared that Mississippi would abide by the compromise measures. The convention also stated that the "right of secession from the Union on the part of a State or States is utterly unsanctioned by the Federal Constitution, which was framed to 'establish' and not to destroy the Union of the States." The final resolutions did explicitly outline the state's right to resist attempts by the federal government that would violate "the rights of people of the State," including any further attacks against the institution of slavery. The overall sentiment among the convention delegates reflected calm unionism and cooperation in "good faith" with Congress. The delegates also decided to include the Constitution and George Washington's "Farewell Address" as appendices in the final published record, potent reminders of Mississippi's connection with the United States and Washington's prophetic caution against factionalism and sectional hostilities that could threaten to tear apart the nation.[30]

The crisis of 1850 split sentiments within Mississippi between two factions eager to establish the South's position on the slave expansion issue. Warring with each other, they used definitions and labels to deride their opponent and maintain a positive group concept. Disunionists and submissionists ultimately resorted to a shared historical narrative of the nation's founding in an effort to build support and unanimity in the state. Mississippians ultimately chose to embrace their common identity as Americans and push aside, at least temporarily, the passions of southern nationalists.

Mississippians continued their unionist spirit throughout the rest of the decade and continued to champion their heritage as Americans. In 1852 Green Callier Chandler, a lawyer and newspaper editor, spoke at a celebration of George Washington's birthday. He remarked that "party spirit is thus for the time being allayed, the petty distinctions in politics and religion forgotten, and fraternal feelings are restored to the community." Chandler said that in commemorating great Americans such as Washington, "we are naturally led to reflect that we all have one common ancestry, one common country, one common destiny." Despite the political bickering of the past few years, Chandler commented that "men do not love their country in proportion alone to the efficiency with which its government protects them in their rights." Rather, "there are other higher springs of patriotism," which Chandler argued came about from celebrating the patriots of years past.[31]

Even during the contentious events the Kansas-Nebraska Act brought about in 1854, Mississippians still relished their connection to the Union. Jefferson Davis, initially tied with the more radical elements in the state, continued to urge his constituents to adhere to unionism. In an 1857 address given at Mississippi City, Davis spoke of Mississippi's early role in the Union and commented that "she had never violated the compact of our Union." Davis explained that Mississippi had "fulfilled her duties to the Union, and thus she has given assurance that, in whatever contingency the future may bring forth, at whatever sacrifice she may be called upon to make, she will tread the paths of constitutional principle and of duty." In a pamphlet addressed to the citizens of Mississippi a year later, Davis reiterated the cause of the South as being akin to the cause of upholding the principles of the Constitution and the Founders' vision. "Habituated to respect the popular judgment, to confide in the patriotism of the people, and to revere our constitutional Union," Davis expounded, "I cling to the hope so uniformly cherished, that the good sense of our generation and its posterity, will not allow the madness and wickedness of fanaticism and sectional jealousy, to destroy the political fabric our fathers erected and dedicated to the happiness, tranquility, prosperity and liberty of their descendents forever."[32]

The division between unionists and ardent states' righters in Mississippi persisted throughout the rest of the decade but were most pronounced during those first few years. As the decade unraveled a series of predicaments over the slave question, the friction between unionists and states' righters within the state softened as they turned their ire northward. Northern attacks on slavery intensified throughout the decade, and southerners took those attacks as personal affronts against their honor. Historians have shown repeatedly that slavery and the relationship between masters and slaves determined much of the South's social and cultural composition. Engrained in every aspect of southern society and culture, the institution of slavery helped maintain a racial hierarchy, determine gender roles, and signify class status—an attack on slavery was an attack on everything southerners knew. The North appeared intent on annihilating the South's most cherished institution, slavery, which composed the centerpiece of southern society and culture. The code of honor that permeated southern culture demanded a response to any assaults, and Mississippians obliged. As northern attacks intensified stemming from events such as the Fugitive Slave Act, Bleeding Kansas, and the Dred Scott decision, Mississippians went on the defensive to protect their sense of honor and the risk posed to the existence of slavery. Defending slavery meant defending their identity as southerners. Governor Quitman reinforced these ideas in his inaugural address in 1850. Speaking about slavery, he declared, "This institution is entwined in our political system, and cannot be separated from it, without destruction to our social fabric." Quitman defended the morality of slavery and stated that "we do not regard it as an evil, on the contrary, we think that our prosperity, our happiness, our very political existence, is inseparably connected with it. We have a right to it above and under the constitution of the United States. We cannot give up that right. We will not yield it."[33]

Congressman and senator Albert Brown defended the institution of slavery on several occasions in Congress. Brown echoed the common defense of slavery that most southerners adopted in the decades prior to the Civil War. Brown regarded "slavery as a great moral, social, political, and religious blessing—a blessing to the slave, and a blessing to the master." In addressing the sectional tensions that existed, Brown rhetorically asked, "Who is at fault, or rather who was first in fault in their fraternal quarrel?" He answered, "We were the owners of slaves; we bought them from your fathers. We never sought to make slaveholders of you, nor to force slavery upon you. When you emancipated the remnant of your slaves, we did not interpose." Brown continued to blame the North: "Content to enjoy the fruits of our industry at home, within our own limits, we never sought to intrude upon your domestic quiet. Not so with you. For twenty years or more, you have not ceased to disturb our peace. We have appealed in vain to your forbearance." Brown insisted that northerners had no right to interfere in slavery's existence, especially since, according to Brown, northerners had initially supplied southerners with slaves. Brown believed that northerners should not concern themselves with the slave labor system in the South; southerners did not try and convert or dismantle the labor system in the North.[34]

The process of defending their institutions helped Mississippians craft their social identity as southerners, but not yet as outcasts to the United States. Mississippians still maintained their unionist underpinnings, while branding northerners as the out-group. One of the many charges Mississippians pinned on northerners concerned their apparent attempts to destroy the Constitution. In labeling northerners as intent on trampling the Constitution, Mississippians reinforced their national identity as Americans and branded northerners as a fallen people.

In a scathing tirade in the House of Representatives following John Brown's raid on Harpers Ferry, Congressman Lucius Q. C. Lamar, from Lafayette County, spit venom at northern politicians for their lackadaisical enforcement of constitutional principles. Lamar reminded northerners that the Constitution, "framed by your fathers and my fathers in a lofty spirit of enlarged patriotism, also made the institution of slavery part and parcel of this Federal Government." He accused northerners of having "taken issue with the constitution and . . . attempting to throw off its restrictions." At the same time, southerners regarded "that constitution as the instrument of our protection," and they were "determined to maintain its sacred compromises." Lamar viewed the sectional rift between the North and the South as stemming from the two divergent attitudes of adherence to the Constitution. He felt as though southerners supported and defended constitutionalism, while northerners viewed it as an obstruction in their desire to exercise power over the entire nation.[35]

At times southerners had harsh words for their northern brethren based on their economic, social, and cultural differences. During the 1850s, though, the intensity increased as southerners went on the defensive against perceived northern aggression toward slavery. Mississippians embraced their American roots and cast northerners as deviators from that heritage. In defending slavery, Mississippians tried to maintain a positive group concept. They frequently touted the benefits of slavery, their aristocratic nature, and their love of liberty. At the same time, they labeled northerners negatively as a way to juxtapose against their positive group identity. Embracing these labels convinced Mississippians that there were more differences than similarities between themselves and the North. The process of creating a positive group concept and social identity often involves the disparaging labeling of an "other." The desire to create a positive group concept means finding an outlier on which to dump unfavorable characteristics. The pressure to defend their institutions resulted in southerners vehemently branding northerners with pejorative labels.[36]

Mississippians reserved the label "abolitionist" as one of the most odious tags that they placed on northerners. While Mississippians frequently used words such as "free soiler" and "anti-slavery" to describe their northern opponents, they reviled the term "abolitionist," which represented something repugnant and inherently antisouthern. Several Mississippi newspapers carried an editorial that originally appeared in the New York *Evening Mirror*, where the editor, southern sympathizer Hiram Fuller, defined the term "abolitionist." In a previous article, Fuller picked a fight with an abolitionist newspaper and pithily remarked that "we have yet to learn that an Abolitionist can be a gentleman." Fuller's characterization elicited a response from an enraged reader, an abolitionist, who wrote a letter voicing displeasure. The abolitionist asserted that he would no longer advertise in Fuller's paper. Fuller redounded with another editorial, this time expounding on the meaning of "abolitionist." "What, then, is it to be an 'Abolitionist?'" Fuller asked. "It is in the first place, to be a traitor to the Constitution, which recognizes Slavery. [. . .] It is to be an instigator to servile rebellion—a stealer of negroes—a distributor of the peace—a promoter of bloodshed—a destroyer of the Union of the States." Fuller explained that the word was of the "blackest reproach."[37]

When Mississippians spoke of abolitionists, their definition mirrored Fuller's and expanded on the idea. The *Yazoo Democrat* published a letter by A. H. Brisbane where he declared that "every man who believes that slavery is an evil, must be an abolitionist, or a contemner of the laws of his maker." Educator Ebenezer Elliott detailed the unholy and ungodly character of abolitionists. In an essay Elliott quoted 1 Timothy 6:1–5, where the apostle Paul urged masters and servants not to blaspheme the name of God. Paul counseled servants not to despise their believing masters, because "they are brethren." Paul offered a warning for those who would "teach otherwise," saying they were "proud, knowing nothing, but doting about questions and strife of words, whereof cometh envy, strife, railings, evil surmisings, perverse disputings, of men of corrupt minds and destitute of the truth, supposing that gain is godliness; for such withdraw thyself." Elliott asked, "Can any words more accurately and vividly portray the character and conduct of the abolitionists, or more plainly point out the results of their efforts?" Elliott charged abolitionists with "repudiat[ing] the authority of God's law" and perverting God's word by "wresting the Scriptures from their plain and obvious meaning to compel them to teach abolitionism."[38]

In 1853 an anonymous author known as Seraiah the Scribe published a satirical book chronicling the fire-eaters and their attempts to spread their secessionist ideas in the early 1850s. Writing in pseudo-scriptural form, with stylized chapters and verses, Seraiah championed the unionist cause and criticized the states' rights positions and actions during those heady days. While he had choice words for his rivals, particularly John Quitman and Jefferson Davis, he saved some of his choicest bile for northerners. Seraiah also accused northerners of abandoning God's will and purpose. Citing the Hamitic myth, Seraiah wrote, "[K]now ye not that the children of Ham were given us as a lawful heritage even from the days that Noah came forth from the Ark and drank of the fruit of the vine?" Seraiah criticized the "Yankees," because they "have not regarded the covenants of their fathers, which were made in the days of old, when this land was delivered from the oppression of our British rulers, when the Free Soilers held the children of Ham in bondage, as we now do." In parting, Seraiah added a few further descriptions besides covenant-breakers to his list of northern characteristics: "Are they not the white-livered, cold-blooded, and brazen-faced Yankees, that deal and traffic in notions, and all sorts of wares and brazen clocks, and blue vessels and wooden nutmegs?" He continued in his biblical stylings: "They think of naught but gain, they are full of treachery and deceit, their words are smooth like oil, but under their tongues is the poison of asps, and their cry is as the horse-leech, 'give, give.'" Mississippians labeled northerners with any undesirable trait that they could imagine.[39]

In 1851 the *Mississippi Palladium*, a newspaper in Holly Springs, printed an essay by an anonymous author from Alabama, where the writer warned of the abolitionist influence. The author stated that the abolitionists "tell office-seekers they ought not to take office, because their oath to support the Constitution is an oath to support slavery." Beyond that, "they disorganize parties and disturb election calculations." The author summarized his views on abolitionists when he said, "[I]n a word, they disturb the indolent repose, the fat slumbers, of the self-satisfied; they wound the self-complaisance of the timorous and compromising; they interfere with the selfish counsels and courses of the worldly-minded; they embarrass the policy of the discreet, moderate and circumspect."[40]

Initially, Mississippians did not label all northerners as abolitionists. Instead, they viewed abolitionists as "visionary and mad fanatics," and that "a large society at the North, would gladly be rid of them." As the decade progressed, Mississippians worried as political parties appeared to institutionalize abolitionist policies into their party's platform. When the two-party system collapsed in 1854 over the Kansas-Nebraska Act, several organizations sought to take the place of the Whigs. The Know-Nothing or American Party emerged as one of the early, and more prominent, of the national organizations that reached the southern states. The other, the Republican Party, confirmed Mississippians' fears that abolitionism had taken ahold of northern sympathies. After a few years, the Republican Party supplanted the initial success of the Know-Nothings, fueling southern concerns that the entire northern population embraced abolitionism.[41]

Some former Mississippi Whigs initially supported the Know Nothings due to their antiparty attitude and detachment from the old party system. The Know-Nothings famously adhered to strict principles of secrecy, pledges, and nativism to create a fiercely loyal following. Yet suspicious Mississippians looked upon the new party warily. The *Ripley Advertiser* declared that "ABOLITIONISM has triumphed at the North, *through the instrumentality of the Know Nothing Organization.*" It listed abolitionists the party organization in the North elected who opposed the Kansas-Nebraska Act a year earlier. The paper stood by the claim that the Know-Nothings intended to effect the means "of destroying the friends of the South at the North and promoting Abolitionism." A year later the *Advertiser* carried an article titled "Let the South Beware!" in which they claimed that the Know Nothings "at the North, are anti-slavery at heart." They warned that in the general election, the northern Know-Nothings would fall into the Republican camp for president.[42]

Mississippians accepted the Know-Nothings initially but greatly feared the "Black" Republican Party. From the beginning, Mississippians regarded the Republican Party as an abolitionist organization. Southerners usually referred to Republicans as Black Republicans; a derisive way to indicate the pro-black policies the party supposedly espoused. When the Republicans ran a candidate in the 1856 presidential election, they adopted an antislavery platform that supported Congress's authority to prohibit slavery in the territories. Southerners quickly linked the Republicans with the abolitionist cause and tried to find direct ties between the two. One paper said that the Republican Party denied "that any constitution can give the power to hold slaves; and they insist that our federal constitution must be construed so as to forbid it." Educator Ebenezer Elliott warned "of a party in the North organized for the express purpose of robbing the citizens of the Southern States of their property." Henry Foote indicated that the Republicans "proclaimed to the world that *'the Constitution confers sovereign power over the territories of the United States for their government; and that, in the exercise of this power, it is both the right and duty of Congress to prohibit in the territories those twin relics of barbarism, polygamy and slavery.'"*[43]

In a satirical poem reminiscent of *Paradise Lost*, anonymous Mississippi author Lacon recounted a council between Satan and his angels in their attempts to destroy America. After the demons of Mormonism, alcoholism, women's rights, and sectarianism had instigated their deviousness, the Demon of Abolitionism had a turn to unleash his fury. He decided to destroy the South and the rest of the nation through the Black Republicans. In a response to Satan, the Demon of Abolitionism laid out his plan:

> In doctrines these are Black Republicans,
> But claim to be the Union-loving men,
> Who wish their plans all carried out in peace,
> And so come in to make a compromise,
> Resolved that if the South will but submit
> The Union shall be saved, and peace preserved,—[. . .]
> And if the Black Republicans succeed,
> And once can get the government in hand,
> They will be forced to carry out their plans,
> Their principles maintain, and threats fulfill,
> Or fall before a party fiercer still.
> In either case the South will be destroy'd,
> And in her ruin that of her foes involved,
> Or in her majesty she must arise,
> And with a mighty hand her rights maintain,
> And, at expense of Union, save herself.

The demon continued to explain that once in power, the Black Republicans would free the slaves, resulting in further treachery when the freedmen would resort to a life of banditry and vagabondism.[44]

The branding of northerners as abolitionists resulted in Mississippians' growing nativist tendencies, not toward foreigners, but toward northerners and any outside influence. Betty Beaumont, British by birth, moved to Mississippi when her husband received a job as a machinist working on the railroad in Woodville. Upon arriving to her new home, Beaumont hired a black servant, Aunt Charity, and asked her to borrow some flat irons from their neighbor, Mrs. Conrad, since their belongings had not yet arrived from Philadelphia. "I noticed that [Aunt Charity] was talking to herself in an angry manner," Beaumont explained. "Calling her, I asked the cause of her vexation. She replied that Mrs. Conrad said that she did not want to lend to Yankees, and we'd better send for our own things if we had any to send for." Beaumont expounded on the treatment she and her husband received in Mississippi: "It was a time of great political agitation, and every stranger, especially from the North, was looked upon with distrust. I knew that there was some sort of current against me, but what that current was I could not understand." She continued, "I did not think I could be in any way mixed up with anything at all connected with politics, for I had never given any thought to such matters. Neither was Mr. Beaumont a politician in any sense of the word; and yet, as we long afterwards discovered, we were at this time constantly under the eye of suspicion." As the years passed, Beaumont noted the growing distrust of northerners and those "not in favor of slaveholding." She commented that her "husband really cared nothing about the matter one way or the other; he did not consider that he had anything to do with it." Despite this, their neighbors misconstrued "his indifference on the subject [. . .] and it was hinted that he was secretly an abolitionist. This impression worked against him and made us many enemies long before we had any suspicion of it."[45]

The fear of northerners and outside influences struck panic in Mississippians who worried about the possibility of incited violence. In 1850 newspaper editor W. B. Tebo warned against the "imminent danger from the attacks of northern abolitionists and home emancipationists." Tebo further cautioned that the "enmity between the white and the black race is rapidly maturing, and that it would require only the hand of some daring and master spirit to pluck the fruit, bitter as it is, and plunge our State into servile troubles." Tebo proposed severe restrictions against the free black population, with expulsion as the best option, because "it is now well known that the free blacks are employed by the abolitionists of the north, as active agents to spread the poison of their doctrines among our slaves, and to run off all who listen to their syren song."[46]

Southerners constantly feared slave insurrections, especially after Nat Turner's rebellion in 1831, but the sectional hostilities made those fears more palpable as constant attacks against the institution of slavery came flooding from the North. Of course, Mississippians' worst fears came to life in 1859 with John Brown's raid on Harpers Ferry. The failed plot to incite a slave rebellion only confirmed to Mississippians their perception that abolitionists desired to destroy the South. Word quickly spread that Brown had a map that contained areas throughout the South of high slave concentrations. In her diary a planter's wife, Susan Darden, noted the places Brown marked with crosses in Mississippi as potential sites for slave uprisings: "Warren, Claiborne, Jefferson. Church Hill, for this county, not far from here. Franklin, Adams & Wilkinson." Darden commented, "It is dreadful to think of a set of white scoundrels rising & killing persons with the plea to liberate the slaves. They ought to be hung; burning would be nothing but right. It was providential that it was not carried into execution." A newspaper in Natchez entreated readers that they "cannot be too vigilant" and continued to remind Mississippians of abolitionist machinations aimed at the South.[47]

As information concerning Brown's raid unfolded, more newspapers commented on the raid and its implications. The *Mississippi Baptist*, a religious newspaper that rarely commented on local or national events, finally produced an editorial that exclaimed that "it was time that [the North] should begin to reap the harvest which they have so abundantly sown." The paper continued that "if they cease not, there is but one course for the South to pursue [. . .] the arm that holds the dagger must be broken in the North." The paper hoped that northerners would silence the "unholy" abolitionists in their midst and warned that the South will not "fellowship with a whimpering alliance with those who continually hold over our heads the assassin's dagger."[48]

Mississippi newspapers linked Brown's raid with the Republican Party and the abolitionist tendencies emanating from the northern states. Ethelbert Barksdale, newspaper editor and politician, commented that the Brown incident should "carry with it an instructive lesson to the South." Barksdale wrote, "It warns them of the sleepless activity and fiendish hate which the leaders of the anti-slavery party cherish for her institutions, and bids her be ready at a moment's warning to repel the blow which they are preparing to strike." John Bosworth, editor of the *American Citizen*, admitted the difficulty in trying to convince southerners that "no man of any pretension to sagacity had any thing to do with it." Bosworth stated that many in the South believed that the raid was "but a prelude of that 'irrepressible conflict' so eloquently depicted by the great leader of the extreme wing of the Republicans—Senator [William] Seward." He also lamented that many in the South "attempt to fasten upon the entire North the responsibility of the scheme." Many in Mississippi echoed the declaration of the *Mississippi Free Trader* to "hold the Republican leaders responsible for the treason they have mediated, uttered and actually by the aid of Old Brown accomplished."[49]

The conclusion of the decade brought greater uncertainties for Mississippians concerning their place within the Union. Mississippians continued to divide between disunionists and submissionists, and by the time of Brown's raid, many had chosen the former. Although the two factions existed within the state, Mississippians still clung to an American identity and championed federalism, entwined with state sovereignty, as the primary defender of constitutional liberties. Mississippians remained proud of their national heritage and increasingly viewed northerners as prodigals to the revolutionary cause and constitutionalism. As Mississippians defended the institution of slavery and the social structure of the South, they vilified northerners and cast them as an out-group. By the end of the decade, the tumultuousness of the 1850s convinced Mississippians that northerners embraced or sympathized with the abolitionist cause. The rise of the Republican Party's popularity in the North and West, combined with the apparent ties between the political party and the abolitionists, compounded the fear that slavery's existence was imperiled. Mississippians waited anxiously for the impending presidential election in 1860 to confirm their status and place within the United States.

"THOSE WHO SHOULD BE BROTHERS"

The Southern heart is fearless,
The Northern heart is cold,
The one has justice on her side,
The other's false and bold,
Should civil strife sweep o'er this land,
We'll breast the storm and then,
We will unite with all our might,
And we will fight like men.[. . .]
Oh! woe betide the traitors,
Who now seek their countrie's fall,
They've deserted her Bright Banner,
Her Glory, Pride, and all.
They desecrate God's temples,
With impious harangues rude,
They seek like Demons, not like men,
To plunge this land in blood.[1]

Speaking to a crowd at Enterprise, Mississippi, on southern interests during the 1860 presidential campaign, Greene Callier Chandler warned his audience that "anti-slavery feeling" had "taken possession of the northern mind." Chandler declared, "Abolition is there taught from the husting, in the schools, from the pulpit, indeed, everywhere, and is embraced by two-thirds of the people in some form or other." Chandler saw an "irrepressible conflict" and believed that abolitionists "banded together for the one avowed purpose of destroying the peace of fifteen States." In a Fourth of July address the same year, Chandler cautioned that "it is not with foreigners, but those who should be brothers, who have a common history, lineage, and destiny, that trouble is to be apprehended." Chandler felt abolitionists subverted southern rights and that "the national democracy, the bulwark of southern defense against northern fanaticism, has shown its incapacity to withstand longer the immense abolition pressure upon it." Chandler believed the northern states rejected the Constitution and sought to impose their control on the southern states.[2]

Henry Foote, a senator from Mississippi, referred to the difficult decisions placed before the citizenry of the state and the South in 1861 as choosing between the classical Greek monsters Scylla and Charybdis. Mississippians eventually chose to leave the Union in an attempt to protect slavery. Southerners believed that the threat of slavery's demise was an attack on the social fabric on which they based their society. Planters gained social standing through their ownership of slaves, the demonstration of paternalistic qualities, and their ability to manage their large estates. The planter class derived their hegemony through the formation of racial slavery and by preaching that all whites had the opportunity to rise through the ranks to become like them, their social superiors. Southerners believed the Constitution granted and protected their right to their slave property. When those rights fell under attack during the 1850s, southerners believed northerners blatantly subverted the authority of the Constitution. Throughout the decade, though, southerners sought redress through the Constitution and the federal system. Although they tended to champion a specific political ideology based on the concept of states' sovereignty, they continued to place their faith in the republican government the Founders devised. The election of 1860 shattered the continual hope of rectification in the federal system and opened the door to southern nationalists and fire-eaters, who quickly secured leadership and promised to rejuvenate the South's fallen national status by leaving the Union.[3]

Mississippians continued to maintain their American identity during the secession crisis of 1860 and 1861. The act of secession resulted in the creation of a southern nation, but most Mississippians did not view their actions as an attempt to create a separate, southern nation out of a strong sense of southern nationalism. Mississippians viewed their efforts as a continued revolutionary process that started with the Founders. Despite the act of secession, Mississippians retained an American identity and justified their actions as patriotic. In many instances, Mississippians compared the situation between the southern and northern states as akin to what the colonists faced with Great Britain nearly one hundred years earlier. Acting against political tyranny gave America its unique institutions and character, and Mississippians contended their actions constituted a continuation of that same theme. Mississippians touted secession as an act of preservation against a people who corrupted the national government and trampled on constitutional rights, and they insisted that the act of separation would preserve those rights that they cherished.[4]

The 1860 presidential campaign marked the beginning of the secession movement. Traditional party structures broke down following the Kansas-Nebraska Act when the Whig party fractured and never recovered. As other political parties vied to take the place of the Whigs, southerners struggled to create a national party coalition that supported the expansion of slavery. Northerners increasingly appeared ambivalent and even hostile concerning property rights in slaves and the institution's growth. As the Republican Party grew in numbers in the northern and western states, southerners had limited national party options to satisfy their demands concerning the slave problem. In local southern politics, the Democratic Party remained, and those who constituted the former Whigs and Know-Nothings started to operate under the banner of the Opposition. Despite concerted attempts, southerners failed to establish a new conservative party that gave them the desired vehicle to protect slavery. As party conventions met in the spring of 1860, the party structure fractured even more and left southerners feeling alienated from the traditional political process.[5]

The Democrats held their convention on April 23, 1860 in Charleston, South Carolina, to nominate a presidential candidate and political platform. Southern delegates went to the convention with the charge to have the party implement a platform that guaranteed slaveholding rights in the territories. Jefferson Davis proposed a series of resolutions in the United States Senate in February 1860 that he desired the Democratic Party to adopt. Most notably, Davis's fifth resolution stated that Congress should have the ability to protect "constitutional rights in a Territory" if the territorial government, executive, or judicial branch of the federal government failed or refused "to provide the necessary remedies for that purpose." Southern delegates believed in the necessity of explicit guarantees for slavery's expansion in the West and that potential-nominee favorite, Stephen Douglas, would undermine their goal. Douglas perhaps prevented civil war ten years earlier after securing the passage of Henry Clay's compromise measures. While this furthered his political career, several southerners felt less than satisfied with the outcomes. In recent years, southern Democrats had cringed when Douglas sided with Republicans concerning the fraudulent pro-slavery Lecompton Constitution drafted in Kansas. The southerners knew that Douglas supporters would not welcome a slave code in the party's platform.[6]

Southern delegates, including all those from Mississippi, walked out of the convention after a stinging defeat of their pro-slavery platform. Northern Democrats said they could not endorse a party platform they knew their constituents opposed. The dismissal of the southern convention members left a northern majority large enough to elect a candidate for president. Douglas did not receive enough votes after fifty-seven ballots, leaving the remaining tired and weary Democrats torn asunder. The Charleston Convention ended with a sectional split in the Democratic Party. Eventually the two factions held their own conventions and nominated their own candidates for the presidency: Stephen Douglas won the nomination among the northern Democrats, and John Breckinridge of Kentucky won in the southern convention. The split in the party confirmed the fears of many southerners that they had few allies in the North. One Mississippi planter condemned the northern delegates for desiring "to force upon the South a candidate for her support who has openly and avowedly declared himself opposed to the very rights that she is trying to maintain and a question that is threatening the very basis of our organization in this 'Union.'" He hoped that "this action was no creature of the people of the North" and felt confident that the southern delegates would still unite the Democratic Party and rally the North behind their cause for "the Constitution and laws."[7]

The split in the party left Mississippi Democrats disappointed with their northern compatriots, but they quickly united behind Breckinridge and his running mate, Joseph Lane, as states' rights nominees. One newspaper optimistically declared that "the nomination of Breckinridge and Lane is received throughout the Union with huzzas, firing of cannon and the greatest enthusiasm." A Jackson newspaper reported that the citizens of the city "signalized [their endorsement] by the blazing of rockets, the firing of cannon and other evidences of joy." The paper lauded Mississippians and their role in the presidential nomination process, stating that from the beginning "neither friend nor foe has entertained a doubt as to where [Mississippi] stood. It was known that no sort of influence could induce her to accept either Douglas or his heresies." The editor predicted an easy Breckinridge victory, because they could not name more than five counties in which they could find a "Douglas Democrat."[8]

By 1860 most disunionists in the state supported the Democratic Party, while submissionists acted under the Opposition banner. Those of the Opposition in Mississippi supported the candidacy of John Bell, the Constitutional Union nominee. The Constitutional Union Party drew much of its membership from former Whigs and Union Democrats. They convened in Baltimore on May 9, 1860 to establish their platform and nominate their presidential candidate. William Sharkey led the eleven delegates from Mississippi. The delegates to the convention decided that since "platforms adopted by the partisan conventions of the country have had the effect to mislead and deceive the people, and at the same time to widen the political divisions of the country, by the creation and encouragement of geographical and sectional parties," they would simply adopt the political principles of "The Constitution of the country, the union of the states, and the enforcement of the laws." The Constitutional Union Party decried secession as illegal but mostly operated as the primary opponents to the southern Democrats.[9]

The one candidate for president that vexed Mississippians and southerners the most was the Republican nominee for the presidency, Abraham Lincoln. The *Eastern Clarion* newspaper, edited by J. G. Markham, covered the Republican Convention, held on May 16, 1860, and Markham revealed his anxiety over Lincoln's nomination. Relieved that prominent Republican and antislavery advocate William Seward did not receive the party's endorsement, Markham warned that the Republicans remained "as sectional and as hostile to the rights of the South, and as dangerous to the existence of the Union, with Lincoln as its candidate, as though Seward himself [carried] its standard." Markham described the Republicans' agenda as "based upon the simple ground of hostility to the South—the idea of an 'irrepressible conflict' between Northern and Southern social institutions, and a determination to place that which most distinguishes the latter under the ban of the Federal Government, and finally to destroy it." Markham expressed his desire for the Democratic Party to reconcile so that together they could defeat "the Black Republicans" and preserve "the Union upon the principles of the Constitution."[10]

Mississippians expressed concern over the perception that abolitionists controlled the Republican Party and that Lincoln intended to destroy the institution of slavery. In his diary Flavellus Nicholson, a Mississippi farmer, explained that the Republican policy was "to prevent the slave holding states from ever acquiring any more territory, and by this means indirectly, and by Legislation—directly, to finally destroy the institution of Slavery in the South." One newspaper warned that the "Black Republicans have boldly published their programme and they will steadily carry it out if the South submits, to the bitter end. They have proclaimed the 'irrepressible conflict.' They have said these States and Territories must be all free or all slave." Another paper blatantly decried "outrages which abolition fanaticism has

continued year by year to heap upon the South, [that] have at length cul-
minated in the election of Abraham Lincoln and Hannibal Hamlin, avowed
Abolitionists, to the Presidency and Vice Presidency—both bigoted, unscrupulous and cold-blooded enemies of the peace and equality of the slaveholding States." Speaking in the House of Representatives, Lucius Lamar
candidly stated that "it is a unanimous sentiment in the South that the existence of this Republican organization is a standing menace to her peace
and security, and a standing insult to her character." Scholar Henry Hughes,
writing for a Mississippi paper, predicted that "if Lincoln is elected, Abolition will be effected in eight years." Hughes explained that "Black Republi-
canism is 'anti-slavery,' and therefore revolutionary. Its essential dogma is
that our peculiar labor system is essentially evil." Hughes contended that
Republicans desired to "totally abolish" evil and that they wanted "to revolutionize our labor system."[11]

Abraham Lincoln and the Republican Party threatened more than just
the institution of slavery; they threatened constitutionalism. Several weeks
before the election, a group of citizens in Carroll County organized a meeting to deliberate "upon the perils that environ us, as a people." After appoint-
ing Colonel William Booth as president of their convention, they adopted a
series of resolutions. They affirmed their commitment to the United States
and the Constitution but resolved that if outsiders imperiled the "terms
of the compact of [the] Union," they "should take measures to secure our
rights." One resolution declared that "a Black Republican President will be
a violation of the spirit and substance of the compact, and, if submitted to,
will result in the overthrow of our institutions, and our subjugation to an
intolerable oppression." The citizens reaffirmed their commitment to the
United States and believed that many northerners were "willing to do us full
justice." Not only that, but they believed that many in the North who associated with the Republican Party perhaps did not understand the "dangers
which surround" the South. If they did, they would no doubt "come to the
rescue and faithfully observe the compact made between their fathers and
our fathers." For many in the state, elements within the Republican Party
endangered the Constitution and jeopardized the existence of the United
States.[12]

The news of Lincoln's victory produced a wide array of emotions and
reactions within Mississippi. Southern nationalists in the state pounced in
an attempt to build momentum for secession. The southern nationalist fervor did not lead Mississippians to abandon their American identity; instead,
it reaffirmed it. Even the most ardent fire-eaters continued to embrace their

American identity. They often argued for the preservation of the Constitution and republican principles against northerners who had corrupted the system of government. They appealed frequently to American patriotism as a means to gain support for secession by drawing direct parallels to the American Revolution. In many instances, southern nationalists made the argument that secession was necessary to save their American identity.

Southern nationalists argued that further connection with the Union under a Republican president would result in a violation of their constitutional rights. A few weeks after the election, a planter wrote in an editorial of his unwavering support for the cause of the South. He challenged the patriotism of the Republican Party and denigrated them as "exterminationists" who sought "to pervert the Federal Government into a power opposed to our equal right to enjoy our Constitutionally advised system of property in the common territories." The planter chided southerners for the divisiveness that engulfed the region over the question of secession. He lamented that "instead of fighting the common enemy in solid, serried and unbroken phalanx, *as we should have done, we have been quarreling among ourselves*, thus insuring the election of an avowed enemy, beyond a mere prediction." The planter concluded, "For if we remain in a Union, whose Constitution has been time and again set aside by Northern negrophilists, we must remain as men who will yield to less than their rights." According to the planter, remaining in the Union meant giving up on the Constitution and accepting subjection to northern demands.[13]

Even unionists made similar arguments concerning the Republican ascendancy. In late November unionists gathered in Vicksburg to devise a way to stem the tide of secession. They urged calm and conciliation rather than a rash impulse to abandon the Union. However, they did issue a resolution in which they declared that "'in the election of Lincoln to the Presidency the SPIRIT OF THE CONSTITUTION WAS VIOLATED.'" They further acknowledged that "'his nomination and election were effected by a combination of a portion of the States, conspiring together to obtain possession of the government for SECTIONAL PURPOSES in avowed hostility to the interests and institutions of the other portion." For those gathered at the meeting in Vicksburg, Lincoln and the Republicans posed a clear danger to the Constitution of the United States.[14]

Ethelbert Barksdale, newspaper editor and politician, drew parallels between the situation the South currently faced and that which the American colonists confronted decades earlier. In an editorial Barksdale reminded his readers that "when Government ceases to regard . . . the rights of the citizen . . . it perverts itself from its original purposes, and is no longer entitled to his allegiance." He explained that it "was under the influence of this idea that our forefathers threw off the rule of the mother country and established for themselves a government of their own." The South faced a similar crisis because, according to Barksdale, the northern states wielded "the vast machinery of the Federal Government as now constituted, for destroying the liberties of the slaveholding States." As such, the southern states had a "duty to dissolve their connection with it, and establish a separate and independent government of their own."[15]

Newspaper editor Howard Falconer also drew allusions to the revolutionary generation to justify secession. Falconer took exception to the unionists in the state who frequently referred to the many attempts of the colonists to reconcile their differences with Great Britain before their act of separation. Falconer insisted that the "Union-shriekers" wanted to convince the people of the state that the "Revolution did not commence until the 4th of July, 1776." As Falconer pointed out, however, "they ignore the fact that the affair of Lexington, the battle of Bunker Hill, and the expedition to Canada, all took place the year before the colonies declared independence, and that a state of war had long existed when that declaration was put forth." Falconer suggested that over the course of the past decade, the South and the North engaged in a "state of war" and that secession, like the act of independence, was the next, natural step.[16]

Prominent unionist John Wood mocked the trend among secessionists in the state who appealed to American patriotism in order to promote secession. He stated that "a great effort had been made by the leaders of the secession movement to assimilate the revolution they were about to inaugurate, to the revolution of our ancestors, which established American independence." Sarcastically, Wood explained that "young Patrick Henrys" sprang up "in every county, and [appealed] to the patriotism of the people . . . which far excelled all the powers of eloquence ever displayed by 'the forest-born— Demosthenes.'" Continuing his rant, he said the "many young orators, who had never before appeared upon the stump, made such strained efforts, that the hearer was irresistibly reminded of the young Shanghai rooster, . . . that crows so hard, that he seems to be in imminent danger of crowing himself out of his knee joints!" While Wood thought such parallels to the Founders foolish, secessionists continued to couch their arguments in a language that invoked their American identity and heritage.[17]

Unionists also appealed to their American identity and heritage in their calls for tranquility and rational action. Unionist papers tried to quell the calls for secession by reminding readers that the South still had the Supreme Court, the Senate, and the House of Representatives for protection. The South had "three distinct ramparts against aggression [by] the President." Editor John Bosworth indicated that the president of the United States was not "a Ruler, a King, a Prince, or Autocrat," but "the servant of the people. He is elected by them, and holds his office but four years." Although Bosworth cringed at the thought of a "Black Republican President," he stated that the president's duties "are prescribed by the Constitution of the United States, and he is amenable to the laws as the humblest citizen in the land." Not only that, but Bosworth plainly stated that "being in the Union does not compel us to have [direct] intercourse with the North. We need never go North of Mason & Dixon's line."[18]

Unionist William Smedes addressed a crowd gathered in Vicksburg to discuss the issue of secession. Smedes had little good to say of the Republican Party or Abraham Lincoln. He noted that a Republican victory "would degrade one half the nation" and that "no patriot should vote for him." Smedes even acknowledged that the citizens of Mississippi would find Lincoln's election "offensive," because the Republican Party put on airs of "moral and social superiority." Yet Smedes argued that Lincoln's election "will occasion no imminent danger to us or our section." Instead, "the good citizen who regards *Government* as sacred . . . will find no justification or excuse in raising the standard of rebellion, merely because a man of obnoxious and dangerous sentiments has been elected according to the forms of the Constitution and in the mode prescribed by it." Smedes believed the laws of the country and the Constitution would protect southerners and that the mere election of a sectional president could not significantly alter the place of the South in the Union.[19]

John Aughey, a prominent unionist and minister, wrote a memoir shortly after escaping from a Confederate prison during the middle of the Civil War. Detained for his unionist sympathies, Aughey claimed that the state had many Union men even after the election of Abraham Lincoln. Aughey described the feeling of unionists in the days after the revelation of the presidential contest. "The conservative men were filled with gloom," he wrote. "They regarded the election of Mr. Lincoln, by the majority of the people of the United States, in a constitutional way, as affording no cause of secession. Secession they regarded as fraught with all the evils of Pandora's box, and that war, famine, pestilence, and moral and physical desolation would follow in its train." Aughey grieved that when the citizens of Attala County learned of Lincoln's victory, "there came a day of rejoicing."[20]

Late in 1860 Aughey preached a sermon to defend the unionist cause and appealed to a sense of patriotism and connection with a shared American identity. Aughey asked, "Why should we secede, and thus destroy the best, the freest, and most prosperous government on the face of the earth? the government which our patriot fathers fought and bled to secure. What has Mississippi lost by the Union?" Aughey hoped to strike a chord of commonality that would somehow manage to hold the North and South together. He boldly proclaimed, "I deem it the imperative duty of all patriots, of all Christians, to throw oil upon the troubled waters, and thus save the ship of State from wreck among the vertiginous billows." Aughey took his appeal to patriotism a step further and audaciously invoked the desire of Deity. "I have a message from God unto you, which I must deliver, whether you will hear, or whether you will forbear," Aughey warned. "As to the great question at issue, my honest conviction is (and I think I have the Spirit of God,) that you should with your whole heart, and soul, and mind, and strength, oppose secession. You should talk against it, you should write against it, you should vote against it, and, if need be, you should fight against it." Using the same rhetoric that appeared ten years earlier over the compromise measures, Aughey contended that true patriots, true Americans, would condemn the cause of secession.[21]

Despite the pleading of unionists, fire-eaters managed to convince many in the state that Lincoln's election to the presidency had forced the South to make the decision to secede. A current of support for secession swept the state. A Jackson paper claimed that, after talking to several persons attending a fair a few days after the presidential election, "almost without division, the people are in favor of immediate withdrawal from the Northern States and the establishment of a Southern confederacy. In this great conservative movement for self-preservation, men of all parties are joining with a zeal and enthusiasm which we have never before seen equaled." Henry Craft, a lawyer near Pontotoc, commented on the rising secessionist sentiment in his diary. "The feeling seems to pervade the whole south that we cannot longer remain united," Craft wrote. "I have always been a Union man but now I go for immediate secession." Craft further elucidated his position: "I regard Mr. Lincoln's election as conclusive proof of the existence of the 'irrepressible conflict' and of the existence of a majority party which will war upon the south until disunion will be inevitable. This party might not precipitate this result for some years, but seeing that it is inevitable we should, I think, wait no longer." Susan Darden, noted in her diary that citizens in Jefferson County had raised a "pole on the Public Square. It is called 'The Anti-submission Pole'; will have a flag on it."[22]

Mississippi had a fire-eater at the helm in 1860, just as it had during the issues over the compromise measures in 1850. Governor John Jones Pettus, a planter from Kemper County, won the gubernatorial election in 1859, supported by the state's prominent disunion men. Pettus spewed his fiery rhetoric during the 1860 electoral season and, at one point, declared that if Lincoln won the election, then Mississippi would no longer celebrate the Fourth of July. Shortly after hearing the outcome of the ballot returns, Pettus issued a decree demanding that the state legislature meet on November 26 to address how Mississippi would handle the recent results. Many throughout the state praised Pettus's actions and believed his leadership would help Mississippi weather the storm the Republicans had thrust upon it through their fanaticism.[23]

On November 26, 1860, as the state legislature convened according to the governor's orders, Governor Pettus issued a message for the political body and citizens of the state. Like other secessionists, Pettus used the language of American patriotism and identity as his rallying cry for separation. He maintained that the South still supported the principles upon which the Founders built the nation, and that the same Providence that assisted the revolutionary generation would assist southerners. Pettus began by declaring that the North had dragged "the institutions of the South" before a tribunal "in violation of every principle of the Constitution and common sense, and tried before a Court having no jurisdiction, and a jury ignorant of the law and the facts; and the verdict thus obtained is that slavery is sinful and must be destroyed." The problem, as Pettus saw it, was that the "Northern mind will never rest satisfied until slavery is placed in such a condition as will insure its ultimate extinction." Drawing upon biblical imagery and appealing to patriotism, Pettus utilized a stunning analogy. "Then go down into Egypt while Herod reigns in Judea," he declared. "It is the only means of saving the life of this Emanuel of American politics, and when in after years it shall be told you, that they who sought the life of this Prince of Peace and fraternity are dead, you may come out of Egypt, and realize all the fond hopes of patriots and sages, of peace on earth and good will among men, under the benign influence of a re-united Government deriving its just power from the consent of the governed." Herod (the North) had threatened to destroy Jesus and everything holy (the Union), which resulted in Joseph and Mary (the South) fleeing temporarily to Egypt to save the life of their precious child. In Pettus's metaphor, the life of the Union, just like the life of the Savior of the world, depended on escaping evil and returning triumphant once that evil had dissipated. As the only true bastion of American republican principles, the South, out of necessity and preservation, needed to break away from the North and stand as an exemplary pillar so that one day, when northerners changed their hearts and minds, the restoration of the Union could finally take place.[24]

The state legislature issued a call for an election to convene on December 20 to elect delegates for a convention. The convention would meet in Jackson to decide Mississippi's place within the Union. Each county could elect the same number of delegates as they had representatives in the state legislature. Most potential delegates ran on nonpartisan platforms and declared their intention as either a "southern co-operationist" or a "separate state secessionist." Southern co-operationists did not necessarily oppose secession but believed that the state should first exhaust all means of preserving the Union before making the decision to secede. Voter turnout significantly decreased, since the elections occurred on the heels of the heated presidential campaign. Only about 60 percent of those who turned out in the November election (voter turnout for the presidential election exceeded 80 percent) participated in the December vote. Despite gaining support for secession, the delegates elected to the convention did not heavily represent the same sentiment. The delegates who openly advocated for immediate secession totaled 43 percent of the delegates elected. Co-operationists composed 31 percent, with the remaining 26 percent of delegates representing a coalition ticket or those whose views were uncertain. With the wide-ranging election of delegates, secession was not necessarily imminent, except for the fact that, unknown to Mississippians at the time, South Carolina had officially severed ties with the Union the same day the polls opened in Mississippi.[25]

The Mississippi delegates assembled in Jackson on January 7, 1861 to discuss the appropriate measures for the state to enact. South Carolina had already seceded from the United States, leaving some moderates relieved that Mississippi would not act alone if it reached the decision to separate from the Union. Those representing the various counties came from nearly all the social classes in the state, with a majority belonging to the yeomanry. Only four delegates of the one hundred members owned more than two hundred slaves. Fifty-five owned fewer than twenty, and fifteen of the delegates were not slaveholders. The delegates had turned in favor of immediate secession, emboldened by South Carolina's example. In the opening invocation, Reverend C. K. Marshall alluded to the almost inevitable decision of secession when he prayed, "Forgive all our sins; let them not be visited retributively on our homes, or our country. Make us Thy people and deliver us from all evil—and may we never have occasion to regret the steps we are about to take in the great work that now lies before us." Those opposed to secession knew they had an uphill battle and devised ways to decelerate the rising fervor. James Lusk Alcorn, supported by former Whigs and Opposition, introduced an amendment that would require Mississippi to wait until other southern states took action before the state left the Union. In spite of all his efforts, he failed to stall the secessionist spirit.[26]

The convention decided quickly that Mississippi would secede from the Union and issued a declaration to expound upon the reasons for the dissolution. The delegates began the document by stating that their "position is thoroughly identified with the institution of slavery—the greatest material interest in the world." Espousing the ideas of King Cotton, they stated that "a blow at slavery is a blow at commerce and civilization." While the document outlined northern attacks against slavery over the course of the nation's history, a thread occurs throughout the declaration: in the view of Mississippians, northerners estranged the South from their American identity and place within the Union. The delegates wrote that northerners had trampled "the original equality of the South under foot" and had "utterly broken the compact which our fathers pledged their faith to maintain." Abolitionists had "recently obtained control of the Government, by the prosecution of its unhallowed schemes, and destroyed the last expectation of living together in friendship and brotherhood" by breaking "every compact into which it has entered for our security." Drawing on their shared heritage, the delegates maintained that "for far less cause than this, our fathers separated from the Crown of England," and that they would "follow their footsteps." The act of secession was neither an act to create a new southern country out of a sense of southern nationalism, nor an act of rebellion. Instead, the delegates viewed secession as an act of preservation and a way to "maintain their rights" afforded by the Constitution.[27]

Further evidence for the belief that northerners had stripped the South's American identity comes from the speeches by the state's secessionist commissioners. Governor Pettus sanctioned commissioners to travel to other slaveholding states shortly after the November presidential election to persuade state legislatures to pursue the course of secession. William L. Harris, commissioner to Georgia, spoke to the state legislature days before Mississippi voted on its secession convention delegates. He began his speech by reminding the Georgia lawmakers that "the violation of our constitutional rights, which has caused such universal dissatisfaction in the South, is not of recent date." Speaking of the 1850 compromise measures, Harris declared that "nothing but [the South's] devotion to the Union our Fathers made, induced the South, *then*, to yield to a compromise." Harris warned that under a Republican administration, the federal "government [now] stands *totally revolutionized* in its main features, and our Constitution broken and overturned." What bothered Harris, as well, was that the Founders had "made this a government for the white man, rejecting the negro, as an ignorant, inferior, barbarian race, incapable of self-government, and not, therefore, entitled to be associated with the white man upon terms of civil, political, or social equality." Yet, Harris continued, the "new administration comes into power, under the solemn pledge to overturn and strike down this great feature of our Union, without which it would never have been formed." Harris alluded to the Founders who "secured to us, by our Constitutional Union, now being overturned by this Black Republican rule, protection to life, liberty, and property, all over the Union." Harris argued that the North had destroyed the principles upon which the nation had rested. His fear resided in the belief that Lincoln's government would steer the nation in a new direction toward racial equality without the consent of the South.[28]

Assigned to Virginia, secession commissioner Fulton Anderson spoke to the state convention in February 1861 after Mississippi had formally left the Union. Anderson first wished to differentiate the "patriotic and conservative men of the Northern section" who had "manfully defended the constitutional rights of our section" from the "dominant faction of the North." Anderson harangued the convention with biting accusations against the northern people for allowing a Black Republican to come to power. "It cannot, therefore, be presented that the Northern people did not have ample warning of the disastrous and fatal consequences that would follow the success of that party in the election," he asserted. "Impartial history will emblazon it to future generations," Anderson proclaimed, "that it was their folly, their recklessness and their ambition, not ours, which shattered into pieces this great Confederated Government, and destroyed this great temple of constitutional liberty which their ancestors and ours erected, in the hope that their descendents might together worship beneath its roof as long as time should last." Anderson spoke of northern hatred and fanatical passions that had "practically disfranchis[ed] the whole body of the Southern people." He railed against northerner voters who placed Republicans in office who "avowed its purpose to take possession of every department of power, executive, legislative and judicial, to employ them in hostility to our institutions." Republican control of the federal government meant that "the descendants of the leaders of that illustrious race of men who achieved our independence and established our institutions, were to become degraded and a subject class, under that Government which our fathers created to secure the equality of all the States—to bend our necks to the yoke." Anderson finished by stating that abolitionist doctrine had percolated into "the school-room, the pulpit, on the rostrum, in the lecture-room and in the halls of legislation." Northerners now held "hatred and contempt of us and our institutions, and of the Constitution which protects them."[29]

While many celebrated and supported secession in Mississippi, some lamented the severed ties to the Union. On 10 January 10, 1861, Susan Darden commented in her diary, "News came to Fayette from Jackson that Mississippi had seceded from the Union. It is sad to think that we are not one of the United States; all alone." G. W. Bachman, a Methodist Episcopal minister, noted in his journal, "I received the sad intelligence that my native state, Mississippi seceded from the Union yesterday at 2 P.M. I fear they have acted hastily." After later hearing news of Jefferson Davis's election as president of the Confederate States of America, Edward Fontaine, a planter near Jackson, bemoaned that "the United States of America—This once glorious Republic is now no more." Speaking of the United States, he wrote that "its origin[,] progress, [and] decline . . . have no parallel in History. Unlike all other Governments, which have passed away, it has fallen without the shock of foreign or civil war." Fontaine's unionist sentiment swelled: "The glorious banner which has waved victoriously even [*sic*] so many battle fields" now had "scattered stars, broken arrows, and a dead eagle—we weep over each."[30]

Mississippi federal politicians also expressed their regret over the decision of the state to secede. Serving as a senator, Jefferson Davis tried to ward off secession and find compromises to alleviate the fears of the South over Lincoln's election. In Washington, D.C., Davis pled for patience and hoped that Republican leaders would do something to assuage the concerns of southerners about slavery. On December 20, Davis along with twelve other Senators formed the Committee of Thirteen in an effort to find a solution to the national crisis. Composed of five Republicans, seven Democrats, and one Know-Nothing, the committee agreed (with Davis's urging) that any action would require majority support among the party lines within the group. John Crittenden of Kentucky, the Know-Nothing, proposed a series of compromises aimed at protecting slavery in the South by re-extending the Missouri Compromise line (except through California). He also endorsed constitutional amendments that guaranteed slavery's existence. The committee failed to agree on the compromise; the Republicans would not support the expansion of slavery.[31]

When secession officially came, Davis, along with Mississippi's other congressional representatives, resigned. Davis marked the occasion with a farewell address in which he continued to espouse his American patriotism and the North's stripping of that identity away from the South. Davis evoked the history of the country and said that King George III "endeavored to do just what the North has been endeavoring of late to do" to the South: deprive them "of the rights which our fathers bequeathed to us." He defended slavery and argued that the Founders recognized and perpetuated the rights of slave ownership. Davis claimed that by electing a Republican, northerners now sought to incite slave insurrection just as the British government did during the American Revolution. Congressman Reuben Davis also retained a sense of American patriotism and devotion. He wrote his feelings of leaving the nation's capital for the last time. As he looked at the American flag, he commented that "around that flag the whole South had rallied, not many years before, with passionate pride and devotion. Our proudest recollections were of the days when our gallant youth had followed it to victory."[32]

By the middle of January, the Deep South states seceded and met at a convention on February 4 in Montgomery, Alabama, to draft a new constitution. The Constitution of the Confederate States of America mirrored the Constitution of the United States except for the inclusion of explicit defenses of slavery as well as a few minor changes to support a states' rights ideology. The next order of business for the Provisional Congress was to appoint a provisional president to serve until later that fall when the Confederacy would hold elections. Since several slave states had yet to follow the Lower South, the Congress decided to find a moderate voice to represent the Confederacy. Jefferson Davis, not a participant in the conference, quickly emerged as the front-runner when prominent political leaders from Virginia (who had yet to secede) made known their preference for the former Mississippi senator. Davis, a West Point graduate and military leader during the Mexican-American War, also served as the secretary of war under Franklin Pierce in addition to his service as senator. As a states' rights Democrat and moderate, Davis supported secession but did not invoke the fiery rhetoric of men such as William Lowndes Yancey and Robert Barnwell Rhett. On February 9, Davis received word that the Provisional Congress unanimously elected him president of the Confederate States of America and requested his presence in Montgomery. Hesitant but willing to serve, Davis set out for Montgomery, where his inauguration occurred on February 18 at the Exchange Hotel.[33]

In his inaugural address, Davis still spoke of his reverence for the American identity and the shared heritage as Americans. He declared that the North had "perverted" the Constitution of the United States and "the purposes for which it was ordained." Davis explained that "the impartial and enlightened verdict of mankind will vindicate the rectitude of our conduct, and He who knows the hearts of men will judge of the sincerity with which we labored to preserve the Government of our fathers in its spirit." According to Davis, the North caused the southern states to secede by overthrowing the principles upon which the nation stood and trampling carelessly on the constitutional rights of southerners. Davis made it clear that the "Constitution formed by our fathers is that of these Confederate States, in their exposition of it, and in the judicial construction it has received, we have a light which reveals its true meaning." Rather than appeal to southern nationalism, Davis spoke of the dissolution of southern rights within the Union and declared that the purpose of the Confederacy was not to revolutionize politics but to defend the rights already established in the founding documents of the United States.[34]

For most within the state, the secession movement did not occur out of a strong southern nationalist impulse. Instead, the desire for separation stemmed from the belief that northerners violated their constitutional rights. They also believed the election of a Republican for president would result in their inability to seek redress for any grievances in the federal system. Since their whole social structure and social concepts relied so heavily on slavery, they feared that any threat to the institution would result in a forfeiture of their social fabric. Although Mississippians seceded from the United States, they did not immediately drop their American identity; rather, they argued the necessity of secession to carry on the legacy of the revolutionary generation and protect the principles upon which the nation stood.

"LIKE PATRIOTS OF OLD"

— • —

We are a band of brothers, natives of the soil,
Fighting for our property we gained by honest toil;
But when our rights were threatened the cry rose near and far,
Hurrah for the Bonnie Blue Flag that bears a single star. . . .
Then here's to our Confederacy, so strong we are and brave,
Like patriots of old, we'll fight our heritage to save:
And rather than submit to shame, to die we would prefer,
So cheer up for the Bonnie Blue Flag that bears a single star.[1]

Like many southerners, Greene Callier Chandler adopted a states' rights political ideology to justify the act of secession. Chandler believed that the "national Union was a simple confederacy of independent and sovereign States, with powers limited by the Constitution." Even after secession, Chandler still embraced the principles of the Constitution and blamed northerners for wrongfully acting out of concert with the compact between the states. Chandler reasoned that "African slavery [was] embedded in the Federal Constitution as one of the compromises, and whether slavery was right or wrong in the abstract, I fully believed that it was the imperative duty of all the parties to the compact to carry it out in good faith and give the amplest protection to slave property." Chandler argued that when northerners failed to offer constitutional protection to slavery, southerners had the legal right to separate from the Union. "There is no doubt, in my mind," Chandler declared, "that this is the precise kind of Federal Government that the majority of the Constitutional Convention intended to make, and actually did make." Even outside the Union, Mississippians still retained a sense of their American identity and justified their actions as fitting under the constitutional and federal structure of the United States.[2]

The popular Confederate anthem "The Bonnie Blue Flag" even retained a strong sense of an American identity and shared heritage. Shortly after the Mississippi Convention issued its ordinance for immediate secession, the women of Jackson presented the legislature with the Bonnie Blue flag. The flag was solid blue with a single white star in the center representing the newly formed Republic of Mississippi. After seeing the flag flying over the state's capitol building, Henry McCarthy wrote the lyrics for "The Bonnie Blue Flag." In a treatise that explained the principles upon which the new Confederacy stood, McCarthy wrote that northerners attempted through "treachery" to "mar" the rights of southerners. Alluding to the American Revolution, McCarthy penned, "Then here's to our Confederacy, so strong we are and brave, / Like patriots of old, we'll fight our heritage to save." Wrapped in their new identity as Confederates, lingering vestiges of their American identity remained.[3]

As fighting erupted and the Civil War commenced, Mississippians began to forge a new Confederate identity, which varied only slightly from the American identity that they still protected. The Confederate identity that emerged relied heavily on Mississippians making stark contrasts between themselves and northerners. How they labeled Union soldiers and northerners during the war helped to foster the creation of an "other," thus bolstering what it meant to be a Confederate. As Mississippians interacted with various social groups throughout the war, they solidified their identity as Confederates. For many Confederates in the state, northerners were the antithesis of everything southern, and they tried to control that image in how they spoke about northerners and how they acted around them. By interacting with southerners, northerners unknowingly helped form a new Confederate identity, as much as those who created cultural symbols and disseminated their ideas of the Confederacy in their writings. Much of the new Confederate identity did not rest solely on allegiance to a political body or even allegiance to the Confederate States of America. Instead, their identity concentrated heavily on their juxtaposition to what they considered "northern." Their identity as Confederates remained intact even when their support for the Confederate government waned, because of the stark contrasts that they painted between themselves and their Yankee invaders. While Confederate nationalism diminished over the course of the war, white Mississippians' identity as Confederates did not.[4]

At the same time, Mississippi lacked homogeneity despite efforts to make it appear otherwise during the war and in Lost Cause treatises. Unionists and Union sympathizers constantly interfered with the establishment of a dominant Confederate identity in the state. Some Mississippians maintained loyalty to the United States, did not support the Confederacy, or decried the war effort. Non-Confederate Mississippians undermined the desire of Confederate officials for unity. The changes brought to the institution of slavery resulted in slaves carving out their identity as Americans. Not only did they start acting differently toward their masters, but they embraced the idea of their place as citizens within the American republic. They flocked to the Union lines in droves and volunteered to fight for their freedom and the Union.

War provided the first major context for producing a unified Confederate identity. When Abraham Lincoln called for 75,000 volunteers to suppress the rebellion in the South, Mississippians flooded recruiting stations to join local militias. Lincoln's call for volunteers not only resulted in other states joining the Confederacy but produced the beginnings of Confederate patriotism and a Confederate identity. Ezekiel Armstrong, a young law student, noted in his diary that "Lincoln's Proclamation calling out 75,000 men drew out my latent patriotism and on the 6th of April, 1861, I attached my name to a company." Sophia Boyd of Kosciusko grieved over the prospect of war and "did not think it time yet for college boys to volunteer." Her brother, however, chided such sentiment and said his sister "was not patriotic." M. Ryan traveled to Corinth to join a company and worried "that the Yankees would be whipped before I could get there." Betty Beaumont, British by birth and suspected abolitionist, commented in her memoir that she could not contain the enthusiasm of her boys to go off to war. Beaumont explained, "I wanted to keep my boys secluded, but to this their young spirits could not submit. Their sympathies were with the Confederate cause." She continued, "My sons eagerly caught the drift of the times and warmly espoused the Confederate side, giving such aid as lay in their power and ready to make any sacrifice for what they deemed right." In a letter to her daughter, Sarah Watkins, a planter's wife living near Carrollton, stated, "Hardly anything is talked about but war, nearly all the nice beaux have gone off to war."[5]

While fighting the war, Confederate soldiers vilified their enemy and further produced a strong notion of "otherness" from the North. As young men embarked to fight, many of them had to make sense of why they fought against their own countrymen. Most of the soldiers had not taken part in the political wrangling that consumed the nation during the 1850s. Upon enlistment, soldiers developed a perception of the enemy as something antithetical to themselves and what they knew. They labeled northerners with undesirable characteristics that, at the same time, reinforced what it meant to be a Confederate. Robert Moore, a yeoman farmer's son, noted that several of the men in his unit went so far as to believe that a Yankee did not "look like a man." The long and bloody war only strengthened the sentiments that the North and the South were fundamentally different.[6]

In a sermon delivered to his company on a Confederate Fast Day in March 1863, Edward Fontaine, a planter, summarized the baseless, ungodly traits inherent in northerners. "[They are] the blasphemers of God, his Bible, and his divine institutions," Fontaine claimed, "the violaters of the Constitution; the perjurers who swear to support it, and break it in all their acts; the hirers and employers of thieves and assassins; the stealers of poor slaves; the robbers of churches; the pillagers of helpless women and children; the plunderers of tombs and graves." Many other Mississippi soldiers shared Fontaine's construction of a northerner as vile, immoral, and unholy. Flavellus Nicholson, a farmer and soldier, charged northerners with greed when he commented that the victory at Bull Run "only tended to excite the pride and jealousy of the North and urged her to greater efforts to retrieve her fallen fortunes." Alluding to the exodus of the children of Israel in ancient times, one soldier, Jesse Sparkman, hoped that the "earth might engulf them as the wicked were in the Red Sea," since the North brought a curse upon both sections because of "their own evil doing." The perception among many Mississippi soldiers rested on the idea that the North, wicked and carnally minded, embraced the traits of sinners who opened their arms to immorality.[7]

Many in Mississippi viewed northerners as the fallen progeny of Providence and therefore believed that they alone had become God's chosen people. For many soldiers, the belief that God's will would direct the outcome of the war in their favor helped sustain them through stinging defeats and morale-crushing conditions. A large number of soldiers maintained that the war effort was bigger than just securing southern independence—it was akin to building the kingdom of God and necessitated wresting power away from the fallen North. William Nugent stated in a letter to his wife, "If God be for us, as I firmly and conscientiously believe he is—who can prevail over us[?]" In his diary, Joseph Garey, a native Pennsylvanian and recent Mississippi resident, commented, "[W]e can & will be free, God in his infinite wisdom & mercy would never consent to see his people downtrodden & crying to him for help in their hour of peril. So we will rest the cause with Him. Knoweth that He does all things well." In a letter to his mother, William Nelson acknowledged that God allowed the war to happen "as a means of settling definitely and conclusively the question of slavery." Regardless of the outcome, Nelson knew God would help the Confederate cause and declared that he had "the greatest confidence in the wisdom of God, and believe[d] that all things work together for good to them that love God." Even after decisive defeats, Mississippi soldiers continued to believe God supported their cause. In 1864, after hearing of intense battles near Richmond, one soldier prayed, "Oh my God, wilt thou be with our army in this great struggle which is now going; oh give us our liberty again, so that we all can return to our homes in peace, harmony and worship god under our own vine fig tree."[8]

Still retaining a solid bedrock of their American identity, Mississippi soldiers commented frequently on the North's apparent denunciation of the principles and compact of the Constitution. In his journal, Edward Fontaine sullenly lamented that northerners adopted the policies of fanaticism by supporting Lincoln. He consistently referred to the Union president as a tyrant and his administration as a "military despotism." In March 1863 Robert Moore noted that "the Yankee Congress has adjourned after clothing their President with absolute power. He now has the finance, the judiciary & the military of the country in his hands." William Nugent pondered the outcome of a possible Union victory and declared that he would rather join England or France as a colony or live under the "Russian yoke" than submit to "close fisted" Yankee rule. William Chambers, stationed along the Mississippi River near Vicksburg, noted in his diary that on July 4, 1862 "two Federal fleets . . . fired about 150 shots in commemoration of Independence Day, I suppose. Alas! How it is perverted!"[9]

Mississippians spoke of the corrupt government under Lincoln's administration. One newspaper editor stated that the new government at Washington employed "fanatical Abolitionist[s]" and "cod-fish-eating Yankee[s]" rather than the "high-toned, chivalrous men" of the Border States. The editor further informed readers that "the accounts from Washington show that every department of the Government is to be thoroughly Abolitionized" and that "the 'Nigger worshipers' have the full swing." According to the editor, the northern government only accepted "miserable, mercenary wretches" and those with "a clear Abolition record." William Howard Russell, a correspondent for the *London Times*, traveled through Mississippi in the summer of 1861 and noted that "press politicians and speakers" clumped "black Republicans, and . . . the whole of the North together as the Abolitionists." In an address to the Congress of the Confederate States in May 1861, Jefferson Davis complained that Lincoln and northerners had corrupted "the principles of the Constitution" in their desire to "govern the minority."[10]

Soldiers still relied heavily on their American heritage and past to build a Confederate identity. Using past American holidays, southerners imbued them with significance for the Confederacy as well. Writing while in a Union prison, William Peel commemorated George Washington's birthday in 1864, saying that southerners still hailed the occasion "as a day of rejoicing and feasting." Confederates also marked "the anniversary of the birth of the great founder of our once 'Glorious Republic'" as the "day upon which Jefferson Davis, who bore the same relationship to the [Confederate States], was inaugurated." At winter quarters in Virginia in 1862, Robert Moore sarcastically wrote, "The enemy commenced the firing of a salute very early this morning celebrating the anniversary of the birth-day of George Washington, the fruits of whose labor they are now attempting to destroy. Very consistent they pretend to be." He further commented on the double significance the day had for the Confederacy, since it was the "day set apart for the inauguration of our first president, Jeff Davis, than whom a truer patriot never lived." Soldiers also drew on the imagery of the War for Independence and compared themselves to the revolutionary patriots. During the first winter of the war, Joseph Garey described the grim scene of the Confederate camp. "Our camp reminds us to day of the picture painted by historians of the Valley of Forge during that dark period of the revolution with the exception of our being better clothed than they were," Garey described, "for we have no barefooted or naked soldiers; but otherwise it presents the same dismal aspect."[11]

Women helped fashion a Confederate identity as much as or more so than men. Women wrote frequently of the war and left their impressions of the North in their writings. Many women in Mississippi also interacted regularly with occupying forces. Determined to defy northern soldiers, women assumed the role of a "southern rebel" with impressive vehemence, leaving many northern men to conclude that the characterization they had heard so often of the genteel southern lady was a myth. In conveying their new Confederate identity, many women bent previous notions about gender and gender roles. Known during the antebellum period as refined and high-class, women during the war embraced the labels of rebel, independent, and fiercely aggressive.[12]

Southern women actively participated in the war effort. Many yeoman and planter-class women formed sewing clubs in order to make clothes and flags for the soldiers. Such organizing had not taken place among southern women previously and marked one of the crucial developments during the Civil War that contributed to the creation of a new feminine identity in the South. Sarah Watkins wrote to her daughter that "several of the ladies have joined to have a sewing society in Middleton to make up clothing for the troops." Annie Harper of Natchez remarked that "The Court house & other public buildings were turned into sewing rooms, where the ladies daily gathered to sew for the soldiers." Harper claimed that "Women knit riding in their carriages & at all visits, ever were the busy needles flying, and some even discussed the propriety of knitting during prayer meeting." Some women found other ways to support the soldiers in the field. One group of women in central Mississippi held a concert to collect money to purchase winter clothing for two local companies. "The girls who will give the concert are to represent the different Confederate States," explained Mary Watkins "with each girl having the name of the state which she is to represent printed distinctly on the white sash which she wears pinned on the right shoulder, extending across her breast and back and tied in a bow in the left hip." The girls performed numerous musical pieces which included singing, playing piano and guitar.[13]

Mississippi women assisted in the war effort in various ways from the outbreak of hostilities and even expressed a desire to fight. Writing to her friend in the summer of 1861, Cordelia Scales commented, "It seems so hard that we who have the wills of men should be debased from engaging in this great struggle for Liberty just because we are ladies. The love of liberty is the truest & noblest aspiration which can ever inspire the human heart." Sophia Hays of Kosciusko wished in her diary, "O could I speak an army into existence, how soon would I annihilate [the North]." Stationed as a nurse in Corinth during the battles of 1862, Kate Cumming spoke with many Union soldiers. One revealed that he did not believe the South was united as a people, to which Cumming curtly replied that "if the men did not fight, the women would."[14]

Confederate soldiers commented in letters and diaries about the support they received from the women of the South. Before boarding a train carrying soldiers outside of Mississippi, William Pitt received a gift from a young lady—a small Confederate flag with a piece of paper pinned next to it. The paper read, "'Compliments of Anna Collier to a Soldier. This represents Mississippi. Hurrah for the Confederacy and Davis! May an ever watchful eye be over thee! Anna Collier. Near Brandon." While marching through Tennessee, Robert Moore noted in his diary that despite many in the state expressing Union sympathies, "there are a few ladies who dare to wave &

present us with bouquets." William Nugent, writing to his wife, exclaimed, "God bless the women of the South, God bless them!" Nugent continued his eulogizing: "With delicate frames not made to face the pitiless storm of battle, they yet uncomplainingly bear the brunt of privation at home, and hover, like ministering angels . . . [they rally] from the effects of each reverse they gather courage in misfortune, and inspire us with the ardor of their patriotism and the enthusiasm of their souls."[15]

The zeal of women for the Confederate cause emerged unrestrained when confronted with the enemy. After the fall of Corinth in October 1862, Union forces began to raze Mississippi. Natchez fell shortly after New Orleans in the spring of 1862, and by the middle of 1863, Port Gibson, Jackson, and Vicksburg hosted numerous Union forces. Although several areas of Mississippi remained unimpeded by Union troops, the North had possession of most of the state by 1863. Mississippi women interacted with Union soldiers on a regular basis in the occupied areas. Often in these interactions, Confederate women reinforced their identity and continued to label northerners with undesirable traits. After the fall of Vicksburg, a young lady, Miss Mary, encountered a Confederate soldier on a well-traveled road. She asked the young man if he was a rebel, and he responded affirmatively. A nearby Union soldier questioned Miss Mary: "'You told that man it was right to be a Rebel, didn't you?'" In a "fierce manner," Mary shouted back, "'I said Washington was a Rebel, and that was right.'"[16]

Living in Holly Springs, Cordelia Scales and her family unwillingly hosted Union officers after the town capitulated in 1862. One officer, Captain Flynn, asked Scales to sing "My Maryland." She quickly retorted that she "did not play for Federal officers." Scales's father persuaded her to sing for Captain Flynn. She relented, and after she finished the number, the captain asked Scales if she would write out the words of the song on paper. Scales agreed, but at the top of the piece she drew a Confederate flag, under which she scrawled, "'no northern hand shall rule this land.'" Young and impudent, Scales insisted on waving a Confederate flag outside the family home. Several soldiers threatened her and repeatedly asked her to take it down. One officer told her that if she continued to wave the flag, he would "blow [her] dam brains out." Scales persisted. One day, overhearing a captain speaking to his men about a passage in the Bible that stated the South would drive the North into the sea, Scales commented, "I hoped I would be at the jumping off place & see the last blue coat go under."[17]

In addition to defying Union forces, Confederate women assumed a more masculine role in describing the endurance of their sufferings and also contrasted themselves with northern women. By employing masculine language, Confederate women elevated themselves to a more dominant position over their enemies by emasculating them. Hoping to rouse the occupying Union troops, Cordelia Scales alluded that the women of Mississippi would be willing to take up arms against the North. One soldier replied that southern ladies were "too good natured," to which Scales responded that indeed they were good natured, but that "when our soil was invaded & by such creatures as they were it was enough to arouse any one." Writing in her diary, Emma Balfour of Vicksburg decried the dire situation of the city in May 1863. Despite the shelling and the constant cannonading, Balfour asserted that the women and children of Vicksburg would not surrender and would be "content to suffer martyrdom." Anne Martin commented in her diary that she went to a friend's home and "spent an agreeable time talking over the Yankees, laughing at Yankee women." She also mused gleefully about the "Battle of the Handkerchiefs" that occurred in February 1863 in New Orleans. As Union officers transported captured Confederate military leaders to Baton Rouge, the women of the city stood near the levee and waved their handkerchiefs in support of the southern cause. The Union soldiers hoped to disband the crowd, but the women responded to the Union soldiers with continued resistance, followed by a brief melee and unremitting handkerchief waving. The incident was widely heralded throughout the South, demonstrating the notion that southern women could also whip the Yankees.[18]

Mississippi women proudly embraced the masculine characterization with which Union soldiers frequently labeled them. Emilie McKinley, a governess residing near Vicksburg and a northerner by birth, recalled a conversation held between Victoria Batchelor, one of her friends, and General Dennis, a Union officer. General Dennis said that "there was one circumstance he had noticed among Southern ladies he had met, and that was a great many were always bright and cheerful, even gay and lively, and that under misfortunes which could crush many people." McKinley was proud to note in her diary that Dennis believed a "Northern lady under the same circumstances would hardly be able to speak for her tears." Colonel James Peckham wrote a report that contained other anecdotes of Victoria Batchelor and her role as a "spirited rebel." Peckham noted that "Vic is a stubborn traitor . . . [and] declares she will fight against us when her brothers cease fighting and thinks (at least she says she does) that Yankeedom is gone up." Peckham commented that many of the people in the area, including Victoria and her friends, "openly denounce and abuse us."[19]

Even after the fall of Vicksburg in July 1863, Confederate women helped buoy the sunken spirits of their brothers, sons, husbands, and fathers by retaining faith in the Confederate cause. Hearing the rumors of the impending surrender at Vicksburg, Natchez resident Kate Foster maintained faith that God still supported the Confederacy. "And if this our glorious little city does fall," Foster wrote, "have we not Hope still left us in the goodness of God and we all believe He is for us and having this faith how can we doubt for an instant." Even when confirmation of the city's capitulation reached Adams County, Foster still held to her previous convictions: "Now our struggle will last longer but not for a moment do I think we will be unsuccessful." She believed "God has let it fall to show us our cause does not rest upon the mere fall or holding of any one city." Elizabeth Brown, also a Natchez citizen, shared similar sentiments with regard to the defeat at Vicksburg. "We have got to fight the war harder, that is all," she reasoned, "and trust that God will be with us, and enable us to free our poor Country yet." Belle Edmondson wrote in her diary, "Vicksburgh, surrendered this morning and an exulting foe, madened by success, imagines the Rebellion crushed—poor deluded fools—tis just begun." Her prayer-like soliloquy rested in the belief that "our faith is perfect. God will bless us. No matter how dim the Star of Liberty may grow. . . . God is our Sun and Shield, and we will yet come out victoriously free." Writing to her husband, Maria Giles commented on the loss of Vicksburg and stated, "They say that the darkest hour is always just before day, and I will try to hope that through all the clouds which now envelop us, will soon break the day dawn of our young Confederacy." For many of these Confederate women, the finality of southern independence was almost inevitable, as long as they bore their sufferings well and trusted in the Lord.[20]

Mississippians swiftly adopted a Confederate identity because it varied only slightly from their American identity. It also arose quickly because they had a ready villain in the North, whom they used as a counterpoint and labeled with negative characteristics. The acceptance of a Confederate identity did not necessarily translate into unwavering support of the Confederate government or of Confederate nationalism. As historians have demonstrated, war weariness, Confederate government policies, and crushing losses, all mounted on the southern citizenry and often resulted in high desertion rates, illegal cotton smuggling to the North, and open denunciation of the Confederate leadership in Richmond, Virginia. Mississippians accepted their Confederate identity because they based it on antipathy to the northern states and northerners. Regardless of whether the southern states won or lost the war, or whether they supported the Confederate government or the war effort, they built their identity as Confederates on the belief that they were fundamentally different from the North.[21]

Of course, not all Mississippians adopted a Confederate identity. Mississippi already had a significant unionist population prior to the war. A sizable anti-Confederate contingent existed throughout the state, especially in the northeastern and southern counties. They openly defied Confederate authority and aided federal forces when opportunities arose. Many of these unionists were non-slaveholders and decried secession. Others became anti-Confederates after they witnessed the horrible devastation of war, both in loss of life and economic hardships. Jones County became a hub of unionist sentiment under the leadership of Newton Knight, who openly defied the state's Confederate government. Newton and his followers waged a war to retain their connection with the United States. State officials made numerous attempts to regain control of the county, but all efforts proved costly and futile. Unionists in the state rejected the Confederacy as a nation and what it stood for.[22]

Many Mississippi dissenters did not just disagree with the act of secession but opposed several aspects of southern society and culture as well. John Aughey, a clergyman and unionist, faced intense scrutiny after openly opposing secession in 1861. Eventually moving from Attala to Tishomingo County, Aughey helped transport his friends' cotton to sellers in the North. Arrested shortly afterward, Aughey spent time in a Tupelo prison and, with the aid of fellow sympathizers, escaped before his scheduled execution. In his memoir Aughey railed against the slaveholding class, characterizing them with "idleness, vanity, licentiousness, profanity, dissipation, and tyranny." Praising the yeomanry, Aughey described them as "industrious, frugal, hospitable, simple in their habits, plain and unostentatious in their manners." Aughey painted a picture of Mississippi as one controlled by the slavocracy in which "poor whites are forced to obey." According to Aughey, those who chose to resist the slaveholders were "denounced as abolitionists, and are in danger of death at the hands of Judge Lynch, the mildest punishment they can hope for being a coat of tar and feathers." By branding someone as an abolitionist or a Yankee, slaveholders applied a label of "reproach" that would negatively "stigmatize" those accused. Aughey believed that many Mississippians opposed the planter class and claimed that only slaveholders manifested "considerable antipathy against the Yankees." Writing for a northern audience, Aughey blamed the plantation owners for espousing anti-American attitudes and leading the secession movement that caused the war.[23]

John Wood, another unionist, criticized the state for pursuing the course of secession and denounced those who embraced the foolish doctrine. Writing midway through the war, Wood compared the general condition of the state antebellum to that in wartime. Starvation, economic collapse, and a complete disruption in commerce plagued the state because a fringe group of radicals adopted an extreme states' rights ideology. Wood said that disunionists duped Mississippi's young men into thinking that unless they "took part in the revolution, they would be regarded as the Tories of the Revolutionary War." Wood believed that throughout the course of the century, those "political parsons have seized upon the subject of slavery as a Divine institution, and have rivaled the most fanatical enthusiasts of the North in their extreme views and zealous exertions." He asserted that their fanaticism fueled the belief that "Providence is on their side, and whether in victory or defeat, they have an ample fund of scriptural quotations at hand, with which either to rejoice or to cheer up the weak and faint-hearted." Wood also worried that the extremists introduced a delusional concept concerning the "great superiority" of the southern soldier versus that of a northerner. The false idea led to the death of thousands of boys who believed the pernicious lies and rushed off to war. Wood contended that by bowing to these radicals and their propaganda, Mississippi faced certain destruction at the hands of the North. Wood urged his readers that "a love for the Union should be cherished" and that "the ardent desire of every American patriot should be to see a re-union in feeling among the people of the United States."[24]

Confederate Mississippians sought to silence any anti-Confederate or unionist thought. A number of unionists, some of them parolees from Vicksburg, fled to Jones County in the southeastern portion of the state. The rascally Newt Knight led his military unit, the Jones County Scouts, as they evaded arrest, stole from the Confederacy to feed the hungry, and proved an embarrassing thorn in the side of the Confederate government. William Howell, a soldier in a militia unit, had orders to march to Smith and Jones Counties to ferret out Knight's band. Referring to the hostile attitude present in the southern counties, Howell commented in a letter to his mother that "it is a disgrace to the state that Mississippians should act in such a manner." William Walton wrote a letter to his father-in-law in which he confessed, "We have an element amongst us which is neither southern in sentiment nor gladsome at heart when success attends the efforts of our brave men." Walton stated, "He who is not for us, is against us. He who is against us cannot and shall not, be on any other terms with me than those of enmity. The friendship of such persons brings ruin upon the true southern man." Confederates in the state pursued whatever course they deemed necessary to suppress those that opposed the Confederacy or expressed unionist sympathies.[25]

At the same time, Confederate Mississippians greatly worried about the slave population in the state and what an impending Union victory would mean for those in bondage. The Civil War marked the creation of an American identity among the slave population. The nearly 450,000 enslaved men and women in Mississippi, composing roughly 55 percent of the state's population, supposed that God brought war upon the nation for the purpose of securing their freedom. Slaves knew and understood the implications of a northern victory versus that of southern independence. Many slaves hastened emancipation when they ran away from their masters and joined the Union army. Others secretly provided food and information to Union forces, while some simply refused to work. As slaves clamored for freedom, they encountered several difficulties in trying to fit into a white supremacist American society.[26]

Many slaves knew from the beginning of the war that a northern victory could result in their freedom, which emboldened slaves to act decisively to secure that opportunity. Shortly after the surrender of Fort Sumter in 1861, slaves from several plantations in Adams County conspired to revolt against their masters. The initial planning for the insurrection occurred while some of the male slaves fished along the banks of Second Creek in May 1861. Hearing rumors of abolitionists plotting to attack the South to help liberate the slaves, the insurrectionists wanted to hasten the work of emancipation. While specific details of their plot remain unknown, one white resident of the area, J.D.L. Davenport, wrote to Governor Pettus that "the plans as developed are of the most diabolical character, the white males were all to be destroyed—such of the females as suited their fancy were to be preserved as *Wives* and they were to march up the river to meet 'Mr. Linkin.'" Several years later, one of Davenport's slaves, Charlie Davenport, recalled the episode. "When I wuz a little boy they wuz a slave uprising planned," he remembered. "De slaves had hit all worked out how dey wuz goin to march on Natchez aftah slayin all dare own white folks." The white inhabitants closely guarded their knowledge of the plot and kept the story away from the press for fear that it might embolden their enemies. Between

May and September 1861, the citizens near Second Creek held trials under the jurisdiction of a vigilance committee and hanged somewhere between twenty-seven and forty slaves for conspiracy. Whatever the details of the plot, the fact remained that slaves in the area understood that the agitation between the two sections stemmed from an argument about slavery. They were not about to let the opportunity pass without doing something to gain their freedom.[27]

Slaves knew that Abraham Lincoln's election caused a rift within the country, and they believed God intended it for the purpose of emancipation. Slaveholders tried to keep information from their slaves, but, as Maria White recalled, "They couldn't keep that from our ears. There was so much talk going on." Lincoln became a latter-day Moses to them, the man God destined to lead His captive people out of bondage. Former slave Frank Hughes compared Lincoln to the ancient patriarch. "I thinks about him jes like I did about Moses," he said. "I think it was de will of de Lawd to talk to Abraham Lincoln through de spirit, to work out a plan to set the niggers free. I think he carried out God's Plan." One former slave went even further and declared that "we all thought [Lincoln] was a young Christ come to save us." Like a modern-day prophet, Lincoln "did what God put him here to do, took boundage [*sic*] off the colored people and set them free." Jim Allen believed that "Abraham Lincoln worked by 'pinions of de Bible. He got his meanings from the Bible." Lizzie Norfleet commented that "there wasn't much said about Jefferson Davis. According to the Bible, he was wrong. The Lord said 'The World was made sufficient for all to have a living.' He never intended bondage for nobody. That's why he made the world big enough for everybody to have a home." Slaves quickly embraced the image of Lincoln as emancipator and the Union as friend to the slaves.[28]

From the start of the war, slaves took the opportunity to challenge their status as chattel. Many whites complained that slaves acted impudently and were unruly. Masters and overseers had a difficult time maintaining any order or control on their farms and plantations. Alfred Quine, overseer of a plantation in Warren County, kept a plantation journal to track progress and production. Beginning in May 1863, many entries simply stated, "Negroes all doing nothing." Samuel Agnew, pastor of a Presbyterian church, noted in August 1862 that the "negroes is the absorbing topic. Our negroes seem to be restless and hard to please." By October, Agnew and his family lost eleven slaves who escaped to Union lines. Agnew understood the futility of forced submission and conceded that "every one, with but one or two exceptions will go to the Yankees." He recorded that one of his slaves "does not conceal her thoughts but plainly manifests her opinions by her conduct—insolent and insulting." Those who stayed on the plantation often put on airs of defiance. One slave girl, Susan Snow, overheard the white children singing a popular Confederate song:

> Jeff Davis, long an' slim,
> Whupped old Abe wid a hick'ry limb.
> Jeff Davis is a wise man, Lincoln is a fool,
> Jeff Davis rides a gray, an' Lincoln rides a mule.

In response, Snow sang her own version:

> Old Gen'l Pope had a shot gun,
> Filled it full o' gum,
> Killed 'em as dey come.
> Called a Union band,
> Make de Rebels un'erstan'
> To leave de lan','
> Submit to Abraham.

Unfortunately for Snow, the plantation mistress overheard her song and beat her with a nearby broom. The fact remained, though, that slaves understood their freedom neared, and they would not let the chance to secure it elude them.[29]

With the outbreak of fighting, many black men clamored for the opportunity to enlist in the military and fight for their freedom. As Union troops pushed into the South, they quickly encountered runaway slaves who desired to assist in the war effort. Considered contraband, they were often employed by the Union forces to perform menial tasks such as cooking and cleaning in camp. By the summer of 1862, the United States passed the Confiscation Act, which gave the president the authority to allow blacks to enlist in the military. Many segregated black units led by white officers fought during the Civil War. One battle that involved two black regiments occurred at Milliken's Bend, located just north of Vicksburg. Hoping to distract Grant's forces during the early weeks of the siege, the Confederates launched an attack against the federal garrison at the bend to cut off Union supply lines. The Union army stationed over a thousand Mississippi and Louisiana blacks who, just weeks prior, received their commission to defend the garrison at the bend. Ill equipped, the federal troops managed to repel the attack after engaging in brutal bayonet and hand-to-hand fighting. Eventually, two federal gunboats floated close enough and fired on the Confederates, expelling them from the area. General Henry McCulloch, leader of the Confederate detachment, later reported that "while the white or true Yankee portion ran like whipped curs," the "negro portion of the enemy's force [resisted the charge] with considerable obstinacy."[30]

After the fall of Vicksburg, Grant stationed black troops in the city and even distributed confiscated land to former slaves. Whites complained bitterly about the actions of the former slaves and commented with disgust concerning the parading of black soldiers in their Union uniforms and "making a fine show." In an episode dripping with overt symbolism of the changing social order, Grant seized Jefferson and Joseph Davis's plantations south of Vicksburg and allowed just under two thousand freedmen to settle on the property. Robert Melvin, a friend of the Confederate president, wrote to Davis in July after visiting the plantation home and describing the devastation. "Boxes were torn open and emptied of their contents," Melvin relayed, "books and papers were strewed over the yard and scattered through the woods for miles; fine carpets were cut to pieces and carried off for saddle blankets and saddle covers; . . . in fact everything useful or ornamental was plundered and destroyed with a ruthlessness worthy of Attilla [*sic*] himself." For the next several years, former slaves operated the Davis plantation and produced a significant amount of cotton under a self-established, democratically oriented, communal government. Within the state, blacks started to taste freedom and their changed status within society.[31]

Former slaves expected whites to accept them into society as equals and felt emboldened in Union-occupied areas. Oftentimes, blacks expected Union soldiers to protect them against angry whites in the area when they behaved in a fashion the residents believed unbecoming. Kate Foster recalled an incident that happened at a local Natchez church during the summer of 1863. While in the middle of a service attended by the regular congregants and Union soldiers, a black man walked into the chapel, strode up the middle aisle toward the pulpit, and proceeded to sit in one of the front pews. Infuriated, one attendee loudly asked what the man wanted, and in reply the "impudent scamp said he came to church and wanted a seat." Another in attendance arose and escorted the man to the gallery reserved for blacks; the Union soldiers laughed during the incident. Elizabeth Brown of Natchez wrote in her diary that Union forces arrested her father after he threatened to beat a black man who wandered into their garden. Brown resentfully commented in her diary that she hoped the former slaves "will be made to suffer for their impudence."[32]

Former slaves hoped to take full advantage of their newly acquired freedom. Some expressed the simplest desires after their emancipation. Lewis Jefferson explained that "de slaves wanted to be free so dey could come an' go places like de white folks an' de Patroller wud not git dem. Den dey wanted some money to buy deir own clothes." Charlie Moss believed that "God Almighty nevah ment human beings to be lak animals." He continued saying, "Us niggahs has a soul, an' a heart, an' a mine an we is'nt lak a dawg or a horse. I didn't spec' nothin' outten freedom septin' peace an' happiness an' the right to go my way as I please." Slaves wanted a chance to secure basic rights and live in a fashion similar to what whites lived, and they started to envision a life that included their full participation in white society.[33]

The Civil War produced the right conditions for white Mississippians to birth a Confederate identity, and former slaves to embrace an American one. As Mississippians fought and interacted with Union forces, they projected negative identifiers on their enemies, which allowed them to reinforce positive traits on themselves. As they did this, they drove a wedge between themselves and northerners and firmly believed that the two regions were incompatible. Mississippians still trumpeted their American heritage and the basic concepts of Americanness as they understood it, and they incorporated these ideas into their Confederate identity. At the same time, freedom allowed former slaves to test the waters of American citizenship and rights previously not afforded to them. Freedmen rallied quickly behind the Union cause and started to fashion their own identity as Americans. Despite not having a shared American historical narrative to draw upon, blacks forged their American identity in their efforts to fight against the Confederacy and end their enslavement. The end of the war resulted in a collision between various social groups with different social identities that had many incompatible features, which led the state into a dark period of violence and uncertainty.

"DYING DIXIE"

— • —

Yes, I'm dying Dixie, dying,
Mother Southland, for thy sake,
For thy holy cause I'm dying:
Take me to thy bosom, take!
See, my glassy eyes are closing,
See, my bosom gasps for breath,
Soon 'twill end in sweet reposing
On thy bosom—welcome, death!
I am dying, Dixie, dying,
Still'd my heart within its breast,
Hear the angel voices crying—
Dixie—mother, Heaven, Rest![1]

"The war took away the very flower of our population," Greene Chandler recalled. "Hundreds of young men in all the counties of the State, who were capable of great achievements, perished in battle or in hospital." Chandler described what soldiers saw when they returned from war: "thousands of widows and orphans and disabled soldiers, business suspended, starvation and mourning everywhere—stark tragedy indeed." Chandler grieved for the "bleeding and helpless" South. Recognizing the utter senselessness of further resistance to northern will, Chandler conceded to be "faithful to the Government." Mere obedience to the United States, though, was not as drastic as his overall outlook after the Civil War. "I confess a change from early convictions," Chandler admitted. "I can now see, that the slavery of human beings, except as a punishment for crime, was wrong and inde-fensible, despite the pulpit and its interpretation of the Bible." Prior to the war, Chandler had commented that "the condition of the African, in the slavery in which I found him, was far better for him than the barbarism from which it rescued him." Months before the 1860 presidential election, Chandler openly advocated for the state militia to mobilize and prepare for war to repel the "northern fanatics" who threatened southern property rights. Yet once the war concluded, Chandler quickly aligned himself with the Republican Party, denied any active involvement in the secession movement, and eventually campaigned for universal male suffrage.[2]

The end of the war presented serious obstacles for Mississippians. They no longer recognized the South they fought to preserve. The "holy cause" for which hundreds of thousands of southerners died was completely lost. For the next several years, major transformations caused distress and upheaval. Mississippians no longer had their Confederacy, and they did not know how they would fit back into the United States. The years immediately succeeding the war witnessed a period of anxiety and confusion, as Mississippians underwent a collective identity crisis; planters were no longer planters, elite white women were no longer genteel belles, the yeomanry were no longer planters in waiting, blacks were no longer slaves, and Mississippi sat in a state of limbo in its relation to the United States. The Old South was dead.[3]

Mississippians reacted differently following the close of the war in terms of how they viewed their relationship to the Union. Most white Mississippians tried to find a way to retain their Confederate identity while trying to become "American" again. The changes brought about during Reconstruction, though, made doing so difficult. The end of slavery dramatically altered the social structure in the state and challenged the traditional hierarchy. The influx of carpetbaggers from the North, combined with white unionists and black political participation, caused a revolution in state politics. Republican dominance in local politics, boosted by black votes, forced white Mississippians to adjust to the new political climate. In finding their place back in the Union as Americans, conservative Mississippians had a difficult time trying to reconcile with the North as they watched Radical Republicans in Congress take the helm of Reconstruction. Transitioning from a Confederate identity back to an American identity proved much more difficult than the transition that occurred following secession.

At the same time, the freedmen found it easy to embrace the opportunities presented as citizens. They passionately reveled in their granted legal and political rights. Freedmen formed Loyal Leagues and committed themselves to the Republican Party. They met frequently in political meetings, held parades and celebrations, and turned out in droves at the polls for elections. Black Mississippians desired the ability to enter white society and expected that opportunities for self-improvement would follow their emancipation. Many hoped for land grants from confiscated property; others expected ease in obtaining land for rent or eventual ownership. Blacks believed that the promise of freedom granted them immediate access to all the perks of citizenship.

For white Mississippians, the close of the war brought intense fear and uncertainty as they waited to hear the terms of peace and how the federal government would assimilate them back into the Union. In the early months of 1865, most Mississippians recognized that defeat loomed on the horizon and that they would have to lay down their arms and reenter the Union. Many retained their belief in the justness of their cause. "Every day I feel more and more what a waste of life this is," Charles Roberts wrote to his wife in the spring of 1865. "I know our Cause is just and this is the only thing that at all reconciles me to the great sacrifice I am making." What bothered him the most, though, was the thought that northerners would completely displace all that was southern, all that they had become over the past four years. William Chambers, a schoolteacher before the war, imagined the transformation likely to come to the South after the hostilities ended. "It is an unpleasant thought," Chambers mused, "but one that often suggests itself, that when the contest is ended in our defeat, hundreds—nay thousands—of the Northern soldiers will find homes in the South and make wives of our sisters and our daughters." What brought more sorrow to Chambers was that "where one [southerner] would remain true to principle and be faithful to a memory, many will be ready to forget it all." Edward Fontaine, a planter from Hinds County, shuddered to think that with the fall of the Confederacy "no monuments will be erected by this generation for the graves of the hundreds of thousands of our heroes who have fallen in the defence of our native land." Some feared the North would control the memory of the war and erase the South's identity.[4]

White Mississippians retained their Confederate identity immediately following the war and hoped to enter the Union with that identity still intact. Speaking to a friend about the events of the past four years, James Neilson revealed that he "hoped yet to see a Southern Confederacy, and hoped to see the Yankees humbled." Neilson's friend scolded him that such attitudes would prevent feelings of unity replacing those of old sectional hostilities. Neilson responded that he could not trust or unite with those who opposed and fought against the South. Kate Foster of Natchez also could not see herself reconciling with the North after losing her brothers during the war. Foster, reflecting on her continued support of the Confederacy, grieved, "Not ever our loved Confederacy shall wave the banner under which so many brave have fought and so many fallen to protect." Commenting on the Fourth of July in 1866, Edward Fontaine noted in his journal, "I think of the heroes of the South the descendants of the heroes of 76 who died in a vain defence of the liberty they bequeathed to us. How can we, or the people of any [of] the States which were independent a few years ago, rejoice on this memorable day?" Fontaine defended his decision not to celebrate the Fourth since "a corrupt oligarchy rule the United States, who look upon Virginia and her sisters of the South as conquered provinces, which the [avarice] and blood-thirsty fanatics who sway the Federal Congress delight to plunder, insult and enslave!" Instead, Fontaine wished to indulge in "painful memories of the past, and gloomy anticipations of the future."[5]

In the years following the end of the war, Mississippians desired to rec-oncile with the North and reenter the Union without delay. In an address at the University of Mississippi, Oscar Bledsoe declared that "the primary object of desire with the South at the present time *is restoration of coequal rights in the union of the States.*" He recognized some of the "barriers which stand between us and it" but argued away any potential stumbling block. Bledsoe expressed confidence that southerners recognized the end of slav-ery and the illegality of secession. He affirmed that the "South now stands, in common with all Americans . . . upon the platform of the great general principles which underlie our governmental polity." Bledsoe argued that even though differences over certain issues drove a wedge between the two sections, that the South "has always been devoted to Constitutional Ameri-can Liberty . . . [and] never aimed a blow in wrath at the Constitution." He believed reconciliation possible and without any major setbacks.[6]

Initially, many whites in the state shared Bledsoe's hopes about a fluid reentrance back into the Union, especially after President Andrew Johnson outlined his plan for Reconstruction. In June 1865 Johnson appointed William Sharkey as provisional governor over Mississippi. Johnson instructed Sharkey to summon a convention to draft a new state constitu-tion that recognized the abolition of slavery. In addition, former Confed-erates in the state needed to sign and abide by a loyalty oath. When these tasks were completed as outlined, the federal government would grant full rights to the state and citizenry as members of the Union. The process of reconciliation appeared practical and simple, yet in practice it proved much more problematic.[7]

The emancipation of the slaves and the end of the institution of slav-ery proved one of the difficult hurdles in allowing a quick reconciliation with the North. White Mississippians had a problem with accepting the permanent demise of slavery. In addition to providing a labor system, slavery seeped into every aspect of southern society, including conceptions of honor, paternity, and even independence. The institution of slavery defined everything that it meant to be a southerner. The fear of losing their slave property influenced the decision years earlier to leave the Union. Pastor Samuel Agnew willingly took the oath of loyalty, which said, "I, Samuel A. Agnew, do solemnly swear in the presence of Almighty God that I will henceforth faithfully support, protect and defend the Constitution of the United States and the Union of the States thereunder, and that I will in like manner abide by and faithfully support all laws and proclamations which have been made during the existing rebellion with reference to the emancipation of slaves." He commented, though, that "he did not fancy the latter part of this oath" in reference to abolition. Some still hoped that slavery would continue to exist and looked for ways to keep it intact. In the summer of 1865, Lieutenant Colonel H. R. Brinkerhoff reported to the Freedmen's Bureau that most planters believed blacks would return to bondage shortly, through either a Supreme Court ruling or a constitutional amendment. Brinkerhoff wrote that one planter said, "These niggers will all be slaves again in twelve months. You have nothing but Lincoln's proclamation to make them free." Later in his report, Brinkerhoff stated that many of the whites in the area labored "assiduously for a restoration of the old system of slavery, or a system of apprenticeship or some manner of involuntary servitude."[8]

The slave issue took center stage during the state's constitutional convention in the summer of 1865. Provisional Governor William Sharkey addressed the convention and explained the charge issued by Andrew Johnson for the state to create a new constitution and government so it "may be able to resume its place in the Union." Sharkey advised the convention on matters they needed to address in order to promote "reconciliation between the Northern and Southern people." He outlined eight points for the convention to consider; the last, and most lengthy, dealt with the slave issue. Sharkey expressed concern over further attempts at rebellion against the Union and refusals to take the amnesty oath of loyalty to the United States. He knew that some in the state declined to sign the oath because "they believe the emancipation proclamation unconstitutional." Sharkey plainly asserted that "whether it be constitutional or not, is a question the people have no right to determine." He wondered why some would not accept the amnesty oath, "since slavery has ceased to be a practical question." The simple fact, according to Sharkey, remained that slavery, as the "ostensible cause of the war . . . has been decided against us." Not only that, but it was "too late to raise technical questions as to the means by which" the slaves secured their freedom.[9]

Despite Sharkey's pleas for the convention delegates to leave the slave issue alone, most of the recorded convention debates centered squarely on how slavery ended in the state, its legality, and the status of the freedmen. James Harrison, of Lowndes County, who served on the Committee on Constitutional Amendments, proposed a motion on the fifth day to strike out sections in the constitution that spoke of slaves. Hugh Barr, of Lafayette, proposed a substitute that, in part, stated, "Slavery having been abolished in this State by the action of the Government of the United States, it is therefore hereby declared and ordained, that hereafter there shall be neither slavery nor involuntary servitude in this State." Barr's simple substitute ignited days of debate concerning his wording about how slavery ended in Mississippi.[10]

J. Shall Yerger, of Washington County, immediately addressed his concerns with the preamble. Yerger disagreed that the United States government abolished slavery. Rather, he asserted that the consequence of war resulted in abolition. He explained that after secession, the president "warned them, if they would not discontinue the war, and return to their allegiance, their slaves would be emancipated." The South, though, "declined the proposition, and continued the war, until they were overcome, and slavery was destroyed." Yerger's objection to the substitute stemmed from his belief that the preamble "asserts as a fact, what . . . is historically untrue": that the sole act of abolition came directly from the United States government. He believed that the convention should "deal with [the fact of slavery's demise] in a practical way . . . and not impair the usefulness of our action, by the assertion of things as absolutely true, which some assert and others deny."[11]

A flurry of substitutions flooded the convention floor that altered the language of the preamble. One proposal suggested the language should reflect that the abolition of slavery resulted from the "consequence of the war, resulting from an Ordinance of Secession." Unionists submitted another proposal, in which they chided the disunionists and stated, "African slavery in the State of Mississippi, has been abolished by the power and authority of the United States Government, and the loyal people of the State [will] faithfully support the proclamations of the President . . . in reference to the emancipation of slaves." The disunionists countered with their own statement that blamed "certain authorities of the United States [who claimed] by force of certain proclamations of the President, and of certain acts of the Congress of the United States [that] all colored persons, heretofore held as slaves, in this State, are, of right, free; which said claim is now enforced by military power, against children of tender years, and other innocent persons, as well as against those implicated in the recent rebellion." The old animosities that existed in the state prior to the war surfaced as they debated an issue that extended beyond the abolition of slavery.[12]

For the delegates at the convention, the issue of how slavery finally abated focused primarily on Mississippi's place in the Union and the authority of the federal government to oversee Reconstruction. When George Potter offered the disunionist rejoinder, he followed with a speech to the convention concerning his understanding of Mississippi's national status. He commented that "our State to-day, notwithstanding the acts of secession, notwithstanding the war of rebellion, is still a State of the Union, with all her rights and privileges under the Constitution." Potter refused to submit to any conditions the federal government placed on the state, believing those "dictations" fell short in their constitutionality. Instead, he urged his fellow delegates to abide by the Constitution and let the other issues play out. Since, according to his understanding, the Constitution still protected property rights, Mississippians would do best to wait and see how the abolition of slavery would play out in the federal system. He further argued that President Andrew Johnson had not explicitly demanded that the states abolish slavery as a condition of readmission—Johnson only suggested it. Potter feared that elements in the North desired to elevate the freedmen to equality with whites and would impose strict measures before allowing Mississippi full rights in the Union, specifically the formal recognition of emancipation. He also cautioned that even Abraham Lincoln admitted that the courts might annul the Emancipation Proclamation. Potter held out hope that the federal government would offer compensation to former slaveholders, perhaps through tax relief. Abolishing slavery outright would hurt the state's chances of receiving any monetary consideration from the government.[13]

Others added their voices to the debate over the slavery issue and whether the convention should recognize the means by which slavery ended. Many reasoned that slavery in practice was dead, but nothing legally pointed to its termination. Some suggested that waiting for federal compensation was foolhardy, since the ruling party in Congress would never assent to such a thing. Others refused to make a "bargain with the Abolition party of the North," because that party opposed "the rights of the South." In many instances most of the delegates agreed that even though the state rebelled against the federal government, they currently were not in rebellion; therefore, neither the president nor Congress had the power or authority to dictate what they should include in their state constitution.[14]

For the delegates, the issue at stake in the debates centered on the constitutional authority of the federal government, whether congressional or presidential, to constrain a state to abide by measures that appeared contrary to the Constitution. Any admission that the federal government eliminated slavery would leave open the possibility of forced equality for blacks, strict loyalty oaths, and other extreme measures to reenter the Union. While the demise of slavery as a social institution offered a significant blow, the fear of granting a Republican-dominated federal government dictatorial power over the state loomed even greater. After the heated debates, the delegates overwhelmingly voted for the awkwardly worded section, written in the passive voice, to say, "The institution of slavery having been destroyed in the State of Mississippi, neither slavery nor involuntary servitude, otherwise than in the punishment of crimes, whereof the party shall have been duly convicted, shall hereafter exist in this State."[15]

Other Mississippians also expressed concern over federal authority and the relationship between the state and the federal government. In 1866 one Mississippian remarked that "the North forced the South into an unconditional surrender, and the Southern States are now held as conquered provinces and governed by the will of their Northern masters." Newspaper editor John Bosworth worried that northerners in the southern states intentionally "misrepresented and maligned us." He said that following the war, the South admitted defeat "gracefully" and endeavored to "live in amity and concord with their 'Northern brethren.'" Yet in the ensuing months, the North began to act aggressively against the South. Bosworth cited examples of the state passing laws that the federal government "annulled with the velocity of lightning," because "those laws are not in consonance with the views of the 'the powers that be' at Washington." Other examples included the federal government confiscating southern land, taxing the southern people without representation, and the imprisonment of Confederate officers. According to Bosworth, attempts to "inaugurate the 'era of good feeling'" failed because the North refused to offer a "corresponding spirit of conciliations" and "reciprocity."[16]

Further efforts at reconciliation failed because white Mississippians took offense to the way that northerners characterized them as traitors and rebels. Edward Fontaine of Hinds County traveled to the northern states in the years following the war. While in New York, he lashed out against northerners who routinely "denounced as a *rebellion*" the Civil War, and "stigmatized as traitors . . . Lee, Jackson, and the heroic hosts they led." It bothered him when "fanatical or hypocritical pulpit orators" claimed that southerners fought "a barbarous war against the Union and in defence of negro slavery." A few months later he took issue over the part of the commemoration ceremony of Washington's birthday. In a public display stood a medallion with the portraits of George Washington, Abraham Lincoln, and Ulysses Grant. Latin inscriptions below each profile labeled "Washington the *founder*, Lincoln the *liberator* and *Grant* the *preserver* of the *Republic*." Fontaine thought those portraits should remain "as an index to mark the degeneracy and decay of the Republic—It should be labeled Washington *the founder*, Lincoln *the destroyer*, and Grant the *disgracer* of the Republic of the *United States*."[17]

For Mississippians, in the immediate aftermath of the war, the terms "traitor" and "rebellion" connoted dishonorable traits. In the constitutional convention, William Stone of Copiah County addressed the problem with using the term "rebellion" to describe the war. He surmised that if the southern states "were in rebellion," then all those in the state "are to be treated as traitors and liable to the penalty of treason, which is death." Stone preferred the term "civil war" to describe the conflict, since it meant a contest "between two independent nations." John Bosworth echoed similar sentiments when he wrote an editorial addressing the use of the term "traitor" as applied to southerners. Bosworth claimed that "the late war was a civil war," not a rebellion. He argued that northerners, especially Radicals, could not substantiate the claims of treason and rebellion on the part of the South, despite their attempts. Bosworth considered it "mean and dishonorable" to call southerners treasonous and place them in the company of men like Benedict Arnold.[18]

Mississippians continued to brand northerners with unflattering characteristics and harbored animosity toward them. Russell Conwell, a Union veteran and Boston newspaper correspondent, traveled throughout the South shortly after the war. He stopped just below Vicksburg and stayed with a family who put on airs of amicability. Conwell's host defended the South's actions during the war but claimed that no animosity existed on the part of southerners toward the North. "'The people of the great and noble North are our friends,'" the host commented, "'and we have nothing but the purest love for them. . . . We love our Northern brethren.'" Later that day, after Conwell left the family to resume his travels, he noticed the host and his neighbor speaking to each other in town. The neighbor scolded the host for welcoming a northern man into his home, stating, "I love the South too much to fraternize with her enemies." The host replied quickly, "I want him to say a good word for me in the radical papers. That's just what I want. I may need them to use in Washington." The host aspired to run for office as a revenue collector and hoped good press would help him achieve his goal. He proceeded to tell his neighbor what he actually thought of northerners: "As for the d—d fool of a Yankee himself, to tell the truth, I felt like cutting his throat every time I looked at him. I would just like to hang up every cussed Yankee that comes down here. For they only stir up the niggers to insolence and deviltry."[19]

Whitelaw Reid of Ohio made similar observations when he toured Mississippi following the war. He wrote that "their old prejudices against Northern public men seemed unchanged by the war." He noted that they continued to speak of Charles Sumner "with loathing," William Seward as a "first-class devil," and Salmon Chase as ambition-driven to defeat the South for a side "he knew to be wrong." One northerner recounted similar reviling against northern leaders, often hearing Mississippians refer to Abraham Lincoln as a "baboon," William Seward a "traitor," Charles Sumner a "miscegenationist," and Edwin Stanton the "bloody tyrant." Another traveler, J. T. Trowbridge, visited Corinth and other major battlefields in the state. He ate a meal with a group of people at his lodging, including a "white and delicate" lady "wrapped in shawls." Trowbridge commented that "she was bitter against the Yankees," which amused him. He informed her that he hailed from the North. The lady asked, "From what State are you, Sir?" No doubt with a smile, he informed her he was from Massachusetts. Her immediate response came with a shudder: "Oh! . . . they're bad Yankees!" The lingering animosities and negative traits Mississippians had given to northerners over the previous years still clouded their views and restricted their attempts at readopting their American identity.[20]

Some northerners decided to settle in Mississippi permanently and proved a major obstacle in Mississippians' efforts to restore their relations with the North. Disparagingly called "carpetbaggers," these interlopers not only attempted to make Mississippi their home but to alter the state's political and social institutions. White Mississippians viewed carpetbaggers as manipulative, self-serving, money-hungry, and exploitive. Carpetbagger Henry Warren recalled that the press "poured out the vials of their wrath upon their devoted heads with all the bitterness the English language is capable of expressing." He said that, overwhelmingly, whites believed "that the so-called Carpet-Baggers were in fact a set of thieves and robbers devoting themselves exclusively to plundering their patriotic brethren of the South." Overwhelmingly Republican in politics, carpetbaggers profoundly influenced and shaped Mississippi's national identity during Reconstruction. Carpetbaggers worked closely with the black population and made Mississippi a Republican stronghold for a brief period of time. Most whites in the state reviled the carpetbaggers and heaped on them much of the blame and scorn over Reconstruction politics and the major transformation the state encountered during the 1870s.[21]

In the first years after war's end, carpetbaggers did not exert much political influence in the state. That changed, however, when Congress wrested control of Reconstruction from Andrew Johnson. As the political showdown over Reconstruction measures started to take shape in early 1866, white Mississippians watched nervously as the political landscape transformed. Senator Lyman Trumbull of Illinois presented the Civil Rights Bill to Congress that aimed to displace the restrictive Black Codes the state legislature enacted in 1865 to control the black population. Johnson's veto only slowed the bill from becoming law—Congress managed to secure enough votes for an override. Congress also secured passage of a bill to give the Freedmen's Bureau, an organization operated through the military to provide relief and support to the freedmen, more leverage in their authority and jurisdiction. Radical Reconstruction followed a year later when Congress passed the Reconstruction Acts of 1867, which divided the southern states into five military districts and outlined the process required for full admittance back in the Union. The act mandated that southern states allow black political participation in the creation of a new state constitution that granted full legal rights, as well as suffrage, to the black population.[22]

Mississippi underwent significant changes when General Edward Ord assumed military control over Mississippi and Arkansas in March 1867. Ord helped rectify the flailing Freedmen's Bureau in the state, filled some government vacancies, and promised to deal swiftly with the pervasive violence. Ord and the Freedmen's Bureau created a new electorate in the state by registering voters for the purpose of holding another constitutional convention. Much to the chagrin and disappointment of conservative whites, the new electorate consisted of 79,176 blacks and 58,385 whites. Knowing the disparity, some whites hoped to create a biracial coalition to combat the Republican influence. Those attempts largely failed, as blacks made it clear they desired to support the Republican Party. Carpetbaggers and scalawags (unionist southerners) led the Republican organization and managed to solidify a black voting bloc.[23]

Black Mississippians started to form their own national identity during the war, as they fought for the Union and gained their freedom. Most blacks expected their emancipation granted them opportunities as equals in white society. Lucy Thurston, a former slave, said as much when she stated that "some niggahs got in their haids de' wuz' equal like the white folks an' they spect they wuz gwine hev' fine homes' an' lib like dere Marsters." Many expected social and economic mobility, especially after rumors floated that the federal government intended to give them "forty acres and a mule." In November 1865 a Freedmen's Bureau agent wrote to his officer that "nearly all of them have heard, that at Christmas, the Government is going to take the planters' lands and other property from them, and give it to the colored people." Joseph Warren, the superintendent of black schools, "spoke of the great eagerness of the blacks to buy or lease land, and have homes of their own." The freedmen also clamored for an education. Although their success was made difficult by rigorous work hours and white resistance, the number of black schools reached fifty by the summer of 1866, with 5,407 students.[24]

Race relations in the state experienced a dramatic shift following the war. Whites continued to expect subservience from the freedmen, but blacks failed to reciprocate. Instead, many blacks tested the limits of their freedom, maintained high expectations, and sought redress if they believed someone usurped their rights. In a telling example, planter Edward Fontaine wrote of an incident that occurred between his family and his hired workers. Fontaine's young son and one of the freedmen's sons, John, ended up in a physical confrontation. Mrs. Fontaine first heard the commotion, rushed outside, and separated the two children. She grabbed John and dragged him to his mother, Fanny, expecting disciplinary action. Fanny blatantly refused to punish her child. Furious, Mrs. Fontaine marched hastily to a nearby cedar tree dragging John behind her, broke off a branch, and whipped him a dozen times around his legs. Upset over the incident, Fanny took her family and headed to Jackson to issue a formal complaint with the Freedmen's Bureau.[25]

The next day, Edward Fontaine traveled to Jackson to take care of some business. He walked into the Freedmen's Bureau office to lodge some grievances about his laborers. Lieutenant Myers, acting provost marshal, welcomed Fontaine and started to write a report based on Fontaine's allegations. When Fontaine mentioned the whipping of the previous day,

Myers interrupted him and informed him that Fanny and her husband had already relayed the incident and that formal charges were pending against Fontaine and his wife. Taken aback, Fontaine informed Myers that "negroes will often tell any sort of lie to accomplish an object." He continued, saying, "This complaint is an infamous lie told by Fanny to justify her coming to Jackson without leave and to prevent you from sending her home." Myers looked up at Fontaine and replied, "Yours sir is a very common accusation made against the colored people: but permit me to say, as far as my experience and observation enable me to judge I have found as much, or even more honor among them, than I have ever found *among the white people of the South*." Myers told Fontaine to expect a heavy fine and a prison sentence for the corporal punishment. Fontaine "only smiled" and left the office.[26]

Although a judge later dismissed the charges, the episode reveals the changing social order within the state. White Mississippians had a difficult time conceiving of a social order in which blacks received equal protection under the law. Emancipation did not change white attitudes toward blacks. For the most part, whites in the state believed emancipation worsened the condition of blacks, and they leveled claims that the freedmen were brazen and ungovernable. Flavellus Nicholson stated flatly that the freedmen "are a lazy set as a general thing—some are inclined to be insolent." Justifications for compulsory labor laws stemmed from the belief that blacks would not work without intense scrutiny and regulation. Traveler John Trowbridge commented that "it seemed impossible for the people of Mississippi . . . to understand the first principle of the free-labor system." He noted that slavery had "rendered labor disreputable" and that white Mississippians "could not conceive of a man devoting himself voluntarily to hard manual toil." As landowners, white Mississippians had the edge in forcing an unfair and unproductive labor system on the freedmen in sharecropping, but the control had its limits.[27]

After emancipation black Mississippians wanted to test their freedom and exercise their rights. With the backing of the Freedmen's Bureau, blacks had some options when entering into labor contracts. Agents often noted that many blacks "would not contract" with southern plantation owners but "are very eager to engage with Northern men" or others they felt they could trust for a fair wage. Some freedmen asserted their freedom when they left their old masters and found new employers. Others acted in a brasher manner. Charles Davenport related an incident in which several freedmen decided to attend an "entertainment" at Memorial Hall in Natchez. "Dey dressed deysef's fit to kill," Davenport later recalled, "an' walked down de aisle an' took seats in de very front." The whites in the audience, including the performers, took offense, stood up, and walked out of the hall, leaving the freedmen alone in the empty building. For blacks in the state, emancipation meant the ability to exercise their liberty as free and independent members of society.[28]

The ability to participate in politics solidified a black national identity. Loyal or Union Leagues started to emerge within the black community and offered the mobilizing mechanism to support the Republican Party. Once Freedmen's Bureau agents explained to blacks the purposes of the voter registration in 1867, blacks embraced their role as electors. Freedman Louis Davis claimed to have voted "heaps of times." William Francis Fitzgerald, a white farmer in Warren County, commented that "in matters of politics the negroes are more enthusiastic than any other race of people, I presume, on the face of the earth; they will stop anything in the world to go to a political meeting or to hear political speeches." Superintendent Joseph Warren noted in a report that blacks sang "patriotic songs" in school, which ultimately led to the arrest of the black teacher who allowed it. Passionate black participation in politics continued for the next several years as they held rallies, political meetings, and supported campaigns.[29]

The November 1867 vote for the purpose of calling a constitutional convention offered blacks the first opportunity to exercise the right of suffrage. When election day came, blacks "thronged the streets" and "crowded and monopolized the side walks." Voter turnout among the freedmen reached 80 percent as they "came into town by squads, platoons and companies." Whites hoped to derail the call for a convention by refusing to vote. Congress required majority showing among the state's electorate to call for a constitutional convention. One newspaper reported that "not a single Southern white man approached [the polls] for the purpose of voting." Due to the high participation among the freedmen, though, a majority of the state's electorate turned out, with 69,739 voting to hold a convention and 6,277 opposing. Ord called for the convention to assemble in Jackson on January 7, 1868, to draft a new state constitution.[30]

Conservative Mississippians called the assemblage the "Black and Tan Convention," because of its racial composition. Ninety-seven delegates showed up for the convention: 79 Republican, 17 conservative, and 1 unidentified in their political persuasion. Of the 97 delegates, only 18 were freedmen, and 23 carpetbaggers. The convention met until May and focused on drafting a new constitution that addressed a myriad of topics, most of which concerned pressing issues in the state such as education, poverty, the collection of debt, black suffrage, and, the most controversial, proscription of former Confederates. Although voters initially rejected the constitution in 1868, Congress and newly elected president Ulysses Grant intervened over concerns of voter fraud and the proscription clause, paving the way for the adoption of the new constitution.[31]

As a whole, the convention expressed a strong unionist sentiment and desire to usher in a new period in the state's history as part of the United States and to rectify past mistakes. President pro tem Alston Mygatt addressed the convention at the outset and rejected the Old South social structure based on slavery that enriched "the few at the expense of the many" and "built up large landed aristocracies." He lamented the "causeless cause" of secession and war and hoped that the "blood of the thousands of lost soldiers" would "cry out against those who signed that treasonable instrument." Later in the convention, Benjamin Orr of Harrison County offered a resolution that completely distanced Mississippi from its past actions. The resolution disavowed the "perverted theory of State rights," rejected the idea and practice of secession because it resulted in "confusion, anarchy, and national destruction," and maintained "that our primary allegiance is due the government of the United States; that the Constitution and laws of the United States are the supreme law of the land."[32]

The new constitution and continued black political participation ensured Republican dominance within the state's political structure. Republicans started to define the state's national identity. Peter Bailey, a carpetbagger, gave a speech outlining the virtues of the Republican Party. He noted that "it was the Democratic party in the South that carried the Southern people into rebellion against their government." Bailey also commented that "whatever a man in the South may have been before the war, whether Whig or Democrat, if he became a rebel he is a Democrat to-day, for all rebels seem to be Democrats now; all secessionists are Democrats; all State sovereignty men are Democrats." For men like Bailey, the Republican Party offered Mississippians the clearest path to rectify its image as an outcast in the Union. Bailey contended that the political faith of the Republican Party was "based on the everlasting truths of the Declaration of Independence." He said that the Republican Party wanted to "keep the controlling powers of the country in the hands of men who never sought by open rebellion . . . to destroy the government." James Alcorn, famous scalawag and candidate for governor in 1870, wanted to "build up in accordance with the spirit of the age, in accordance with the will of the Nation, a party, new to the history of Mississippi—a party, determined, while raising the State from her prostrate position under the foot of power, to erect it, not upon its point, but upon its base—the masses of its citizens."[33]

The political character changed in Mississippi as well, causing great consternation among conservatives. Although most blacks held only local political office, some did serve in the state legislature and even in national offices. Hiram Revels, a black carpetbagger from Ohio, finished an unexpired term in the U.S. Senate starting in 1870, and became the first black senator. In 1874 the state legislature voted Blanche Bruce to serve in the U.S. Senate. John R. Lynch of Adams County served several terms in the House of Representatives, starting in 1873. Black-majority counties throughout the state elected a number of black officials to respected positions. The political landscape transformed dramatically.[34]

Conservatives feared the shifting tides in the state as the Republican Party started to infiltrate and promote adjustments to political and social institutions. One of the major concerns that conservatives had was the alliance between carpetbaggers and freedmen, and social changes promoted by that interaction. W. B. Jones of Natchez explained that "the object of the Radical party who are the white as well as the black negroes of the land endeavor only to bring about social equality, and the plan they are pursuing is to bring down the whites of the south to a level with themselves, by making us as poor as they are." Pastor Samuel Agnew sarcastically declared that with the infusion of northerners into the state, "the negroe is a sacred animal. The Yankees are about negroes like the Egyptians were about cats. Negrophilism is the passion with them."[35]

Albert Morgan, a prominent carpetbagger and radical who settled in Yazoo County, found himself in serious jeopardy when rumors spread shortly after his arrival that the freedmen considered him their friend. Colonel Black, the plantation owner from whom Morgan and his brother rented, approached Morgan on the subject and gently told him that he should make a greater effort to become more popular with "our people." Colonel Black condemned Morgan's treatment of "the nigros on the street" and also his "manner of speech while among them." Mrs. Black defended Morgan, believing that he would not engage in the behavior the colonel outlined, because it was "unbecoming a gentleman." The colonel's chastisement had little effect on Morgan; he continued to work on the plantation and interact with the freedmen. After a few weeks, Black approached Morgan again, this time with fire in his belly. "Well, sir, by G—d, sir, yo' may not understand the effect of youah own example," the colonel began. "It was only a few days ago that I saw you as I passed by Tokeba at work with some nigros repairing a fence. And Mistress Black says that the other day she drove on to Tokeba to see how things wor' going, and, by G—d sir, yo' brother was working at the mill with the nigros." In a huff the colonel continued, "I took yo' for a *gentleman*; yo' are only a *scalawag*." By interacting openly with the freedmen, carpetbaggers challenged the established social order to which white Mississippians adhered.[36]

Some conservative Mississippians resorted to violence after they lost their ability to control the political and social transformations. During the 1868 convention, the Ku Klux Klan made its first appearance in Mississippi. The Klan represented a group of disaffected men intent on resisting radical Reconstruction and preserving white social superiority. Six ex-Confederates founded the Klan in 1866 in Tennessee. The Klan boasted Nathan Bedford Forrest as their Grand Wizard. White Mississippians praised Forrest as a war hero who spent the last few years of the war evading Union forces and inflicting havoc on Union positions throughout Mississippi. Former Confederate soldiers composed a bulk of the Klan's membership and used intimidation and violence to counteract the social and political changes produced by the war's end. Many whites in the state sympathized with the Klan and passively endorsed their methods. Robert Somers, a newspaper reporter from Scotland, commented while touring the state in 1870 that "the power with which the 'Ku-Klux' moved in many parts of the South, the knowledge it displayed of all that was going on, the fidelity with which its secret was kept, and the complacency with which it was regarded by the general community, gave this mysterious body a prominence and importance seldom attained by such illegal and deplorable associations."[37]

One of the first reports of the Klan in the state came from the *Corinth News*, which reported in March 1868 that "some mysterious communications have been sent to individuals, concluding with the fearful admonition—'fail not at your peril.'" Disguised men on horseback rode through the streets during the night, causing "amazement and consternation" among the freedmen, who believed the "great object of the Klan was to wage war upon all Africans, and to show no quarter." Several blacks throughout the state who received visits from these hooded men described the terrifying ordeal. Sylvia Floyd said that "mos' o' de time in de woods, dey would ride through dressed in long white hainty looking robes wid white masks all over deir head an' faces, dey even went up in a [point] at de top ob de head. Dey had big holes cut out fer de eyes." She continued: "Dey sho' wuz scary looking an' mo' so to de colored folks for dey never did know what dey might do next. What dey wuz fer, wuz to keep de colored folks scared up, an to make 'em do what dey wanted 'em too." Sam McAllum remembered one night while at a party several members of the Klan rode up asking for one man in particular. "I don't know'm what he done," McAllum recalled, "dey say he done some'pen bad." The Klan found their man, carried him off into the woods, and "killed him dat very night." Several murders, performed in vicious and animalistic fashion, occurred throughout the state that went uninvestigated or unsolved.[38]

The Klan targeted educators and blacks attending schools in hopes of preventing freedmen from elevating themselves to an equal (or higher) intellectual plane than whites. Major Klan offenses in Monroe and Pontotoc Counties centered on stopping the operation of black schools. In a letter addressed to her sister, Jennie Shaw wrote of the Klan's activities in Monroe County. "[The Ku Klux Klan] have whipt several white men whipt and killed several negroes," she recalled, "they whipt colonel Hugins the superintendent of the free schools nearly to death and every body rejoiced when they heard it for every body hated him he squandered the public money buying organs sofas and fine furniture for the negro schoolhouse in Aberdeen." Despite the Klan's violent actions, Shaw ended her letter saying she was openly "in favor of the KKK." J. E. Robuck, a white citizen of Lafayette County, related an incident in which a lady from "the Northern slums" had opened a school for the freedmen in which she used "high pressure efforts to convince the negroes that they were not only equal to, but far superior to the Southern white people." According to Robuck's account, the schoolteacher "received a written notice to vacate and abscond, otherwise she would positively be 'tarred and feathered.'" She left the schoolhouse immediately "for parts unknown." Maria Waterbury, a teacher from Illinois and part of a larger contingent of reformers, recounted a frightening experience after arriving in Mississippi. They boarded with a carpetbag family and one night received a visit from the Klan. Huddled inside, they could hear the pounding of hooves and the tramping of footsteps outside the house. As the terrified teachers grasped one another in prayer, they waited nervously until the men finally left. They learned later that the Klansmen did not enter the residence, believing the teachers were armed.[39]

Congress eventually passed a series of acts to deal with Klan activities in the South, but open resistance and hostility toward blacks and carpetbaggers remained and intensified. Reporter John Dennett recounted the story of an unnamed man from Boston who moved to Mississippi with the hopes of making a fortune as a planter. Initially he "praised his new neighbors highly" but eventually "became convinced that the people were too much opposed to Northern men for him to stay among them with safety." John Moore of the Freedmen's Bureau reported that "the disposition of the whites towards the colored people has lately undergone a radical change." He said that the "line of demarcation . . . has been deeper drawn" as whites "used every effort to gain political control of the freedmen, in order to defeat the present attempt of Congress to restore unity and harmony." Moore later informed his superiors of the worsening attitudes: "The disposition of whites towards the colored people is very flagrant and attended with any amount of hatred. They persecute them in every way possible and annoy to get them to commit some act then have them arrested and put in prison to gratify their hatred towards them."[40]

As Republicans started to shape Mississippi's place within the Union, white Mississippians refused to bend in their convictions and felt cut off from the direction in which the state headed. As such, they started to cleave to their past identity, both as Confederates and antebellum Americans, despite their initial calls for reconciliation. Members of the state legislature called for the creation of a state monumental association to secure funds to erect a monument to honor their Confederate past. They hoped the appeal for funds, lacking in detail, would flood the government offices in Jackson, because the effort "commends itself most strongly to feelings and sympathies of our people." Another effort to preserve their Confederate identity came from Benjamin Humphreys while he served as governor. Humphreys called for the creation of historical societies throughout the South "to preserve the memorials of the recent sanguinary struggle." He hoped that through the historical societies, "durable records in the form of maps, charts and diagrams of the movements and counter movements of both armies . . ., together with the heroic part acted by our brave people, will be transmitted to posterity, to whom we appeal for the vindication of the truth of history and the rectitude of our cause."[41]

Memorial Day marked one occasion when Mississippians celebrated their fallen dead and worked to preserve their Confederate identity. Emmett Ross, a newspaper editor in Madison County, wrote and published several popular poems to commemorate Memorial Day. In one of his published poems, Ross wrote of the North's desire to prevent the South from remembering the killed Confederate soldiers and the difficulty of reconciliation with the northern states who branded them as rebels. He quipped,

Then why will men the sentence pass
And write the stern decree

That holds it a disloyal act
To raise, in memory
Some marble shaft or granite pile,
Whose towering grandeur will
Commemorate the resting-spot
Of Jackson, Polk and Hill?

Ross responded,

The sordid wretches who proclaim
The South an outlaw set—
With Ku-Klux laws, enforcement acts,
The sword and bayonet—
Were not the men who bravely fought,
And, when the fight was won,
Laid down their arms, and said: "Brave boys,
Your fighting was well done!"

Ross's poem implicates a cruel northern people who he believed had more to be ashamed of with regard to the war than did southerners. His frustrations over the inability of southerners to find their place back into the Union emanates from his verses.[42]

Newspaper editor John Bosworth expressed the difficulties of celebrating the Fourth of July because northerners had "wrested from them, by the strong arm of power, almost every vestige of the liberty for which their forefathers fought and died." He still held to the principles of the Constitution and the Declaration of Independence but claimed that a "crazy crew of demagogues and fanatics" flagrantly violated all the principles contained in those documents. Bosworth claimed that all the accusations leveled against King George III in the Declaration of Independence applied presently to those "leading the strings at Washington." He grieved that the "Fourth of July has ceased to be a day hailed with pleasurable emotions by Southern men," and that all the "bright and glorious memories that once clustered around it have departed." For Bosworth, the implications of Reconstruction meant that the South would no longer truly belong within the Union.[43]

Like Emmett Ross, John Bosworth praised Memorial Day as a time to revere their "Lost Cause." Bosworth praised the women who "will deck the graves of the brave men who fought and fell . . . for a cause now lost—for a country now degraded—for principles now deserted—and for a banner now furled forever." He specifically called upon the "fair women throughout the South" to "pay the last sad tribute of affection to those whom we have 'loved and lost.'" Ross also believed that the women of the South had a duty to maintain the memory of the fallen:

> As long as Southern women live,
> Their self-appointed trust
> Will be this special, hallowed task;
> To guard our soldier's dust.
> No Spartan mother ever met
> Her son upon the shield—
> No Thracian maiden ever wept
> Her lover on the field
> With greater pride and greater pain,
> And true, heroic zeal;
> For human hearts have never felt
> As Southern women feel!

Both men expected southern women to be the vanguards of the Old South and preserve the memory of Confederacy.[44]

J. W. Clapp also charged women to uphold the memory of the Old South and pass it along to future generations. Clapp, speaking to the graduating class at Franklin Female College at Holly Springs, declared that there was "one department or sphere of literary labor to which woman is by nature and circumstances peculiarly adapted, and that is, in ministering to the intellectual wants and appetites of the young." Clapp stated that because of Mississippi's current situation during Reconstruction, "we are bound by every consideration of honor for the dead and of respect for the living to see to it that our children shall not, at school or at home, shape their ideas or acquire their information and impressions from books or other sources of a character calculated to poison their minds and their hearts and teach them lessons of humiliation and shame." He warned that "of this there is much danger, unless these books are made to represent facts as they appear from a Southern stand-point." Clapp persisted in explaining that northern-ers desired for southern children to learn that their fathers fought a dis-honorable war and "thereby incurred the guilt of treason or rebellion." He hoped that the women of the South would teach their children "to think and to feel that they are descended from an illustrious line of ancestry, and that the noblest blood that has ever coursed through American veins has been that that was warmed by Southern suns and throbbed in the hearts of Washington's and Henry's and Jefferson's and Madison's and Marshall's and Lee's and other heroes and statesmen and orators." Clapp wanted to make sure that their posterity "be further taught that this blood has not deteriorated, but that the living and the dead of this generation have shown themselves worthy of their exalted lineage."[45]

In addition to preserving the memory of the war, conservative Mississippians wanted to venerate their Confederate heroes. Those in the state still honored American southerners like George Washington, Thomas Jefferson, etc., as evident in Clapp's speech, but they started to add Confederate leadership into their pantheon of national heroes. In a telling letter following the death of Robert E. Lee, prominent politician Lucius Q. C. Lamar compared Lee with George Washington. In his assessment they both possessed unparalleled qualities worthy of adoration. He stated that "both were slaveholders; both, by inclination as well as inheritance, were planters; both possessed in an eminent degree those qualities which ennoble and invigorate the Southern character; and both were inspired by a heroic devotion to liberty and right." Yet, as his letter continued, Lamar showed how Lee trumped some of the qualities of Washington. Lamar noted that Washington "was born with a love for command, and a yearning after it," whereas for Lee, "self-assertion was a thing unknown." According to Lamar, Washington "wooed glory like a proud, noble, and exacting lover," but Lee "sought not glory; he turned away from her."[46]

Lamar also disagreed with the assertion that Lee's memory should belong to both sections of the country. He reviled the northern states who prevented the South from enjoying "real union, concord, amity, and security from oppression" within the nation. He alleged that the northern states would not bring Robert E. Lee into the "common heritage" of America. Not only that, but he believed southerners "cannot, and ought not to, surrender him to America." Even after five years from the end of the war, Lamar still seethed that Confederate men were "branded as rebels and proscribed as traitors to America." Lamar concluded that Lee "has already taken his place in history; not as an American, but as a Southern patriot and martyr, of whom America was not worthy."[47]

Reconstruction, and in particular the rise of radical Reconstruction, made the process of reconciliation more difficult for white Mississippians. Their initial willingness to admit defeat and anticipate full rights back in the Union never reached fruition, as Congress stepped in and dictated the terms for restoration of rights. For conservative Mississippians, the changes brought about by the emancipation of the slaves, full legal and political rights for the freedmen, and a general social reordering, proved too much to handle. Conservative Mississippians felt they could not belong to a Union that recognized black rights, discredited their act of secession as rebellion or as traitorous, and stripped their Confederate heroes of the franchise.

At the same time, black Mississippians started to build their own identity as Americans. Emancipation brought promises and expectations that blacks worked to secure. When Congress mandated black political participation in the Reconstruction process, the freedmen responded with enthusiasm and vigor. They changed the political structure of the state with their unwavering support for the Republican Party. They held rallies, campaigned for candidates, and attended political meetings. Freedmen greatly influenced the tenor of the state's 1868 constitution and precipitated a statewide shift in political alignments. The rapidly changing social and political landscape appeared to offer the infinite ability to act as full citizens within the United States.

"THY BRIGHT SUN WILL RISE AGAIN"

——— • ———

[Dixie]! thy bright sun will rise again,
Though hidden now beneath the pall of night:
Thy struggles and thy throes are not in vain;
Thy banner still is proud, unstain'd and bright.
Thou hast thy cherished names, all glory crowned,
That bid thee still look upward undismayed;
Thou art to Fame by golden fetters bound,
Which never can be cut by hatred's blade:
Though naked, thou art yet in her bright beams arrayed.[1]

In March 1876 Greene Chandler gave the keynote address at the Republican State Convention and spoke of their recent loss of political control following the controversial 1875 statewide elections. He maintained that the party had an "honored and historic name" that he traced back to the "first party organized in this Country during the administration of Washington." For him, the party, then and at present, "was based on the leading idea that this is a government of the people, for the people, and by the people." Chandler rejected the charges the Democrats leveled that "Republicans have destroyed the rights of the States, consolidated all power at Washington, and are looking to ultimate empire." He also defended the stance of the Republican Party "in taking the negroes by the hand, and proposing to give them the rights enjoyed by ourselves." Chandler believed that the Republican Party still offered the best prospects of ensuring Mississippi's place in the Union as an equal.[2]

Years earlier, when Republicans first gained control of the state government, many hoped that Republican rule would secure Mississippi's place in the Union following their restoration of rights within the federal system. Standing before the state legislature in 1870, Reverend A. C. McDonald offered his view of Mississippi's new national narrative and identity. "Nine years ago, in a misguided moment, under the mad excitement and blind passion of the hour," he proclaimed, "the people of our own and other States resolved to break away from the Federal Union, and enter upon the untried paths of separation. For four years they stumbled upon the dark mountains of rebellion. For near five years more they have wandered in the mazy labyrinths of a reluctant reconstruction." McDonald, though, saw a significant change at that moment. Relieved, he stated, "At length the long agony is over, the suspense ended; the blackened ruins of war have been left behind, the uncertainties of reconstruction are passed, and our people are once more treading in the broad paths of our glorious Union." He cherished the direction of the state toward "universal liberty" and a new sense of national identity resulting from the "merging of the provincial pride of each section of the Union into one national sentiment."[3]

Although a majority of Mississippians shared McDonald's new national identity for the state, conservative Mississippians resisted it. From the beginning of Reconstruction, conservative Mississippians sought to define their place within the Union but struggled to fall in line with the national identity a majority of Americans accepted. Conservative Mississippians felt disconnected from the prevailing national narrative that viewed southerners as treasonous and the Civil War as a conflict focused on preserving the Union (which southerners had rejected) and freeing the slaves. Many whites hoped for swift reconciliation and a restoration of rights antebellum. When the Republican leadership in Congress refused to allow southerners to dictate the terms of Reconstruction, conservative Mississippians continued to rebel, resisting Republican rule because it rejected their Confederate identity, stripped them of the old social order, and branded ex-Confederates as traitors and rebels to the United States.

The middle of the 1870s witnessed a concerted effort among conservative Mississippians to redeem their state from Republican rule and alter the narrative of their national identity. Using intimidation and violence, conservatives managed to hamper Republican voting in the 1875 election and send a strong message to scare blacks from the polls in the future. In addition, conservatives started to reconcile their national identity by successfully labeling carpetbaggers and blacks as the out-group rather than northerners wholesale. Playing on racial sentiment still prevalent throughout the nation, conservatives argued that black political participation and corrupt carpetbaggers had hijacked Reconstruction and prevented a true healing of the sections. By labeling the Republican base with undesirable characteristics, conservatives managed to steer the state's national identity in a direction that allowed them to venerate their Confederate and American past and regard the Civil War as a brothers' conflict, not a treasonous act. During the final years of Reconstruction, conservatives started to produce their Lost Cause legend that spoke not only to their justifications for secession and reasons for their loss during the Civil War, but to their place within the nation's historical narrative and identity.[4]

In 1872 William Henry Sparks completed a history of the country, especially the South, at the behest of William Sharkey and other prominent southerners. Having spent a majority of his adulthood in Louisiana and Mississippi, Sparks interspersed his personal history within the context of a larger national narrative. Sparks commented on the contemporary sectional attitudes that plagued the country. Like most white Mississippians at the time, Sparks blamed the North for the present state of feelings during Reconstruction. "Every tie that once united the descendants of the Norman with those of the Saxon is broken," Sparks explained. "They are two in interest, two in feeling, two in blood, and two in hatred. For a time they may dwell together, but not in union; for they have nothing in common but hatred." Reflecting over the nation's history, Sparks stated, "It is painful to look back fifty years and contrast the harmony then pervading every class of every section with the discord and bitterness of hate which substitutes it to day." He said that "then, the national airs of 'Hail Columbia' and 'Yankee Doodle' thrilled home to the heart of every American, [but] to-day, they are only heard in one half of the Union to be cursed and execrated." Sparks believed that "this hatred, this cursed memory of oppressive wrong will live on." He also warned that "we will never forgive, and we will wait; for when the opportunity shall come, as come it will, we will avenge the damning wrong."[5]

After several years of radical Reconstruction, conservatives hoped to force the issue of redemption from Republican rule. They knew that redemption could take place only if the black voting ceased to exist, since the freedmen overwhelmingly supported the Republican Party. After receiving the right to vote, blacks engaged in political affairs with regularity and zeal. Edward Fontaine commented on the frequency of black political meetings and the enthusiasm they generated in the black community. Like many whites, he worried that blacks used the opportunity to drill and arm themselves for a possible race war. He commented extensively in a journal entry in 1874 about the political situation at that time and his fears of an impending conflict. He noted that blacks "all stick together as a race, and

are compactly united against the whites. . . . They are political enemies."
Fontaine believed black attitudes against whites were "becoming daily more
inimical and dangerous." He predicted that on the current course, the "fate
of the negroes in the Southern States will be sealed. They will be extermi-
nated and driven from the country suddenly, or slowly." The present political state created a stark racial divide that Fontaine and other conservatives
believed was unsustainable.[6]

Fontaine did make an observation that conservatives would finally use
to redeem the state from Republican rule: conservatives could use the racial
divide to their advantage. Fontaine compared the current situation in the
South to that of Jamaica's Baptist War (1831) in which a massive slave uprising sparked a strong reaction by British forces. He said that blacks in the
state "imagine they are the most numerous, and powerful. They see here in
some counties that they outnumber the Whites, as they did on that Island."
However, Fontaine commented that those slaves on Jamaica, just like the
blacks in the United States, failed to realize the vast number of whites that
would work to suppress their rebellion. "The negroes of Jamaica counted
a few thousand white people settled among several hundred thousand
blacks," Fontaine explained. "They forgot or knew as little of the scores of
millions of Whites in the vast British Empire, as these 4,000,000 of negroes
in the South do of the 36,000,000 of Whites in the United States." He confi-
dently stated that "the white people want the valuable cotton, sugar, and rice
lands of the fruitful South, which these restless freedmen are making less
valuable year after year." Fontaine assumed that if confronted with choosing between whites or blacks in the South, the rest of the nation would side
with white southerners.[7]

Beginning in 1874, conservatives planned to redeem their state from
Republican rule and emphasized the need for white solidarity. Previous
efforts to thwart the Republican machine failed. Blacks remained loyal to
the Republican Party despite efforts to form a coalition and chip away at the
Republican base. Due to the success of the Republican Party, most of the
whites in the state started to gravitate toward the Democrats. W. H. McRaven commented, "'Democracy' means, just now—all opposed to the Republican National Administration—viz. old line Whigs—Secessionists—States
Rights & the old Democrats." With all the political upheaval the Civil War
and the initial years of Reconstruction caused, the political lines started to
coalesce along racial lines. Traveler Charles Nordhoff noted in 1875 that two
political factions aiming "to create and maintain excitement, bitterness, sus-
picions, fears, and hatred" stood poised to annihilate the other. "On the one

side stands an unscrupulous and determined band of Democratic politicians of the worst kind," Nordhoff commented, "who, in newspapers and by their daily conversations, excite the white Democrats who listen to them to unreasoning and unreasonable fury, and at the same time alarm the timid negroes and bind them together." Uniformly critical, Nordhoff described the "equally unscrupulous band of Republican politicians, with Governor [Adelbert] Ames at their head, who have 'captured' the colored vote, and mean to hold power and plunder by its means."[8]

In the Warren County elections in 1874, Democrats used coercive means to oust much of the Republican leadership, a strategy they adopted on a larger scale in the next year's statewide elections. Conservatives used violence and intimidation to prevent or persuade carpetbaggers, scalawags, and freedmen to stay home on the day of the election. Addressing the state legislature following the election results, Adelbert Ames accused conservatives in Warren County of "appealing to the prejudices of their class, and urging on a war of races, for political purposes." He warned that the "insurrection has its sympathizers and supporters in other parts of the State," and that "they have deliberately and knowingly entered upon this work of revolution." He further prophesied that "one race of our people will be deprived of their rights and remanded back to as unfortunate a condition as they have ever known, or else be compelled to wander forth seeking freedom rather than homes, as is now the case with many of their race in other States." Ames worried that the Democratic strategy, based on white-line voting and black suppression, would significantly degrade the rights of blacks who had "struggle[d] for personal liberty and personal security."[9]

As the 1875 statewide elections approached, conservatives hoped to convince whites to vote the Democratic ticket. When Charles Nordhoff asked one conservative how they intended to align all the whites into one voting bloc, he responded without hesitation, "We'll make it too damned hot for them to stay out." In many instances conservatives informed carpetbaggers and scalawags that the political winds in the state would shift, and if they wanted to retain their relevancy, then they needed to comply. In addition to white-line voting, conservatives committed several acts of voter fraud. In some instances they hijacked Republican ballots, in others they stuffed ballot boxes with Democratic tickets. Others reported having their tickets changed from Republican to Democrat after they cast their votes.[10]

Conservatives also planned to scare blacks away from the polls. Carpetbagger Henry Warren said that "from the outset it was apparent that the Democrats of the County were taking an unusual interest in the campaign."

He said that the Democrats held meetings "at which inflammatory speeches were made." In addition, a "military campaign was organized, called the red-shirt cavalry." Warren explained that the Red Shirts "were riding about the County at night, shooting up the County, so to speak, threatening and intimidating the colored voters in every way possible." Aurelius Parker of Amite County claimed that several freedmen in the area received nighttime visits from whites who threatened to kill them if they registered to vote. J. L. Edmonds of Clay County, a freedman, actively campaigned during the fall of 1875, until five white men with pistols surrounded him in West Point. One of the white men, whom Edmonds recognized, told him "to stop and have no more to do with it" or he would need to put on his "burying clothes." Edmonds testified that the Democrats "at the meetings, on the stumps and at the school-houses, around the various parts of the county, they said they would carry the county or kill every nigger; they would carry it if they had to wade in blood." In Grenada County, on the day before the election, white Democrats organized a procession through the streets. During the parade they dressed like devils and carried empty coffins. On one wagon they built a large platform on which stood a tar-filled cauldron above a bonfire. Several "demons" danced around the cauldron, next to which sat a restrained black man.[11]

Several other incidents occurred during the fall of 1875, including riots in which conservatives disbanded Republican meetings and gatherings with gunfire. J. W. Lee attended several Republican meetings and later testified that Democrats often infiltrated the gatherings and induced the participants to stop. The freedmen used drums to applaud the speakers, and Lee recalled that in such instances a white man in the front would stand up, with a pistol in his hand leveled at the drummer's head, and yell out, "'Stop that; you cannot beat that drum here. This is a white man's country, and we don't allow it.'" Two major riots ensued in Yazoo and Hinds Counties where Republican gatherings ended in gunfire and dispersion at the hands of armed whites. By the day of the election, November 2, 1875, many of the freedmen who normally voted remained at home, while those who ventured to cast their ballot met stiff resistance at the polling station.[12]

The effectively executed Mississippi Plan resulted in Democratic control of the state legislature and eventually the governorship. The final tallies reveal startling irregularities from two years earlier when Mississippians voted for similar public offices. For instance, in 1873 the citizens of Claiborne County voted for the Republican candidate for treasurer with 97 percent of the vote, but in 1875 the majority went to the Democratic candidate with 68 percent. In 1873 Kemper County pledged 61 percent of their votes to the Republican candidate for treasurer, while in the next election the Democrat received 76 percent. The most dramatic example came from Yazoo County, a Republican stronghold, which polled 86 percent (2,427 votes) for the Republican candidate in 1873 yet drew only seven votes for the party in 1875. The statewide totals compared to the 1873 election cycle showed that Republicans experienced a 4 percent decrease in the number of votes obtained. The Democrats, however, experienced a 107 percent increase from the previous election.[13]

Once in power, the Democrats quickly worked to oust the carpetbag governor, Adelbert Ames. They presented twenty-three articles of impeachment against him for fraud and political abuse. The investigative committee produced pages of alleged incidents when Ames failed to fulfill the oath of his office to protect the state constitution and enact his duties as governor. Ames wrote to the House of Representatives in March 1876 and indicated that "if the Articles of Impeachment presented against me were not pending, and the proceedings were dismissed, I should feel at liberty to carry out my desire, and purpose of resignation." The House acquiesced in his request and ultimately dropped the charges. The legislature appointed John Stone, president pro tempore of the state senate, as governor. Democrats would continue to dominate the governor's office until 1992.[14]

A federal congressional investigation launched in 1876 at the behest of Ames sought to verify the validity of the previous year's election in Mississippi. Conservatives used the investigation to mask their brutal and fraudulent tactics and restore their social image and national perception. Conducting several interviews and visits to the state, the committee heard testimony from participants in the campaign and eyewitnesses to particular events. Although a majority of the committee members deemed the election in Mississippi fraudulent, President Grant's unwillingness to intervene halted any federal involvement beyond the investigation. During the interrogations, conservatives did not admit their guilt in intimidating, beating, and killing black voters but took the opportunity to defend their actions and create a positive self-concept. Hints of Mississippi's Lost Cause emerge in many of the testimonies, as conservatives tried to rewrite the narrative of Reconstruction and even Mississippi's antebellum history.[15]

Several of those who testified derided the carpetbaggers and Republican leaders who they claimed defiled the state's political structure. In his testimony, Lex Brame of Clay County accused most of the white Republican leaders in the state of corruption based on their desire for political tyranny.

Brame claimed that several of the leaders had indictments against them for abuse of office, bribery, and thievery. Prominent Jackson newspaper editor Ethelbert Barksdale testified that many of the freedmen had grown weary of the unending promises of Republican leaders, because they failed to deliver on their claims. Reuben Davis of Monroe County accused Republicans of controlling the black vote by telling them that if Democrats came to power, they would reinstitute slavery, disfranchise blacks, and would no longer allow them to sit on juries. Not only that, but according to Davis, Republicans purportedly told freedmen that electing Democrats to office would result in Democrats casting spells and charms on the freedmen that "would fill them with lizards and scorpions and snakes, and bring diseases upon them, so that they would die." Freedman J. R. Strother commented in his testimony that Democrats informed him that "they were not going to allow [blacks] to be elected." Strother said they told him "that it was the 'carpet-baggers' they hated, and that they hadn't anything against me personally only that I belonged to the republican party." Many conservatives who testified reviled the scalawags who came to power through their involvement with the Republican Party. Davis commented that he "never really thought that the carpet-bagger was as bad a man as the scalawags" because the carpetbagger was generally honest, while the scalawag had "universally sold himself to the party for the sake of plunder." In most cases, conservatives spoke of white Republican leaders in unflattering terms and leveled accusations against them as corrupt and manipulative.[16]

Conservatives did not expend all their vitriol on Republican leaders but attacked the freedmen as the real problem. Reuben Davis summarized the feelings of many conservatives in his testimony. "I think that the negro is by nature dishonest," Davis reasoned. "I think the negro by nature destitute of all ideas of virtue, and I think the negro is capable of being induced to commit any crime whatever, however violent, especially if he was encouraged by bad white men." Davis concluded, "I think all efforts at the civilization of the negro, and in putting him on an equality in point of civilization and culture with the white man, will be as great a failure in this country as they have been in other parts of the world." Thomas Walton relayed the sentiments of many conservatives when the committee asked why whites did not want the freedmen to control the political affairs of the state. "One reason is because the negroes are negroes, and another is because the negroes are ignorant and the white people are more intelligent," Walton stated, "and another reason is that nearly all the property [in Leflore County] is in the hands of the white people; and still another reason is that the negroes, when they get the power in their hands, are disposed to monopolize everything themselves." Walton oriented his comments to reflect as negatively as possible on the black population.[17]

When the investigators brought up the topic of voter fraud, many conservatives blamed the freedmen. Joseph Billups of Lowndes County claimed that three of the freedmen on his plantation "did not vote because they were intimidated from voting." When the investigator asked by whom, Billups replied that black Republicans told his laborers that "if they voted the democratic ticket they would be killed . . . that their lives would be in danger if they did vote." William Montgomery of Hinds County testified that many of the freedmen believed "they will receive bodily harm from their own race" if they attempted to vote for a Democrat. Montgomery claimed that several freedmen voted the Democratic ticket when they were able to do so outside the presence of Republicans. John Ellis of Copiah County said he witnessed "some of the leading freedmen, republican freedmen, taking tickets out of the hands of the negroes that wanted to vote the democratic ticket and tearing their tickets up, right before their faces—taking them right out of their hands and tearing them up and giving them other tickets—republican tickets." According to conservatives, the freedmen committed voter fraud in the election by preventing blacks from voting for the Democratic candidates.[18]

Conservatives used the congressional investigation as an opportunity to improve their national image and create a positive group concept. Several of those interviewed sought reconciliation and a reinforcement of their American identity by disavowing any notion that Confederate or rebel influences still existed in the state. Near the end of his testimony, Reuben Davis stated, "I have not to-day one iota of prejudice for any man in this Union. . . . I am to-day as devoted to this entire country as any man in it, and I would make as many sacrifices to-day for the good of the whole country as anybody to bring about harmony between the North and the South." To better illustrate his sincerity, Davis explained, "We thought we were right in the South during the war, and maintained the conflict just as long as we could, and when the war was over we gave up." Despite the massive war that came at a tremendous cost for both sections, Davis "saw no reason why there should ever be a quarrel afterward between the different sections of the Union." He believed that all white southerners were dedicated to making the United States the "greatest and grandest Government upon the face of the earth."[19]

J.A.P. Campbell of Madison County, who sympathized with the freedmen, offered similar convictions. Campbell claimed that "after the flag of the Confederate government was struck the mass of the white people of the South felt that they had no other government than the Government of the United States, and transferred cheerfully their allegiance, I think, (certainly I did myself, after that flag was furled forever,) to the United States." He contended that after the war, the people of the South hoped "to govern themselves according to American ideas, as they had always done," but quickly found themselves "lorded over by little military men with shoulder straps and epaulettes . . . and through parties that sprang out of that state of things, composed mainly of negroes." Campbell suggested that the freedmen, not the conservative elements, prevented sectional harmony within the state.[20]

Despite the testimony of conservatives who hoped to construct a positive national image, the Senate report included several pieces of evidence that showed how conservatives really felt about the act of secession and the subsequent rebellion, and how they viewed northerners. In a section titled "Opinions of New England," the committee included snippets from conservative newspapers that expressed their true feelings toward northerners. One item from an Iuka newspaper included a passage that read:

> The southern people will never follow the crazy God-and-morality, negro-worshiping, spoon-stealing, white-man-hating, outside-of-the-Constitution-standing, black-and-white-blood-mixing, women-crowing, baby-strangling, c-e-o-w-pronouncing, hell-deserving, New-England-Yankee-clock-peddling, chicken-stealing, box-ankled, bandy-shanked, round-shouldered, hypercritical, canting, psalm-singing, cowardly, cut-throat, slandering, vulgar, slimy-mouthed, onion-eating, whisky-drinking, sausage-stuffing scoundrels.

In addition to various other passages, the committee included one, lifted from the *Panola Star*, to summarize the hopes of conservatives in the state. It began, "The northern vagabonds which infest our land will ere long be seen skulking back to the place from where they came—that lovely country of hickory hams and wooden nutmegs—accompanied by a few southern renegades who have rendered themselves extremely odious to former friends by aiding and abetting in their villainy." The editorial ended with a snarky farewell:

> And when these boot-licks of tyranny sneak back, carpet-bag in hand, and think of the ghost of old John Brown marching on, we ask them to think of us as a people—

What hates the Cotton Mather and the Roger Williams stock,
That dirty pile of hell's manure first dumped on Plymouth Rock.

The Senate report contained several other examples of conservative feeling that appeared less than conciliatory to the northern section or even contrite for the act of secession and war.[21]

The congressional investigation into the 1875 election concluded without any sanctions or enforceable measures that would nullify the results. Weariness over Reconstruction contributed to the lack of action on the part of the federal government as well as political considerations. Mississippi congressman John R. Lynch stated that President Ulysses Grant decided not to intervene in the state election due to pressure from Ohio political operatives who warned it might cost Republicans votes in their state. Lynch pressed Grant on the issue, and Grant responded, "If I had believed that any effort on my part would have saved Mississippi I would have made it, even if I had been convinced that it would have resulted in the loss of Ohio to the Republicans." Knowing the realities in Mississippi, Grant conceded, "I was satisfied then, as I am now, that Mississippi could not have been saved to the party in any event and I wanted to avoid the responsibility of the loss of Ohio, in addition." Although the Senate investigation produced insurmountable evidence of voter fraud, intimidation, and violence, northerners generally felt little outrage or need to challenge the result. The disputed 1876 presidential election and its outcome also ensured the Democratic success in the state would stand.[22]

For redeemers, the only way to restore the state in totality was to eliminate black political participation, thus dismantling a major component of black national identity. Black voter turnout started to decrease following redemption—it dropped down to only 16 percent in the 1882 election from a high of over 80 percent prior to 1875. Redeemers knew that recently ratified constitutional amendments prevented outright disfranchisement, but they also banked on national white-supremacist attitudes to help them attain their objective. Agrarians seeking agricultural reform called for a constitutional convention in the 1880s. Poor harvests, falling prices, and a general decline in agriculture brought farmers together under the Greenback Party. Their hope for reform largely centered on disfranchising blacks to propel their political aspirants into serious contention with the Democrats by limiting the number of Republican votes. Governor John Stone signed off on the proposed convention and ordered elections for July 1890.[23]

The constitutional convention met in August 1890, and the delegates gathered in Jackson. A majority of the convention delegates sought to disfranchise blacks to ensure white political dominance. In his opening remarks, convention president Judge Solomon S. Calhoon stated that the "fact remains that there exists here in this State two distinct and opposite types of mankind," which he believed resulted in political disunity, corruption, and power-grabbing. Using the same justifications as conservatives in the aftermath of the 1875 political campaign, Calhoon charged that for "twenty-five long years" white Mississippians had sought for "strictly homologous political relations between those races . . . [but] have failed." He blamed the lack of political homogeneity on the "law of God" and a "principle of human nature." He argued that when "any of the five distinct races encounter the other in the matter of government, that from the instinct implanted in its nature, it desires to be in the ascendancy." According to Calhoon, and echoed in sentiment by many of the delegates, blacks caused political ruptures, produced disharmony and violence in the state, and, with regard to any issue, "one finds them massed on one side to the other whenever it comes to any matter of Government policy." The convention members suggested that the only solution for a peaceful existence between the races was to ensure that political power rested in the hands of whites.[24]

During the convention, the one committee under the most scrutiny was the Franchise Committee. Composed of thirty-five members, the Elective Franchise, Apportionment and Elections Committee proposed measures that aimed to limit black political participation by imposing a two-dollar poll tax and a requirement that each elector had "to read any section of the Constitution of this state; or he shall be able to understand the same when read to him, or give a reasonable interpretation thereof." While not specifically targeting blacks, and thus not technically violating the 14th and 15th Amendments of the Constitution, the provisions made it possible for whites to deny blacks voting privileges by taking advantage of the economic disparity and limited reading skills of most blacks. Those who could meet the qualifying provisions still had to provide a "reasonable interpretation" of the state constitution that whites could easily declare unsatisfactory and thereby deny the individual the right to vote.[25]

To the dismay of black leaders throughout the country, the convention's only black member, Isaiah Montgomery, supported the new franchise laws. According to his estimation, the new laws would disfranchise 123,334 blacks out of a total of 189,890, leaving a black voting force of only 66,550 to a white voting bloc of 107,001, despite a black majority constituting 55 percent of the state's population. In a speech given to the convention,

Montgomery acknowledged "the fearful sacrifice laid upon the burning altar of liberty" but justified his support as an effort "to restore confidence, the great missing link between the two races, to restore honesty and purity to the ballot-box and to confer the great boon of political liberty upon the Commonwealth of Mississippi." Montgomery directed a pointed request at the convention, though, and asked that "the enlightened sentiment of this great State as voiced from the hustings, from the public presses, from the lecture platforms and from the pulpit, shall unite in the determination that the great question shall be settled upon the enduring basis of Truth, Justice, and Equality, that the race problem shall become a thing of the past and cease to vex and alarm the public mind; that the two great races shall peaceably travel side by side, each mutually assisting the other mount higher and higher on a scale of human progress." In exchange for his acquiescence on voting rights, Montgomery hoped to see tangible improvement in race relations in the state.[26]

Montgomery's support of the Franchise Committee's conclusions reflected the accommodationist impulse among several prominent African American leaders in the South at the time, especially Booker T. Washington, who was a friend of Montgomery. It also signaled a transition in the attitudes of black Americans who felt the full potential offered in Reconstruction policies failed to materialize. Redemption stripped away blacks' national identity and removed hopes of ever gaining an equal place within white society. By the end of the century, black leaders decided to pursue other options that could, in the future, improve race relations and fulfill the hopes of equality inspired by emancipation. Washington argued that blacks could achieve a place in white society not through "agitation of questions of social equality," but by "severe and constant struggle rather than artificial forcing." He believed race relations and securing future political rights would come in time as whites and blacks worked together for "mutual progress."[27]

Despite the prevalence of the accommodationist attitudes, Montgomery still received a fair amount of criticism from both contemporaries and future generations, as black political participation decreased in Mississippi. Frederick Douglass charged that Montgomery's support of disfranchisement equaled "disaster to the race" and John R. Lynch, a little more composed, called Montgomery's decision a "disappointment." Others declared Montgomery a Judas. Reactions within Mound Bayou, Montgomery's plantation, remained mixed, with some feeling betrayed and others applauding his statesmanship. Regardless of support or disdain from black leaders,

Montgomery's estimation that the law would disfranchise over 100,000 proved nearly accurate. Black voter registration declined dramatically in black-majority counties.[28]

In addition to disfranchisement, the convention delegates codified segregation based on the already unwritten practice of black exclusion and separation in the public sphere. The new era of Jim Crow, although largely in place prior to the 1890 constitution, ushered in social, political, economic, and judicial practices that reinforced white supremacy. In nearly all matters of life, blacks faced segregation and discrimination. Black schools in the state received only a fraction of the funding of white schools. Blacks charged with crimes did not have the benefit of a trial and often faced lynch mobs. Whites refused to sell land to or to do business with blacks. A code of racial etiquette permeated society, one that required unbending respect toward whites. The stark division in society between whites and blacks formed a barrier between two separate worlds that occupied a shared space.[29]

By the end of the decade, conservatives managed to wrest political control away from Republicans. While redeemers had not completely restored their national image, they had managed to change the narrative of Reconstruction and even secession. Using blacks, rather than the North, as the out-group, redeemers started to modify the perception of the state as one willing to reconcile any lingering sectional hostility. As the century ended, the Spanish-American War swelled American patriotism. Southerners and northerners fought side by side in a brief but successful war. At the same time, Mississippians started to reconstruct their history and national identity by solidifying the Lost Cause legend that managed to celebrate an American and Confederate identity as something compatible and not mutually exclusive. Lost Cause writers left a legacy for their posterity that distorted the act of secession and the Civil War as patriotic and very much American. Instead of vilifying northerners, they decided to vilify blacks and play on the racial stereotypes prevalent in American society at the time.

"LONG AS LIFE SHALL LAST"

—— • ——

The sordid wretches who proclaim
The South an outlawed set—
With Ku-Klux laws, enforcement acts,
The sword and bayonet—
Were not the men who bravely fought,
And, when the fight was won,
Laid down their arms, and said: 'Brave boys,
Your fighting was well done!'"...
Thanks be to God! they cannot still
The throbbings of the heart;
They cannot blot from out our souls,
Or tear from memory's chart
The monuments we've builded there,
Which, long as life shall last,
Will rise above the towering stones,
Mementos of the past.[1]

In December of 1889, Greene Chandler spoke at a memorial service in Corinth to honor the recent passing of Jefferson Davis. Although Chandler previously disavowed secession and the Confederacy, he started by saying that "no man in all our history has been more misconstrued and misrepresented by friends and foes alike." Chandler criticized "Union men" who labeled Davis an "extreme secessionist," as well as southerners who "would make him the scapegoat for troubles and losses" during the Civil War. Chandler, like many southerners, compared Davis to Washington: "[Davis] believed in the right of the States to withdraw from the Union, as Washington believed in the right and duty of the colonists to sever their connection with the mother country." Rather than paint a picture of the former Confederate president as a southern demagogue, Chandler claimed that "the name and fame of Jefferson Davis are the common heritage of the American people." Chandler believed that the legacy of Jefferson Davis belonged to America as a whole, not just to those that seceded from the Union. Davis embodied qualities that defined other great Americans.[2]

Following redemption, white Mississippians rectified their national image to convey a positive group construct through their Lost Cause legend-making. Whites within the state wanted to reconcile with the northern states and also desired to preserve their southern/Confederate heritage as something positive and worthy to pass down to future generations. Lost Cause writings that emerged around the turn of the century reflected a positive Confederate American identity that liberated the South from any treasonous actions while still retaining a strong national identity. In their writing, Mississippians defended the actions of secession and the Civil War as honorable and American. At the same time, and more importantly, they faulted the period of radical Reconstruction as the culprit to explain any lingering negative impressions about the state and its people and used blacks as the scapegoat. In much of the Lost Cause historical narratives, conservatives wrote specifically to future generations to explain and justify the actions of secession, the reasons why their "revolution" during the Civil War failed, and how northerners ruthlessly tyrannized the state during Reconstruction. They justified white supremacy as a necessary measure to ensure peace and tranquility in the future, and often cited the failure of racial amalgamation during Reconstruction as their primary example. By preserving the past in a very deliberate manner, in rewriting their history to maintain a positive social construct, usually at the expense of blacks, white Mississippians managed to reconcile their badly stained image as traitors and rebels while creating a lasting national identity that venerated their lost cause.[3]

Confederates worried about how history would judge them even as they fought in the Civil War. In 1864 William Pitt Chambers wondered "what posterity will think of this war after the last spark of Southern resistance is extinguished in blood." Having survived the harrowing siege of Vicksburg, Chambers pondered the legacy of the war. "Why such wholesale destruction of life and property? Why such rivers of undying hatred?" he asked. "What induced thirty millions of the human race living under the same government, all speaking the same language and having a common origin, to engage in such an unholy strife?" Chambers thought specifically about the outcome of the war in the South where "the wheels of social progress are stopped, religion is retarded and the arts and sciences are laid away and

covered with dust; forgotten are the amenities and all that elevates, ennobles
and adorns." Chambers worried about the prospects of losing the war and
predicted that "nominal freedom will come to some four or five millions
of an inferior race, who will probably be invested with the right of suffrage
without intelligence to use it, thus affording to the world the most conspic-
uous example in all its history—that republican governments are a failure."
Chambers believed that history would not be kind to southerners who had
brought the carnage upon the nation and allowed for the potential collapse
of America's republican government.[4]

In their historical writing, conservatives paid homage to the Old South as
the pinnacle of southern (and even American) greatness. Dunbar Rowland,
writing for the Mississippi Historical Society in 1900, stated that from "1817
to 1861 Mississippi was a garden for the cultivation of all that was grand
in oratory, true in science, sublime and beautiful in poetry and sentiment
and enlightened and profound in law and statesmanship. It was a land of
brave men, fair women and eloquent statesmen." Others endorsed similar
characterizations, including Belle Kearney, daughter of a plantation owner.
She claimed that prior to the Civil War, "The South was in its glory. It was
rich and very proud. Its wealth consisted of slaves and plantations. Its pride
was masterful from a consciousness of power." Horace Fulkerson, an author
and mercantilist, wrote that those who settled the South during the colonial
period came from the "descendants of the very flower of the chivalry of
Europe; of men and women who had braved every danger in the defence of
their religious scruples and political liberties." He declared that these men
and women had flowing in their veins the "blood of the English cavaliers of
Maryland, and Virginia, of the Scotch Irish of North and South Carolina, of
the Hugenots [*sic*] of South Carolina, and of a mixture of all in Georgia." In
his account they had sacrificed all they had in their native land, "had quit-
ted their pleasant homes in the most highly civilized portions of Europe to
dwell in the wilderness solitudes of the New World." Historians of the state
argued their ancestors came from the most prominent stock that Europe
had to offer and that they brought with them their virtuous character.[5]

State history writers frequently commented that the state's character
and glory relied heavily on the "simple" and "homogeneous" social structure composed of the great planters, the merchant class, and the yeomanry.
Describing the antebellum social order, white Mississippians extolled the
role of the planter class as purveyors of civility, genteel society, and progres-
sivism. "The life of the great landowners and slaveholders resembled that
of the old feudal lords," Belle Kearney commented. "Generally, those of this

class served in the legislatures, studied law, medicine, theology; conducted
extensive mercantile enterprises and controlled their private finances,—
seeking recreation in hunting, traveling, entertaining, and in the cultivation of the elegant pursuits that most pleased their particular turn of mind."
Dunbar Rowland depicted the planter as scholarly, with a "passionate fond-
ness for statecraft, oratory and politics." Frank Montgomery of Adams
County wrote that "the highest ambition of all men in the south at that
time, so far as occupation was concerned, was to be a planter, and to spend
the most if not all his time on his plantation." Montgomery illustrated the
typical Old South planter as "a proud man, proud of his wife and children,
proud of his plantation and slaves, proud of his stainless honor, and ready
to exact or give satisfaction for wrongs fancied or real, suffered or done."
Equally virtuous, in the eyes of Montgomery, were the plantation women,
who "were surrounded by refinements and luxury" and participated in "a
time-honored social routine from which they seldom varied; a decorous
exchange of visits, elaborate dinings and other interchanges of dignified
courtesies." Belle Kearney mourned that she was "just two months and six
days too late [. . .] to be a Constitutional slaveholder."[6]

The authors of Lost Cause literature blamed northerners for the demise
of the Old South social structure and for waging an unconstitutional war
of aggression against the South. When the sectional conflict flared in 1850,
Mississippians abhorred terms such as "secessionist" and "disunionist." In
their historical writings, Mississippians did the same, because to call oneself
a secessionist would be an admission that the South started the war. They
declared their unwavering allegiance to the United States on the eve of secession and assumed a role as aggrieved victims of northern machinations.
Referring to the right of secession, Reuben Davis, a lawyer from Aberdeen,
wrote, "From the first, I doubted the correctness of this theory, and universally maintained that secession would prove to be only another name for
bloody revolution." He stated, "I was proud of my citizenship of this grand
Republic, and sorrowed over the possibility of disruption." Annie Harper of
Adams County wrote her history for her daughter at the close of Reconstruction. She claimed that on the eve of the Civil War she continued to maintain
a "Reverence for the United States government [which] was instilled into my
being with the Westminster catechism and when my individuality asserted
itself, I found my self as thoroughly orthodox in matters of church & state,
as tho' I had been reared on Plymouth Rock." Such commentary suggests
that white Mississippians felt happy and content in the United States and had
done little to aggravate the conditions that brought about war.[7]

In order to maintain a positive social identity, many of those who wrote about secession usually devoted an inordinate amount of time justifying the act and portraying it as both a last resort and a noble pursuit. Most did not speak specifically about the actual steps toward secession, since doing so would admit the state's culpability in causing the resulting war. Much of the emphasis on secession centered on how northern actions forced the South to make the decision. Frank Montgomery recalled that "until the John Brown raid I had never for a moment lost my loyalty to the union, but after that I became a secessionist [because of] the manner in which his death was received in the north, for he was looked upon as a martyr to the cause of freedom and was almost deified by many." David Holt, son of a wealthy planter, wrote that following Brown's raid, northerners "under a false idea of Christianity, and with envy, hatred, and malice, shook the red flag of war in the face of the Southerner." Subsequently, Holt explained, the presidential election of the following year pushed many in the state to support secession, because Lincoln represented "the extreme abolition sentiment of the north." Annie Harper argued that Lincoln hated the South, was "opposed to her vital interest," and made it so that southerners were "no longer equal participants in a government which they had had a full share in forming." Instead, she asserted that northerners only wanted "cowardly submission to a ruler elected for no purpose but to oppress [southerners]."[8]

Those writing long after the close of events emphasized how northerners had violated constitutional principles and forced the issue of secession on a patriotic South. Harper maintained that with the election of Abraham Lincoln to the presidency, "the government had failed its original purpose of affording equal rights to all, and we were no longer the *United* states." According to Reuben Davis, the North's desire to abolish slavery through the guise of the federal system violated the "voluntary compact which alone held the States together, and therefore the Southern States were released from bonds already broken on the other side, and had the right to withdraw peacefully from the Union." To highlight the idea of northern aggression, Davis argued that even though the North provided a path for the southern states to leave the Union, their true intentions were manifested when they waged "a war of invasion and conquest." Davis said that southerners had no option except to respond with "a war for the defense of our homes and the maintenance of our constitutional rights." J. E. Robuck closed his memoir confident that "the impartial pen of the historian will not let principles and patriotism of those who exerted themselves for the independence of the South suffer in contrast with those who took the opposite side. And then it will be written that SECESSION WAS NOT REBELLION."[9]

Lost Cause historians and memoirists still maintained the belief in the superiority of the Confederate soldier over his counterparts but had to account for reasons behind an ultimate military defeat. The most popular explanation rested with the sheer vastness of the Union army. Referring to Confederate soldiers, Annie Harper commented, "We deemed them invincible." Former infantryman Samuel Hankins declared, "The Creator never made men equal to the Confederate soldier. For many months none of us had the least hope of success, yet we would stand and be shot at for our country." In justifying Confederate defeat, Horace Fulkerson asserted that the Confederate troops lacked the necessary resources to sustain the fight as long as their enemies. He admitted that "there were occasional desertions" but only "of obscure soldiers," none of whom served as an officer of rank. Fulkerson believed that this fact alone should lift "our common country far above the civilized nations of ancient or modern times, and deserves to be regarded by both parties to the quarrel as a mark of the sincere conviction of each to the righteousness of his cause." James Dinkins, a private in the Eighteenth Mississippi Infantry, blamed southern defeat on the ignobility of northern generals who "could not whip the Southern soldier in battle, but could destroy their homes and starve their families." He boasted that the Confederate Army, composed of "half-starved, but heroic, soldiers . . . stood for four years against the mighty hosts of men, resources, power, and money." Despite defeat, Dinkins stated that "the Confederate army had made a name for bravery and daring for the rank and file, and genius for the leaders, that will challenge the admiration of future generations, and establish a standard for emulation never to be excelled."[10]

No other writing defined how Mississippians and southerners remembered the Civil War better than Jefferson Davis's magnum opus *The Rise and Fall of the Confederate Government* (1881). The federal government detained Davis at Fort Monroe following his capture while Congress and Andrew Johnson fought over Reconstruction and whether to pursue a criminal or civil trial against the former Confederate president. While incarcerated, Davis received an outpouring of support among the citizens of the South, especially after news spread that the prison officials placed Davis in chains. The mistakes the Davis administration made throughout the war that alienated the yeomanry and plain folk quickly disappeared during his prison stay, as assuaged southerners embraced Davis as the symbol of the Confederacy. After eventually indicting Davis on treason, the court allowed him to post bail and permitted him to travel to Canada. By December 1868 Andrew Johnson issued amnesty to all participants in the rebellion, which included Jefferson Davis, preventing the Confederacy's only president from standing trial. With no land and minimal sources of income, Davis tried his hand at business and failed. By 1877 Davis relocated to Beauvoir, a home owned by Sarah Ellis Dorsey on the Mississippi gulf coast, where he lived until his death in 1889. While at Beauvoir, Davis embarked on the task of writing a history of the Confederacy and found a publisher in New York willing to pay an advance and allow for a two-volume edition.[11]

Much to the displeasure of the publisher, Davis spent an inordinate amount of space devoted to the sectional conflict and the causes of the war, as well as the constitutional legality of secession. Davis adamantly and repeatedly declared throughout his work that "no moral nor sentimental considerations were really involved" in the rupture between the northern and southern states, but that they "were struggles between different sections, with diverse institutions and interests." Davis wanted his readers to understand the causes behind the conflict, but, more importantly, he wanted them to realize and accept that slavery did not cause the rift between the two sections. Davis argued that southerners fought for constitutionalism, not the perpetuation of slavery. Davis upbraided early historians of the Civil War who "sedulously represented" the "Southern states and Southern people" as "'propagandists' of slavery, and the Northern as the defenders and champions of universal freedom." He corrected such an interpretation by stating that "whatever extent the question of slavery may have served as an *occasion*, it was far from being the *cause* of the conflict." Davis did not want generations of Americans and southerners to view the Civil War as a struggle fought over the issue of slavery—such an interpretation would dishonor the South. Such a narrative would mean that southern boys and men died to preserve an institution that forced individuals into bondage and denied them fundamental freedoms. Admitting the war started as a fight to preserve slavery would make the southern states culpable for the devastation and loss of life that followed and make heroes of northerners who fought for the freedom and emancipation of the enslaved. Davis provided examples to try and argue that the majority of northerners accepted the peculiar institution, which he described as "the mildest and most humane of all institutions to which the name 'slavery' has ever been applied." He argued that "climatic, industrial, and economical—nor moral or sentimental—reasons" ended slavery in the North. According to Davis, only a few fanatical northerners called for the abolition of slavery, which meant the issue of slavery did not produce the conflict between the states.[12]

Davis narrated the founding of the nation (which he repeatedly referred to as a confederation of independent states), the compact each state entered into upon admission to the confederation, and the machinations of the northern region to usurp power in its quest for lucre. Beginning with the close of the Revolutionary War, Davis explained that after securing independence "the confederation of those States embraced an area so extensive, with climate and products so various, that rivalries and conflicts of interest soon began to be manifested." Episode by episode, Davis traced the history of the United States and all the attempts of the northern states to "appropriate to itself an unequal share of the public disbursements" as the country gobbled up land in the West. He argued that as the United States acquired more land, the greed of the men of the northern states grew. Davis recounted how the Louisiana Purchase substantially increased the size of the country, but northerners limited the amount of land southerners could claim from the transaction. Davis mentioned the tariff issues of the 1830s and how they favored northern manufacturing at the expense of the southern states and chronicled the problems that arose over the Mexican Cession and escalating disagreements that ensued over the next decade. Davis asserted that southerners did not promote the expansion of slavery; rather, they questioned the legality of northerners trying to prevent the "distribution" and "dispersion" of property into the territories. According to Davis, the cause of the war "was not the passage of the 'personal liberty laws,' it was not the raid of John Brown, it was not the operation of unjust and unequal tariff laws, nor all combined, that constituted the intolerable grievance." Instead, he claimed "it was the systematic and persistent struggle to deprive the Southern States of equality in the Union, to discriminate in legislation against the interests of [the southern] people; culminating in their exclusion from the Territories, the common property of the States, as well as by the infraction of their compact to promote domestic tranquillity."[13]

Davis defended a states' rights ideology and squared it with historical examples as fully compliant with the Constitution. In Davis's account, the South acted to prevent the North from an "invasion of the natural and unalienable rights of man." He proudly stated that the Confederate States "drew their swords for the sovereignty of the people, and they fought for the maintenance of their State governments in all their reserved rights and powers, as the only true and natural guardians of the unalienable rights of their citizens, among which the most sacred is, that only the consent of the governed can give vitality and existence to any civil or political institution." Davis defended the act of secession as rooted in the Founders' American political philosophy. He spent over one hundred pages expounding on the rights of secession and giving examples in American history when other states asserted those rights. He did concede that the Civil War "showed [secession] to be impracticable, but this did not prove it to be wrong." Davis stated that southerners did not fight the war to defend the interest in slavery but for "the cause of constitutional government, of the supremacy of law, of the natural rights of man," which were all the same causes that compelled the revolutionaries to break from Great Britain.[14]

In writing about the close of the war and the beginning of Reconstruction, white Mississippians emphasized the major shift in the social and political structure of the state. Historical narratives portray the antebellum era as the halcyon days of the state, but Reconstruction was the opposite. Conservatives wrote with disdain about the elevation of the freedmen into white society and the implications that followed. Narratives tended to underscore the political corruption that immediately followed the franchise of the freedmen and leveled the blame on office-seeking carpetbaggers and scalawags. Many histories and memoirs served as a warning to proceeding generations of the disastrous consequences that would result should blacks receive full equality in the future, often making the case that black social inferiority was both prudent and necessary. To illustrate the point, historical writings elucidated the condition of slaves during the antebellum days as the proper status for the black population.

Many historical writings expounded the myth that masters treated their slaves with great care and that slaves found contentment and satisfaction in their work. In his memoirs J. M. Gibson sought to dispel the perception of the unhappy and discontented slave. He said that "throughout the nation outside the 'Deep South,' there was a common belief that the owners treated their slaves with great cruelty, drove them in their work through long hours in all kinds of weather, provided few clothes and seldom shoes to wear, and forced them to occupy unsanitary huts." Gibson countered that image, saying, "Our Negroes were well-fed and comfortably clothed and given good shoes and boots. . . . The women were not compelled to do heavy work, and no child under twelve years was made to work in the fields or elsewhere other than to carry water or milk to field hands." Historian Dunbar Rowland described black field hands as "happy in their labor." He explained that "their humble and simple lives were free from care. All their wants supplied, and they were contented and satisfied." Annie Harper believed that "of all the races ever held in bondage . . . the negro was the happiest and best treated." She further ratio- nalized that because of their natural disposition, slaves "never felt any degra- dation in [their] position" and were "absolutely content."[15]

Lost Cause writers also perpetuated the myth that because of their sat- isfaction in slavery, most slaves remained loyal to their masters during the Civil War. James Dinkins argued that slaves loved their masters and that only a few instances of slave unrest occurred, usually due to the influences of abolitionists. Dinkins argued that slaves wanted to remain as slaves and used as his evidence the lack of organized slave resistance during the war. "From the beginning to the end of the war," Dinkins reported, "no such thing as an insurrectionary movement was known or heard of, nor the use of any incendiary or insulting language whatever charged, reported, or hinted against the negroes." Dinkins admitted the fact that some slaves left the plantation but contended that "a large majority of the negroes remained at their homes" and cared for their masters' families. In a treatise dedi- cated to understanding the "Negro problem," Horace Fulkerson remarked that "the conduct of the slaves of the South during the war has been the subject of much comment and all of it, it may be said, with approval and highest commendation." Setting out several possible reasons why the slaves remained loyal, which ranged from innate cowardice to lack of knowledge concerning the conflict, Fulkerson believed that "the respect . . . in which the master was held by the slave, and the mild rule at home during the war, had much to do with it, but above these was the good sense, the dignity, and the self respect of the noble women of the South, whose conduct was an ever-present inspiration of good conduct on the part of the slave."[16]

Legend-makers wrote about the lack of emotion or joy that emancipa- tion brought to the slaves; instead, they often argued, it brought devastation. Belle Kearney described the day her father went to the slave quarters to tell the slaves of their freedom. "There was no wild shout of joy or other demonstrations of gladness," Kearney said. "The deepest gloom prevailed in their ranks and an expression of mournful bewilderment settled upon their dusky faces . . . they were stunned. What were they to do? Where should they go? What would become of them?" Kearney apocalyptically explained the effects of emancipation: "Crime swept like a prairie fire over communities. Anarchy triumphed, grinning, red-handed. Desperadoes infested the land. Women were afraid to leave their front doors without being armed or accompanied by a male escort." Kearney's narrative of emancipation portrayed a post-emancipation world where crime and confusion gripped the countryside. Frank Montgomery endorsed such an assessment. He explained that "the negro of that day was a happy and child-like creature. Crime was literally unknown to him." Montgomery rhetorically asked, "Now, what is his condition? Ask the jails, the penitentiaries, the lunatic asylums, which are filled not from the ranks of the old slaves, but their sons and daughters." Montgomery believed that the freedmen appreciated their freedom and handled it well, but the next generations proved emancipation a bad idea.[17]

Writers often commented that carpetbaggers made conditions worse for the freedmen and southerners. They blamed the wandering northerners for manipulating the freedmen and using them for nothing but political and economic gain. "After the war had ended, the South was overrun by a class called 'Carpet Baggers,'" James Dinkins explained. "They were as a general and almost universal thing the scum of the earth. Men who, except in a few instances, had no idea of right, honesty, gentility, or decency, and knew no such law or motto." Dinkins elucidated their primary desire: "They came South to fire the heart of the newly-emancipated negro, and organize a political party, by which they could obtain official control of the different states." He concluded that the carpetbaggers, the "pretended friends" of the freedmen, had "grossly deceived" blacks after the war to attain their own selfish goals. According to Horace Fulkerson, the carpetbaggers infested the land "like the frogs of Egypt" and came "with their divinations and enchantments, and loyal league charters, and their promise of 'a mule and forty acres' to work upon the imaginations and fire the hearts of the lately franchised." J. E. Robuck of Marshall County lamented, "It is a horrid reflection to think what a change the bestowing of the ballot, citizenship, and the diabolical influence of the carpet-bagger and the scalawag had wrought in the disposition of the negro in such a short time." He complained that carpetbaggers hoped "to place the negro permanently above the white population, and thus Africanize the South." He pointed to the passage of the Fourteenth Amendment as the moment when the "friendly relations between the white and black races of the South" turned sour. Robuck asserted that, soon afterward, "hordes of carpet-baggers of a low class were scattered throughout the Southern States organizing among the negroes what they called the Loyal League. This was for the purpose of keeping the white race under foot and an effort to give the negro the ascendancy." Writing for the Mississippi Historical Society in 1901, W. H. Hardy described Reconstruction as a time when "designing carpet baggers and scalawags" indoctrinated freedmen with concepts of social and political equality with whites. Freedmen then became "exceedingly arrogant and insolent," causing violence and a fractured relationship between the races.[18]

Lost Cause narratives expounded on the corruption universal male suffrage brought upon the state. Annie Harper condescendingly wrote of how blacks often went to the polls in complete ignorance: "Every old man who could totter to the polls, hastened to perform the act, of which they comprehended nothing. Whom did you vote for Uncle Granville? I dunno sir, dunno nuthin bout dat, but I got de right color [ballot], & put it in de hole. Why did you take your ax to town. Dunno sir. I never done nothin but what I needed one or tother of em, and I thought mebbe I'd need em in voting." J. E. Robuck believed that the freedmen, inspired by carpetbaggers, had sinister motives to disfranchise whites in the state. "The negro now had literal and practical control of the country under radical carpet-bag rule," he wrote, "and regarded his disfranchised democratic former master as being his worst and bitter enemy, and by the promptings and under the guidance of his political bosses he sought to rush both him and his family out of at least political existence forever, in order to hold his recently acquired ascendancy." Washington Clayton claimed that the black franchise had caused the white citizens "more suffering than our slaves ever endured, mental suffering being so much worse than bodily suffering."[19]

Writers typically lauded the campaigns of the Ku Klux Klan as an effort to free the state from the corrupting influences of carpetbaggers. Lost Cause treatises usually argued that the Klan served to protect both whites and blacks against carpetbag tyranny. J. M. Gibson claimed that the Klan targeted only "obstreperous young Negroes" and carpetbaggers. He stated, "The Ku Klux, I think, killed only one man—that is, one white man. He had defied them, and his conduct had been so ignoble and perversive of peace between the races that it was deemed imperative to make an example of him." Gibson defended the Klan and their actions for providing "good order and peace of the country." J. E. Robuck related several instances when the Klan helped protect unsuspecting blacks from carpetbaggers. According to his account, Robuck and three others decided to infiltrate a Loyal League meeting held at a black schoolhouse in Marshall County. Dressed as freedmen, with coal-smeared faces and wooly wigs, the four men attended the gathering. Reverend Hanks, a carpetbagger, presided over the affair and read passages from the Bible. According to Robuck, Hanks sermonized that blacks were superior to whites and that blacks should think of themselves on equal terms with whites. Robuck claimed that the Klan later captured Hanks during the middle of the night, hanged him, and attached a note to his ankle that read: "Such is the reward a Carpet-bagger gets for teaching Negroes that they are superior to the White People of the South, and that they have a right to marry our White Women. K.K.K." Robuck considered the actions of the Klan prudent and necessary.[20]

Lost Cause writers justified redemption as a revolutionary act aimed to restore the natural social and political order of the state. Most downplayed the intimidation and violence displayed during the 1875 election. Washington Clayton claimed that the plan involved persuading blacks to vote the Democratic ticket. He said that in Lee County "many [blacks] agreed to vote with us" and that "no violence was offered." Belle Kearney believed redemption essential because the franchise "laid a heavy curse on the black race." When writing of redemption, Annie Harper asked, "How would Ohio, Massachusetts, or New York act were the Chinese suddenly poured in over-whelming numbers upon them, and they the property holders allowed no rights but to exist—Do you think they would bear it quietly for twelve years? Think you they would effect as bloodless a revolution as did the South?" Harper claimed that redemption restored the proper balance in the state through whites' magnanimous efforts. She argued that blacks had "been more contented in mind, and more comfortable in body and estate [since the revolution of 1875]." James Dinkins echoed the same conclusion when he stated that after 1875 "the negroes and the whites got along without trouble, and they are getting along harmoniously to this day."[21]

In an address to the Alumni Association of the University of Mississippi in 1902, Dunbar Rowland justified the further redemption efforts of segregation and Jim Crow laws by expounding on the events of Reconstruction. Describing the election of 1875, Rowland explained that after suffering "the bitter humiliation of negro domination" for seven years, "every man swore a solemn oath before high Heaven that he would free himself and his posterity from the disgrace of negro rule or die in the attempt." He declared that the "people felt that they were struggling against infamy and dishonor." In justifying redemption, Rowland said the people of the time believed that "Negro rule [was] ruinous to a State," that "Negro suffrage had been given a fair trial with terrible results," and that "the negro [proved] himself unworthy of suffrage." In his address, Rowland did not attempt to hide the fact that white Mississippians sought to disfranchise the freedmen. Instead, he extolled the decision based on his belief in the inferiority of the African race. "Out of the mass of conflicting opinions there have come two great ideas about which there is no difference of opinion in the South," Rowland explained. "First is the necessity for the absolute social separation and isolation of the negro, [and second], is that the negro will never again be allowed to control the public affairs of a single southern state." Rowland wanted to demonstrate the horrible consequences black suffrage had on the state and urge future generations to prevent the same mistake.[22]

Lost Cause historians and memoirists wanted to make sure that the "horrors" of black suffrage did not repeat themselves in the future. In his book dedicated to explaining the condition and place of blacks within southern society, Horace Fulkerson described the character of the African race prior to slavery, their enslavement in America, and their probable station in future society. Literarily illustrated with scenes of barbarity, cannibalism, and Satanism, Fulkerson declared that the people of western Africa belonged to a loathsome and unprogressive society and culture that wallowed in idleness and heathen worship. While sometimes questioning the moral implications of slavery, Fulkerson believed that the peculiar institution in the South helped elevate Africans above their condition, and, at the very least, brought them to a knowledge of Christianity. Fulkerson argued that freedom stopped black progression toward civility, since they could not comprehend or understand the principles of liberty. Fulkerson cited works by scholars and professionals who provided figures that demonstrated the inability of blacks to amalgamate themselves into civil society, by showing high crime rates as well as high rates of communicable diseases among members of the black community. He further asserted that freedom and suffrage did more than hurt blacks—it threatened the ideals and character of all that was American. "There is an Ideal American founded upon the homogeneity and assimilating qualities of the people who laid the foundation of and built up our system," Fulkerson explained. "The *oneness* of these people in their origin, (diverse as they were in nationalities,) in their mental training, in their historical prestige, and in their religion, *fitted them* for the task of founding on the shores of the New World a great State whose power should be felt among all nations, and whose institutions should bless the whole human family." The homogeneity of the American founders, based on race, had brought the colonists together to form the greatest nation on earth. According to Fulkerson, Reconstruction and "Negro Suffrage shattered this ideal, [and had] broken the unity." He warned future generations of the dangers of black equality and reasoned that the restoration of the divinely inspired American ideal required the continuance of a white supremacist society.[23]

Lost Cause writers managed to create a positive image of southerners by using blacks, rather than northerners, as "the other." They wrote primarily for their descendants in an effort to control historical memory and justify white supremacy. In that process, they crafted a positive national identity of Mississippians that managed to celebrate their Confederate and American heritage as something proud and noble, while blaming the darkest days of the state's history on the black population and a few unprincipled carpet-baggers. At the time of their writing, America as a whole accepted Mississippi's Lost Cause identity more than repudiated it. Vilifying blacks rather than northerners and basing it on white supremacy revealed a common thread the rest of Americans accepted. By the end of the century, reconciliation and sectional healing overshadowed black civil rights as the predominant narrative of the Civil War. Parades dedicated to the "brothers' war" featured veteran Union and Confederate soldiers engaged in mock reenactments that ended in handshakes and unfettered praise for the bravery, valor, and benevolence of southern soldiers. Organizations such as the United Confederate Veterans (1889) and the United Daughters of the Confederacy (1895) ensured the Lost Cause legend remained the standard narrative of the war and Reconstruction.[24]

Northerners accepted the vilification of blacks as "the other" in Lost Cause writings because it played on an already embraced acceptance of white superiority. Northerners tacitly endorsed white supremacy. Homer Plessy's challenge to the Louisiana public transportation segregation law reached the Supreme Court in 1896. The court decided that the separate accommodations did not violate the spirit of the Fourteenth Amendment as long as those accommodations were equal. The seven-to-one ruling featured six justices who originally hailed from northeastern states and two from former slaveholding states. The dissenting opinion came from John Harlan of Kentucky, who offered a stinging rebuttal of the decision and claimed that the constitution did not apply itself separately to different races. In an equally pernicious ruling, *Williams v. Mississippi* (1898), the north-centric Supreme Court once again refused to strike a blow at the state's voting provisions. The court argued in favor of the voting law's constitutionality based on the fact that the law applied equally to whites and blacks. While these rulings alone do not prove complicity or blanket acceptance on the part of the rest of the nation for the South's white supremacist, segregation culture, they do demonstrate the prevalent attitudes among many white Americans that feared racial mixing. Regardless of location, black Americans faced intense discrimination, whether in housing, employment, education, or public accommodation. They also dealt with violence, lynching, and race riots.[25]

As white Mississippians restored a positive national identity, black Mississippians lost theirs. W. E. B. Du Bois explained the identity crisis black Americans experienced near the turn of the century. When he wrote that "the Negro is a sort of seventh son, born with a veil, and gifted with second-sight in this American world,—a world which yields him no true self-consciousness, but only lets him see himself through the revelation of the other world." Du Bois described the frustration of "this double-consciousness, this sense of always looking at one's self through the eyes of others, of measuring one's soul by the tape of a world that looks on in amused contempt and pity." In 1910 sociologist Howard Odum commented on the double identity blacks tended to embody. He explained that the black person has "two distinct selves, the one he reveals to his own people, the other he assumes among the whites, the assumption itself having become natural." Outwardly, blacks tended to conform to white expectations, not due to internalization of the social identity whites prescribed, but to avoid retribution from whites in the form of violence and lynch mobs. Internally, blacks continued to foster and establish a distinct African American identity that started to focus on their African heritage rather than their American heritage.[26]

While many blacks did not write of their experiences as slaves or as freedmen following the Civil War, in the 1930s several acquiesced to interviews conducted by the Federal Writers' Project. Interviewed mostly by white working-class men and women, some blacks performed according to white expectations and mirrored the Lost Cause legend. Strikingly, black respondents often resorted to the narrative arc produced in Lost Cause writings. At times absurd and contradictory in nature, these "reminiscences" demonstrate that blacks tended to spew white racial propaganda without worrying whether it made sense; so long as it was what whites wanted to hear, some blacks were willing to oblige. Oftentimes they could sound just as racist and just as bitter against carpetbaggers as their white counterparts. Their decision to do so reflects one aspect of the double identity they had to create to shield themselves from further suffering at the hands of white society. Their double identity also allowed them to fashion their own identity, on their own terms, at their own time, and in their own sphere.

In their interviews, some former slaves made comments that suggested their proper place in society was either in slavery or in an inferior position, an obvious contradiction to their actions prior to the war to secure their liberty, and during Reconstruction to assert their political rights. They knew enough of Lost Cause historical writings and culture to spout the rhetoric satisfactorily to appeal to white expectations. Some spoke of the widely held belief among whites that only their former masters really understood and cared for the slaves. Louis Davis of Coahoma County declared that "the colored folks . . . needs teaching and caring for [and the] Slave holders cared more for their slaves than the slaves cared for theirself." Isaac Stier of Natchez suggested that northerners, more specifically Abraham Lincoln, did not understand the relationship between master and slave prior to the war. Stier remarked that because of his uneducated nature, Lincoln "never did un'erstan' how us felt 'bout us white folks. It takes de quality to un'erstan' such things." Reminiscing about Reconstruction, Jim Polk Hightower explained that once the carpetbagger entered the state, relations between whites and blacks soured. "The Nigers went off with that class of men," Hightower remembered, "that made the old slave owner mad because they wanted the old slave to do well, for they love him, and it made them mad for the office seeker to come in and steal the hearts of the slaves from them. They wanted the nigger to have confidence in him because they wanted him to do well." Others tried to explain that prior to the war, a filial relationship existed between the slave and master in which each understood his or her role and acted accordingly. "Where I was brought up de white man knowed his place an' de Nigger Knowed his'n," proclaimed Prince Johnson of Clarksdale. "Both of 'em stayed in dey place." Nettie Henry of Meridian said that "things got so unnatchel after de Surrender. Niggers got to bein all kin' o' things what de Lawd didn' inten' 'em for, lak bein' policemen an' all lak dat. It was scan'lous!" Similar to the white Mississippians who expounded the Lost Cause legend, some blacks portrayed the Old South as a time of cordial race relations and peace and posterity until the carpetbaggers infested the land and uprooted the social order.[27]

When many former slaves commented about Reconstruction, they once again echoed the Lost Cause treatises that viewed the carpetbagger with disdain. Within their historically incongruous accounts, blacks tried to distance themselves from carpetbaggers and labeled them negatively, just as whites did in their writings. In addition, they often blamed their suffrage rights for disrupting racial harmony and causing more problems during the Reconstruction period. Jim Allen of West Point said that one man in the area, "a two faced Yankee or carpetbagger," had organized a club for blacks where he tried "to get Negroes to go 'gainst our white people." After receiving counsel from a local white man to–"stop your foolishness—go live among your white folks an' behave–" the freedmen in the area discontinued attending the meetings. Allen said that the carpetbagger wanted the blacks in the area to vote the Republican ticket in order to disfranchise white Mississippians. Pet Franks of Aberdeen recalled that "after de war de Yankees . . . come down here an' wanted all de Niggers to vote de 'Publican ticket. On 'lection day I brung in 1500 Niggers to vote de Democrat' ticket." Clara Young of Monroe County remembered that the "Yankees tried to get some of de men to vote, too, but not many did. . . . We didn' lak de Yankees." Jim Hightower remarked, "Now the worst thing that could have been done for the colored people was to put the ballot in their hands jest after the war." He continued, "The thing that ought to have been done was to have put in the Constitution a clause requiring a Education qualification to become an elector then he would not have come in politics like a rushin mighty wind but as he became qualified he would have come in like a young white man, he had to have twenty-one years of training before he can vote." Hightower even stated that "it is a fact admitted by the leading men of our Race that as a mass we were not competent to have the ballot put in our hands." Offering a similar assessment, Henri Necaise blamed the carpetbaggers who came in and "'stroyed de country." Despite their conservative rhetoric, in the next breath many acknowledged their desire to vote during Reconstruction and hailed the Union forces as liberators during the war. As long as they said what whites wanted to hear, there was a chance that whites would miss or ignore what they did not want to hear.[28]

The necessity for blacks to project a conformist identity centered primarily on the desire to avoid the fierce and unmerciful violence poured out by whites on the black community. Black parents taught their offspring how to act in public and around whites to avoid any retribution. Black children learned how to conduct themselves in a white supremacist world that demanded the proper racial etiquette. When one son queried his father as to why they could not do certain things, the father declared, "Well, son, that's the way it is. I don't know what we can do about it. There ain't nothin' we can do about it. Because if we do anything about it, they kill you." Children quickly found that failure to conform, whether through ignorance or intention, might (and often did) result in violence. Whites continued to use violence to repress blacks, with Mississippi among the national leaders in the number of lynching deaths during the last two decades of the nineteenth century. Between 1882 and 1899, white mobs in Mississippi lynched at least 452 blacks, which averaged just over two deaths per month during the period in question. Although legally free, blacks continued to endure oppressive conditions that relegated them to socially inferior roles, and the failure to maintain those roles often ended in tragedy.[29]

Beginning around the time of the First World War, many blacks emi-
grated away from the state to escape the treacherous conditions of Mississippi's strict, white supremacist social order. With little options for
economic, political, or social equality, those who could afford to leave
moved northward to areas such as Ohio, Michigan, and Illinois. Economic
circumstances prompted many of the moves to northern areas. In letters
to the prominent black newspaper the Chicago *Defender*, many Mississippians wrote what amounted to a job application and pled for help in finding employment. In 1917 one Biloxi resident explained that she was "a good
cook and can give good recmendation." She further explained that her family "are in a land of starvaten" and a "land of sufring." A resident of Vicksburg said that "we are working here at starvation wages and some of us are
virtually without employment willing to accept any kind of work such as
cooking, laundering or as domestics." Several of the letters convey despera-
tion, such as one from a teacher in Lexington who commented, "I am so
sick I am so tired of such conditions that I sometime think that life for me
is not worth while and most eminently believe with Patrick Henry 'Give
me liberty or give me death.'" In many instances, though, blacks cited the
racial conditions and atmosphere as their motivation for leaving. Writing
from Greenville, one resident blatantly stated, "I want to get may famely out
of this cursed south land down here a negro man is not good as the white
man's dog. I can learn anything any other man can."[30]

The diaspora was not an organized event, but rather a constant flow of
migrants out of the South, lasting until the 1970s. In 1910 African Americans
accounted for 56 percent of Mississippi's population, dropping to 50 percent
by 1930, 45 percent by 1950, and 37 percent by 1970. Mississippi's largest cities
also experienced a rapid decline in the African American population starting in 1890 and continuing through 1970. Most experienced at least a 10
percent decline, while Jackson, which claimed 52.8 percent of its population
as black in 1890, declined to 35 percent by 1970. While not everyone had the
means to relocate, the fact that so many did reveals that black Mississippians
refused to succumb to the white supremacist social order.[31]

Black Mississippians experienced difficulties in creating a social identity.
W. E. B. Du Bois described the difficult tug blacks faced as "an American,
a Negro." Du Bois explained that the dual identity of blacks created "two
souls, two thoughts, two unreconciled strivings; two warring ideals in one
dark body, whose dogged strength alone keeps it from being torn asunder." Du Bois continued: "The history of the American Negro is the history
of this strife,—this longing to attain self-conscious manhood, to merge his

double self into a better and truer self. In this merging he wishes neither of the older selves to be lost." Du Bois argued that blacks could not create a true national identity as Americans because "Negro blood has a message for the world." At the same time, blacks could not reject their American heritage, because "America has too much to teach the world and Africa." He said that blacks wished "to make it possible for a man to be both a Negro and an American, without being cursed and spit upon by his fellows, without having the doors of Opportunity closed roughly in his face." In his historical work on Reconstruction, Du Bois showed how blacks in the past managed to create a national identity as Americans. He outlined many examples of whites and blacks working together to form coalitions and to protect and advance black rights. Yet white American acceptance of white supremacy changed the narrative near the end of the century and stripped blacks of their national identity.[32]

In Mississippi, blacks fashioned a social identity and culture that often reflected the dour times in which they lived. Unlike the slave spirituals and the hope of freedom encapsulated in their practice of religion and song in antebellum years, African American culture turned dark in the late nineteenth and early twentieth centuries. Styles of music, folklore, and storytelling became more aggressive, sometimes more assertive, and offered few glimmers of hope or salvation. The emergence of the Delta blues, the ritualized practice of a game of insults called "the dozens," and the venerations of the badman folk hero represented the frustrations and discontent of blacks in the state.[33]

A peculiar musical style emerged in the Mississippi Delta near the end of the nineteenth century that summarized and even symbolized the effects of the Jim Crow era on blacks in the state. In 1903, while at a railroad station in Tutwiler, Mississippi, musician W. C. Handy witnessed a man who played a guitar by sliding a knife along the neck and singing in a somber tone. Handy continued to hear more of this music as he played in locations throughout the state. Later, Handy helped popularize the style as the blues. Scholars believe the blues evolved from field hollers and work songs. The songs often took on a particular style with repeated lines and gloomy, mournful lyrics. Topics covered the loss of a lover, life in the Delta, agricultural disasters, drug abuse, and veiled references to the plight of blacks in general.[34]

Unlike the slave spirituals that contained strong themes of hope and redemption, most of the blues songs had few optimistic moments. Happiness usually came from the bottom of a bottle or narcotic drugs. One common lyrical motif dealt with escape, whether leaving the Delta or a lover, and finding a life elsewhere. Charley Patton, one of the first well-known Delta blues musicians, sang of departing the Delta to "a world unknown" since "every day seem like murder here." In one song, Robert Johnson wailed, "I got ramblin' on my mind." He wanted to run "down to the station / catch that old first mail train I see." In another song, after a lover "mistreated" him, Johnson declared, "Lord I feel like blowin my / old lonesome home." Son House, a contemporary of Patton, made an ultimatum to his lover: "I say look here, baby, you ought not to dog me around / If I had my belongings I would leave this old bad-luck town." The desire to escape perhaps symbolized the longing to flee the harsh and brutal conditions imposed upon blacks. Patton, House, and Johnson grew up working in the fields with their families, either as tenants or as sharecroppers, and had firsthand experience with the economic and social plight of blacks in the Delta. Several of their songs dealt with agricultural themes such as boll weevil infestations and flooding from the Mississippi River. Each artist also made frequent reference to entanglements with law enforcement officials, as well as the dreaded Parchman Farm Penitentiary in Sunflower County that operated as a working farm using convict labor.[35]

Largely secular in nature, blues songs occasionally included religious themes. The way the artists used them demonstrated a marked shift from the spiritual paradigm of the previous generations. Slave spirituals and field songs spoke of endurance and the promise of freedom and redemption, but blues songs tended to focus more on the sinful nature of the narrator and the inescapable bonds of the devil. Although Tommy Johnson initially told the popular story, Robert Johnson became famous for allegedly selling his soul to the devil one night at a crossroad in exchange for mastery of the guitar. He sang frequently about trying to shake the influence of Satan. In one of his more famous songs, Johnson cried, "I gotta keep movin' / there's a hellhound on my trail." In another, Johnson recognized that his desire "to beat my woman until I get satisfied" was because "me and the devil was walkin' side by side." Charley Patton glorified cocaine use and stated that it was "all I want in this creation," and that it was worth killing a man to obtain. Patton sang of redemption in his ballad "Lord I'm Discouraged" but left little hope for gaining any happiness before death. The blues singers from Mississippi had little reason to believe their condition would improve, due to the white supremacist social order.[36]

Other characteristics of African American culture in Mississippi during the late nineteenth and early twentieth centuries also point at signs of pent-up aggression. The lauded exploits of the badman in African American folk culture celebrated amoral characters who committed acts of rebellion and violence without remorse. While scholars have grappled with the origin, intent, and character of these badmen, some have pointed to their actions as targeted against white institutions and laws. The badman symbolized a form of black power against the oppressive racial caste system in the South. Although badmen tended to target other blacks, many times their black victims were those who reinforced notions of white supremacy and accommodationist attitudes, such as black preachers.[37]

African Americans who sought to challenge the racial climate had limited options that allowed a safe means of protest. For black Mississippians, organizational associations that sought redress of segregation and other racial grievances tended to have short lives or operated underground. Initially established in Vicksburg and Mound Bayou in 1918 and 1919, Mississippi chapters of the National Association for the Advancement of Colored People suffered collapse and severe fluctuations in membership due to threats of violence and out-migration. Some Mississippians joined the Universal Negro Improvement Association during the 1920s and '30s, but their numbers appear minor, and they tended not to agitate for radical social change. In the Jim Crow era, black Mississippians had little ability to affect the caste system without significant retribution.[38]

As the twentieth century moved onward, white Mississippians managed to craft a national identity that allowed for a measure of reconciliation while keeping intact a Confederate identity. At the same time, Jim Crow laws, violence, and intimidation stripped blacks in the state of the national identity they created during Reconstruction. The dying generation of Old South planters and Civil War veterans did what they could to ensure that their memory and identity never died. "The old Southern gentleman is passing rapidly away," Annie Harper noted. "That courtly chivalrous dignity which began with the nation with our Washington, and continued to Lee—where shall we find it in a few more years?" Dunbar Rowland had the answer: "The grand and noble men and women of the 'Old South' are rapidly passing away. Their memories, deeds and virtues must be preserved by their sons and daughters." He continued his instructions: "They must be preserved on the living pages of history as a priceless heritage to their descendants. They must be preserved in story, poetry and song, in sculpted marble, and in the glorious beauty of painted canvas so that they will endure forever and forever."[39]

Conclusion
"THOU ART NOT DEAD"

——— • ———

A vestal shrine thou art beloved mother,
A loyal son uncovers at thy bier;
Thou art not dead, but sleepest—yet another,
Thyself transformed, in beauty shalt appear.
Thy naked, bleeding feet shall sandaled be—
Thy golden tresses, all disheveled now—
Again shall crown thy head of majesty,
And richest diadem adorn thy brow.[1]

On November 21, 2009, the Ku Klux Klan held a protest before a football game near the student union building at the University of Mississippi. The Klansmen, in full garb, gathered in response to the school chancellor's ban that prohibited the band from playing a medley titled "From Dixie with Love" at football games. The chancellor nixed the song because several of the fans in attendance would often chant, "The South shall rise again!" during portions of the performance. The Klan issued a statement regarding their decision to assemble, claiming that the chancellor's decision attacked "our Southern Heritage and Culture." The proclamation declared that "this is a direct violation of the right to freedom of speech and will only continue because a hand full of people at Ole Miss want to force change on the University of Mississippi that will destroy the Culture and Heritage on the Ole Miss Campus. Ole Miss should embrace its Southern Heritage and Culture." In an interview before the protest, the Great Titan for the Mississippi White Knights of the Klan stated, "We are coming to Ole Miss to say enough is enough on attacking our Christian, southern heritage and culture." Members of the local Klan decided to gather in what they considered an effort to preserve their southern heritage and what they perceived as components of their southern identity. They manifested a desire to retain the image of the South their forefathers created in their Lost Cause legends. The dozen Klansmen who arrived protested for nearly twenty minutes before leaving. Hundreds of students opposed to the Klan rallied near the student union building, chanting the university's creed, and wore shirts that read "Turn your back on hate." For those gathered in opposition, the southern identity, heritage, and culture the Klan wanted to preserve was full of hate and memorialized slavery, segregation, and white supremacy.[2]

A competing image of southern heritage and identity slowly chipped away at the white supremacist identity as the twentieth century progressed. Black Mississippians took the opportunity to effect change in the wake of the Second World War. As the Civil Rights Movement launched, white Mississippians dug in and resisted the change with a fervency paralleling the Revolution of 1875. Following the *Brown v. Board of Education* decision in 1954, white Mississippians formed Citizens' Councils and implemented means to intimidate any blacks who advocated integration, attempted to register to vote, or claimed membership to any organization that promoted the advancement of equal rights. The state created the Mississippi State Sovereignty Commission, which acted as an in-state intelligence agency. Modeled after the FBI, the Sovereignty Commission sent spies to infiltrate black organizations, collected intelligence on local civil rights leaders, and promoted actions to undermine the Civil Rights Movement. Violence and intimidation reigned once again in Mississippi as blacks in the state tried to reassert their rights. One appalling episode occurred in 1955 when at least two men brutally murdered a teenage boy from Chicago. Emmett Till traveled to the Mississippi Delta to visit some relatives and failed to conform to white supremacist racial etiquette. After supposedly whistling at the wife of a country-grocery owner, the owner and his half-brother kidnapped Till while he slept, brutally beat and shot him, then tied a cotton gin fan around his neck with barbed wire and threw him in the Tallahatchie River. Three days later a young boy discovered Till's swollen and bloated body—an image that circulated in numerous newspapers and magazines across the nation. An all-white jury acquitted the two men after a short trial. The killers even boasted of their activity a few years later to a journalist.[3]

Other episodes of violence occurred as black Mississippians demanded social equality. In 1951 T. R. M. Howard, a prominent black Mississippian, founded the Regional Council of Negro Leadership. His organization focused on civil rights issues and gaining racial equality. One of the members, Medgar Evers, eventually served as the first field secretary in

Mississippi for the National Association for the Advancement of Colored People. Evers played crucial roles in organizing boycotts aimed at white merchants. In 1962 he assisted James Meredith, who applied for admission to the University of Mississippi, setting off a riot on the university's campus. Evers's enormous influence in Mississippi's civil rights movement led to his assassination in 1963 when a gunman shot him in the back on his doorstep. In 1964 when volunteers flocked to Mississippi for Freedom Summer, white Mississippians continued to resist. During the campaign, beatings, murders, and bombings engulfed the state. Despite court rulings and federal laws, white Mississippians continued to resist challenges to white supremacy.[4]

The changes wrought by the Civil Rights Movement may have significantly altered the social structure of the state, but the identity forged in Lost Cause writings still persists. In 2001 voters in Mississippi went to the polls to determine whether they would follow several other southern states and remove the Confederate battle flag from the official state flag. Many whites argued that the emblem represented their southern culture and heritage. When the polls closed, the battle flag remained intact, largely along racial voting lines. Mississippi also continues to celebrate Confederate Memorial Day, designated as an official state holiday on the last Monday in April. Whites in the state still maintain the belief that the Civil War had little or nothing to do with the issue of slavery. The Lost Cause legend persists, nearly untouched, over a century later, unifying whites in a manner that eluded them when their ancestors struggled over the compromise measures, secession, the Civil War, and Reconstruction. The Lost Cause, and white Mississippian adherence to its doctrine, has done more to unify conservative Mississippians than any amount of pseudo-ethnic homogeneity or regional patriotism that swelled during the sectional conflict and Civil War.[5]

While much has changed in Mississippi since the Civil War, much has remained the same. The social identity conservatives forged following the Civil War continues to define the state and some of its people. Lost Cause writers hoping to construct an enduring, positive legacy and social identity for their posterity succeeded in many ways. The dominant narrative of Lost Cause writers continues to define the discussion of the state's "heritage" and "legacy." In 1876, when Annie Harper wrote the history of the Civil War and Reconstruction for her daughter, she closed in poetical adoration for the Old South. She wept over the irretrievability of the Old South. "Beautiful past with its weakness even its sins," Harper wrote, "the world will look in vain for anything that can compare socially with thee." Despite the weaknesses, despite the sins, some Mississippians still cling to that past and identity.[6]

Notes

Introduction

1. "New Presidential Library Hopes to Paint More Complete Picture of Jefferson Davis," http://www.mpbonline.org/news/story/new-presidential-library-hopes-paint-more -complete-picture-jefferson-davis, accessed December 29, 2009; "Work Begins on New Jefferson Davis Library," *Mobile Press-Register* (Mobile), December 6, 2009; Craig Fehrman, "Jefferson Davis' 'Presidential' Library," *LA Times*, June 2, 2013.

2. Fehrman, "Jefferson Davis' 'Presidential' Library."

3. In recent years historians have used memory to understand the Lost Cause legend. I contend that the Lost Cause legend emerged from the social identity that southerners produced in the wake of the sectional conflict, the Civil War, and Reconstruction. Mississippians used the Lost Cause to create a positive group concept that also served to encourage their posterity to maintain a white supremacist worldview. Currently, only one full-length study on Mississippi's Lost Cause exists, Sally Leigh McWhite, "Echoes of the Lost Cause: Civil War Reverberations in Mississippi from 1865 to 2001" (PhD. diss., University of Mississippi, 2003). I have relied heavily on the following works concerning the Lost Cause: W. Fitzhugh Brundage, *The Southern Past: A Clash of Race and Memory* (Cambridge: Belknap Press of Harvard University Press, 2005); David R. Goldfield, *Still Fighting the Civil War: The American South and Southern History* (Baton Rouge: Louisiana State University Press, 2002); David W. Blight, *Race and Reunion: The Civil War in American Memory* (Cambridge: Belknap Press of Harvard University Press, 2001); W. Fitzhugh Brundage, ed., *Where These Memories Grow: History, Memory, and Southern Identity* (Chapel Hill: University of North Carolina Press, 2000); Gary W. Gallagher and Alan T. Nolan, eds., *The Myth of the Lost Cause and Civil War History* (Bloomington: Indiana University Press, 2000); William C. Davis, *The Cause Lost: Myths and Realities of the Confederacy* (Lawrence: University Press of Kansas, 1996); Gaines M. Foster, *Ghosts of the Confederacy: Defeat, the Lost Cause, and the Emergence of the New South* (New York: Oxford University Press, 1987); Richard E. Beringer, Herman Hattaway, Archer Jones, and William N. Still, Jr., *Why the South Lost the Civil War* (Athens: University of Georgia Press, 1986); Charles Reagan Wilson, *Baptized in Blood: The Religion of the Lost Cause, 1865–1920* (Athens: University of Georgia Press, 1980); Patrick Gerster and Nicholas Cords, eds., *Myth and Southern History: The Old South* (Chicago: Rand McNally College Publishing, 1974).

4. Historians have often batted around the term "identity" without providing much definition of the word. Oftentimes, historians have used identity to describe traits, characteristics, or peculiarities of a particular group or region. Psychologist Erik Erikson popularized the word "identity" and argued that identity "connotes both a persistent sameness within

oneself (selfsameness) and a persistent sharing of some kind of essential character with others." Social scientists eventually took the term and contended that identity was primarily external, created and molded by society through social constructs and interaction. This study uses social identity theory as explained by Henri Tajfel and John Turner to understand how Mississippians constructed a national social identity. Tajfel and Turner proposed three theoretical principles on which social identity theory rests: first, "individuals strive to achieve or to maintain positive social identity"; second, "positive social identity is based to a large extent on favorable comparisons that can be made between the in-group and some relevant out-groups: the in-group must be perceived as positively differentiated or distinct from the relevant out-groups"; and, lastly, "when social identity is unsatisfactory, individuals will strive either to leave their existing group and join some more positively distinct group and/or to make their existing group more positively distinct." The sectional conflict, Civil War, and Reconstruction turned Mississippians' world on end and caused situations where their positive group concept turned negative or unappealing. Repeatedly, Mississippians had to fashion and reshape their existing social identity to compensate for the changes occurring all around them. The Lost Cause legend and history writing is the culmination of those shifts and reversals in the creation of their social identity. For quotes, see Erik H. Erikson, *Identity and the Life Cycle* (New York: International Universities Press, 1959), 102; Henri Tajfel and John Turner, "An Integrative Theory of Intergroup Conflict," in William G. Austin and Stephen Worchel, eds., *The Social Psychology of Intergroup Relations* (Monterey: Brooks/Cole, 1979), 40.

Works on southern identity include C. Vann Woodward, *The Burden of Southern History*, updated 3rd ed. (Baton Rouge: Louisiana State University Press, 1960; 2008); James C. Cobb, *Away Down South: A History of Southern Identity* (New York: Oxford University Press, 2005); David R. Jansson, "Internal Orientalism in America: W. J. Cash's *The Mind of the South* and the Spatial Construction of American Identity," *Political Geography* 22 (2003): 293–316; Joyce Appleby, *Inheriting the Revolution: The First Generations of Americans* (Cambridge: Belknap Press of Harvard University Press, 2000); Susan-Mary Grant, *North over South: Northern Nationalism and American Identity in the Antebellum Era* (Lawrence: University Press of Kansas, 2000); Carl N. Degler, "Thesis, Antithesis, Synthesis: The South, the North, and the Nation," *Journal of Southern History* 53 (February 1987): 3–18.

Other theoretical works on identity, identity theory, social identity, and social interaction include James E. Cote and Charles G. Levine, *Identity Formation, Agency, and Culture: A Social Psychological Synthesis* (Mahwah, NJ: Lawrence Erlbaum Associates, 2002); Sheldon Stryker and Peter J. Burke, "The Past, Present, and Future of an Identity Theory," *Social Psychology Quarterly* 63 (December 2000): 284–97; Howard S. Becker and Michal M. McCalls, eds., *Symbolic Interactionism and Cultural Studies* (Chicago: University of Chicago Press, 1990); Marshall Sahlins, *Islands of History* (Chicago: University of Chicago Press, 1985); Richard C. Trexler, ed., *Persons in Groups: Social Behavior as Identity Formation in Medieval and Renaissance Europe* (Binghamton, NY: Medieval and Renaissance Texts and Studies, 1985); Philip Gleason, "Identifying Identity: A Semantic History," *Journal of American History* 69 (March 1983): 910–28; Clifford Geertz, *The Interpretation of Cultures: Selected Essays* (New York: Basic Books, 1973; Herbert Blumer, *Symbolic Interactionism: Perspective and Method* (Englewood Cliffs, NJ: Prentice-Hall, 1969).

The use of "national" social identity in this work does not necessarily equate to nationalism, although it does contain components of it. Like "identity," "nationalism" is a slippery term that scholars use with various definitions. The focus on a national social identity differs from nationalism in that it offers more fluidity and does not limit one's sense of being as confined only to a national perspective. Regional peculiarities seep into a social identity and can incorporate desired traits that may be understood only at a local level. Nevertheless, nationalism plays a part in constructing a social identity, and this study has relied on several works to understand the construction of a national identity. See Paul Quigley, *Shifting Grounds: Nationalism and the American South, 1848-1865* (New York: Oxford University Press, 2012); Peter C. Messer, *Stories of Independence: Identity, Ideology, and History in Eighteenth-Century America* (DeKalb: Northern Illinois University Press, 2005); Gregory T. Knouff, *The Soldiers' Revolution: Pennsylvanians in Arms and the Forging of Early American Identity* (University Park: Pennsylvania State University Press, 2004); Grant, *North over South*; Anthony D. Smith, *The Nation in History: Historiographical Debates about Ethnicity and Nationalism* (Hanover: University Press of New England, 2000); Jill Lepore, *The Name of War: King Philip's War and the Origins of American Identity* (New York: Vintage Books, 1998); David Miller, *On Nationality* (New York: Oxford University Press, 1995); David Hackett Fischer, *Albion's Seed: Four British Folkways in America* (New York: Oxford University Press, 1989); Wilbur Zelinsky, *Nation into State: The Shifting Symbolic Foundations of American Nationalism* (Chapel Hill: University of North Carolina Press, 1988); Benedict Anderson, *Imagined Communities: Reflections on the Origin and Spread of Nationalism*, rev. ed. (New York: Verso, 1983; 1991); Ernest Gellner, *Nations and Nationalism* (Ithaca: Cornell University Press, 1983); William R. Taylor, *Cavalier and Yankee: The Old South and American National Character* (New York: Oxford University Press, 1961; 1993); Carlton J. H. Hayes, *Nationalism: A Religion* (New York: Macmillan, 1960).

"The Southern Phalanx"

1. "The Southern Phalanx," *Mississippian* (Jackson), May 24, 1850.

2. Walter Chandler, ed., *Journal and Speeches of Greene Callier Chandler* (Memphis: Private printing, 1953), 50, 23.

3. "Southern Phalanx"; Eric H. Walther, *The Fire-Eaters* (Baton Rouge: Louisiana State University Press, 1992); John McCardell, *The Idea of a Southern Nation: Southern Nationalists and Southern Nationalism, 1830-1860* (New York: W. W. Norton, 1979); David M. Potter, *The South and the Sectional Conflict* (Baton Rouge: Louisiana State University Press, 1968); William W. Freehling, *Prelude to the Civil War: The Nullification Controversy in South Carolina, 1816-1836* (New York: Harper and Row, 1965); Avery O. Craven, *The Growth of Southern Nationalism, 1848-1861* (Baton Rouge: Louisiana State University Press, 1953).

4. See also Susan-Mary Grant, *North over South: Northern Nationalism and American Identity in the Antebellum Era* (Lawrence: University Press of Kansas), 2000; Carl N. Degler, "Thesis, Antithesis, Synthesis: The South, the North, and the Nation," *Journal of Southern History* 53 (February 1987): 3–18.

5. Washington Lafayette Clayton, *Olden Times Revisited: W. L. Clayton's Pen Pictures*, edited by Minrose Gwin (Jackson: University Press of Mississippi, 1982), 150. Paul Quigley, *Shifting Grounds: Nationalism and the American South, 1848-1865* (New York: Oxford University Press, 2012); James C. Cobb, *Away Down South: A History of Southern Identity* (New York: Oxford University Press, 2005), 21–26; Grant, *North over South*; Joyce E. Chaplin, *An Anxious Pursuit: Agricultural Innovation and Modernity in the Lower South, 1730-1815* (Chapel Hill: University of North Carolina Press, 1993); David Hackett Fischer, *Albion's Seed: Four British Folkways in America* (New York: Oxford University Press, 1989), 207–32; William R.

Taylor, *Cavalier and Yankee: The Old South and American National Character* (New York: Oxford University Press, 1961; 1993).

6. Elizabeth Fox-Genovese and Eugene D. Genovese, *The Mind of the Master Class: History and Faith in the Southern Slaveholders' Worldview* (New York: Cambridge University Press, 2005); Sally E. Hadden, *Slave Patrols: Law and Violence in Virginia and the Carolinas* (Cambridge: Harvard University Press, 2001); J. Michael Crane, "Controlling the Night: Perceptions of the Slave Patrol System in Mississippi," *Journal of Mississippi History* 61 (Summer 1999): 119–36; Stephanie McCurry, *Masters of Small Worlds: Yeoman Households, Gender Relations, and the Political Culture of the Antebellum South Carolina Low Country* (New York: Oxford University Press, 1995); Bertram Wyatt-Brown, *Southern Honor: Ethics and Behavior in the Old South* (New York: Oxford University Press, 1982); Edmund S. Morgan, *American Slavery, American Freedom: The Ordeal of Colonial Virginia* (New York: W. W. Norton, 1975).

7. David J. Libby, *Slavery and Frontier Mississippi, 1720–1835* (Jackson: University Press of Mississippi, 2004); Charles Sackett Sydnor, *Slavery in Mississippi* (Gloucester: Peter Smith, 1935; 1965), ii, 164; U.S. Department of the Interior, *The Seventh Census of the United States: 1850* (Washington, DC: Robert Armstrong, Public Printer, 1853), 449.

8. Michael A. Gomez, *Exchanging Our Country Marks: The Transformation of African Identities in the Colonial and Antebellum South* (Chapel Hill: University of North Carolina Press, 1998); see especially chapter 8; Philip D. Morgan, *Slave Counterpoint: Black Culture in the Eighteenth-Century Chesapeake and Lowcountry* (Chapel Hill: University of North Carolina Press, 1998); Michael Mullin, *Africa in America: Slave Acculturation and Resistance in the American South and the British Caribbean, 1736–1831* (Urbana: University of Illinois Press, 1992).

9. Gilbert Osofsky, ed., *Puttin' On Ole Massa* (New York: Harper and Row, 1969), 66; George P. Rawick, ed., *The American Slave: A Composite Autobiography*, Vol. 7, pt. 2: *Oklahoma and Mississippi Narratives* (Westport, CT: Greenwood, 1972), 12. For more on slave trickster tales and activities, see Lawrence Levine, *Black Culture and Black Consciousness: Afro-American Thought from Slavery to Freedom* (New York: Oxford University Press, 1977), 121–35.

10. The long historiography of slave docility began with early historians generally accepting the premise of slave contentment and other stereotypes promoted alongside it. Stanley Elkins's *Slavery: A Problem in American Institutional and Intellectual Life* (Chicago: University of Chicago Press, 1959) included the Sambo-thesis, which explained slaves' docility as a result of their abusive treatment that reduced them to an infantile state. An avalanche of literature followed that sought to discredit the argument, producing new research into slave autonomy, community structure, slave culture, and slave resistance. See John W. Blassingame, *The Slave Community: Plantation Life in the Antebellum South* (New York: Oxford University Press, 1972), particularly chapter 8; Eugene D. Genovese, *Roll, Jordan, Roll: The World the Slaves Made* (New York: Vintage Books, 1972).

11. Rawick, *American Slave*, vol. 7, pt. 2, 77, 4; George P. Rawick, Jan Hillegas, and Ken Lawrence, eds., *The American Slave: A Composite Autobiography, Supplement, Series I, Mississippi Narratives*, vol. 6 (Westport, CT: Greenwood Press, 1977), 235. On the relationship between slaves and the "plain folk," see Frank L. Owsley, *Plain Folk of the Old South* (Baton Rouge: Louisiana State University Press, 1949).

12. Winthrop D. Jordan, *White over Black: American Attitudes toward the Negro, 1550–1812*, 2nd ed. (Chapel Hill: University of North Carolina Press, 2012); for a general overview

of the period, see Daniel Walker Howe, *What Hath God Wrought: The Transformation of America, 1815–1848* (New York: Oxford University Press, 2009).

13. Christopher J. Olsen, *Political Culture and Secession in Mississippi: Masculinity, Honor, and the Antiparty Tradition, 1830–1860* (New York: Oxford University Press, 2000), 14, 6–14.

14. On the process of creating a positive self-concept, see Henri Tajfel and John Turner, "An Integrative Theory of Intergroup Conflict," in *The Social Psychology of Intergroup Relations*, edited by William G. Austin and Stephen Worchel (Monterey: Brooks/Cole, 1979), 40.

15. *Vicksburg Sentinel*, October 1, 1850; December 3, 1850; *Woodville Republican*, September 4, 1850. Works on gender and gendered language in the Old South include Olsen, *Political Culture and Secession in Mississippi*; Cynthia A. Kierner, *Beyond the Household: Women's Place in the Early South, 1700–1835* (Ithaca: Cornell University Press, 1998); Mary Beth Norton, *Founding Mothers and Fathers: Gendered Power and the Forming of American Society* (New York: Vintage Books, 1996); McCurry, *Masters of Small Worlds*; Victoria E. Bynum, *Unruly Women: The Politics of Social and Sexual Control in the Old South* (Chapel Hill: University of North Carolina Press, 1992); Elizabeth Fox-Genovese, *Within the Plantation Household: Black and White Women of the Old South* (Chapel Hill: University of North Carolina Press, 1988); Wyatt-Brown, *Southern Honor*.

16. Lynda Lasswell Crist, ed., *The Papers of Jefferson Davis*, vol. 4 (Baton Rouge: Louisiana State University Press, 1983), 144–45.

17. *Woodville Republican*, September 4, 1850.

18. *Flag of the Union* (Jackson), December 6, 1850. Several other newspapers in the state changed their names to reflect their states' rights or unionist position; see Olsen, *Political Culture and Secession in Mississippi*, 45.

19. *Flag of the Union* (Jackson), November 22, 1850; December 27, 1850; *Southron* (Jackson), September 6, 1850; *Woodville Republican*, August 6, 1850.

20. *Southron* (Jackson), September 6, 1850.

21. Henry Foote, *Oration Delivered by the Hon. Henry S. Foote on the Fourth of July, 1850, at Monument Place* (Washington: Henry Polkinhorn, 1850), 16.

22. Samuel S. Boyd, *Speech of Hon. Samuel S. Boyd Delivered at the Great Union Festival, held at Jackson, Mississippi, on the 10th day of October, 1851* (Natchez: Book and Job Office of the Natchez Courier, 1851), 3, 16.

23. *Mississippi Free Trader and Natchez Gazette* (Natchez), March 16, 1850.

24. M. W. Cluskey, ed., *Speeches, Messages, and Other Writings of the Hon. Albert G. Brown, a Senator in Congress from the State of Mississippi* (Philadelphia: Jas. B. Smith, 1859), 170, 167, 169.

25. Ibid., 256, 257.

26. Lynette Boney Wrenn, ed., *A Bachelor's Life in Antebellum Mississippi: The Diary of Dr. Elijah Millington Walker, 1849–1852* (Knoxville: University of Tennessee Press, 2004), 96–97, 111, 112, 112–13.

27. *Hinds County Gazette* (Jackson), October 31, 1850. See also Cleo Hearon, *Mississippi and the Compromise of 1850* (New York: AMS Press, 1913; 1972), 47, 172–73; St. George L. Sioussat, "Tennessee, the Compromise of 1850, and the Nashville Convention," *Mississippi Valley Historical Review* 2 (December 1915): 329–47.

28. Olsen, *Political Culture and Secession in Mississippi*, 45–47; Eric H. Walther, *The Fire-Eaters* (Baton Rouge: Louisiana State University Press, 1992), 102–6; Robert E. May, *John A. Quitman: Old South Crusader* (Baton Rouge: Louisiana State University Press, 1985), 236–52.

29. Henry S. Foote, *War of the Rebellion; or, Scylla and Charybdis: Consisting of Observa-tions upon the Causes, Course, and Consequences of the Late Civil War in the United States* (New York: Harper and Brothers 1866), 172–73; Jefferson Davis, *The Rise and Fall of the Con-federate Government*, vol. 1 (New York: Thomas Yoseloff, 1958; 1881), 18–22; William J. Cooper, Jr., *Jefferson Davis, American* (New York: Vintage Books, 2000), 227–39; Bradley G. Bond, *Political Culture in the Nineteenth-Century South: Mississippi, 1830–1900* (Baton Rouge: Louisiana State University Press, 1995).

30. *Journal of the Convention of the State of Mississippi, and the Act Calling the Same; with the Constitution of the United States, and Washington's Farewell Address* (Jackson: Thomas Palmer, 1851), 3, 10, 47, 48.

31. Walter Chandler, ed., *Journal and Speeches of Greene Callier Chandler* (Memphis: Private printing, 1953), 177.

32. Crist, ed., *Papers of Jefferson Davis*, vol. 6, 139, 230.

33. *Port Gibson Herald and Correspondent* (Port Gibson), January 18, 1850. For works concerning slavery's impact on the development of southern culture and society, see Anthony S. Parent, *Foul Means: The Formation of a Slave Society in Virginia, 1660–1740* (Chapel Hill: University of North Carolina Press, 2003); Kathleen M. Brown, *Good Wives, Nasty Wenches, and Anxious Patriarchs: Gender, Race, and Power in Colonial Virginia* (Chapel Hill: University of North Carolina Press, 1996); Fox-Genovese, *Within the Planta-tion Household*; Morgan, *American Slavery, American Freedom*; Genovese, *Roll, Jordan, Roll*; Ulrich B. Phillips, "The Central Theme of Southern History," *American Historical Review* 34 (October 1928): 30–43. For works concerning the code of honor, see Olsen, *Political Culture and Secession in Mississippi*; Wyatt-Brown, *Southern Honor*.

34. M. W. Cluskey, ed., *Speeches, Messages, and Other Writings of the Hon. Albert G. Brown*, 166, 163.

35. Edward Mayes, *Lucius Q.C. Lamar: His Life, Times, and Speeches, 1825–1893* (Nash-ville: Barbee and Smith, Agents, 1896), 622.

36. In creating a positive self-concept and social identity, Henri Tajfel and John Turner argue, "pressures to evaluate one's own group positively through in-group/out-group compari-sons lead social groups to attempt to differentiate themselves from each other." David Jansson showed the process in action using W. J. Cash's *Mind of the South* to show how a national identity emerged by dumping negative characteristics onto the South to excise "undesirable traits [. . .] from the national identity." Tajfel and Turner, "Integrative Theory of Intergroup Conflict," 40–41; Grant, *North over South*, 4; David R. Jansson, "Internal Orientalism in Amer-ica: W. J. Cash's *The Mind of the South* and the Spatial Construction of American National Identity," *Political Geography* 22 (2003): 293. See also McCardell, *Idea of a Southern Nation*, 4.

37. *Southern Standard* (Columbus), April 30, 1853. The article also appeared in *Woodville Republican and Wilkinson Advertiser* (Woodville), April 26, 1853.

38. *Yazoo Democrat*, February 26, 1851; Ebenezer Newton Elliott, ed., *Cotton Is King, and Pro-Slavery Arguments: Comprising the Writings of Hammond, Harper, Christy, Stringfellow, Hodge, Bledsoe, and Cartwright, on This Important Subject* (Augusta: Pritchard, Abbott and Loomis, 1860), x–xi.

39. *Chronicles of the Fire-Eaters of the Tribe of Mississippi by Seraiah the Scribe* (Brandon: Republican Office, 1853), 2.

40. *Mississippi Palladium* (Holly Springs), July 18, 1851.

41. Ibid., quote. For the political crisis brought about by the Kansas-Nebraska Act, see Michael F. Holt, *The Political Crisis of the 1850s* (New York: W. W. Norton, 1978), chapters 5–6.

42. *Ripley Advertiser*, October 18, 1855; March 20, 1856. For Mississippians' embrace of the Know-Nothings, see Olsen, *Political Culture and Secession in Mississippi*, chapter 7.

43. *Ripley Advertiser*, May 15, 1856; Ebenezer Newton Elliott, ed., *Cotton Is King, and Pro-Slavery Arguments*, v; Foote, *War of the Rebellion*, 207. For further information concerning the Republican Party's ideology, see Eric S. Foner, *Free Soil, Free Labor, Free Men: The Ideology of the Republican Party before the Civil War* (New York: Oxford University Press, 1995).

44. *The Devil in America: A Dramatic Satire* (Mobile: J. K. Randall, 1867), 157.

45. Betty B. Beaumont, *Twelve Years of My Life* (Philadelphia: T. B. Peterson and Brothers, 1887), 52, 57, 105–6.

46. *Mississippi Free Trader and Natchez Gazette*, January 19, 1850.

47. Susan Sillers Darden, Susan Sillers Darden Diary, part 1, Mississippi Department of Archives and History, 253–54; *Natchez Daily Courier*, November 1, 1859.

48. *Mississippi Baptist* (Jackson), November 17, 1859.

49. *Semi-Weekly Mississippian* (Jackson), October 21, 1859; *American Citizen* (Canton), October 29, 1859; *Mississippi Free Trader* (Natchez), January 23, 1860 (third quote). See also Adrienne Cole Phillips, "The Mississippi Press's Response to John Brown's Raid," *Journal of Mississippi History* 48 (Summer 1986): 126–27.

"Those Who Should Be Brothers"

1. Chas. Williams, M.D., "A Bugle Blast from the South," *Macon Beacon*, January 4, 1860.

2. Walter Chandler, ed., *Journal and Speeches of Greene Callier Chandler* (Memphis: Private printing, 1953), 198, 189–90, 197–98.

3. For works on the development of slave society see Anthony S. Parent, *Foul Means: The Formation of a Slave Society in Virginia, 1660–1740* (Chapel Hill: University of North Carolina Press, 2003); Kathleen M. Brown, *Good Wives, Nasty Wenches, and Anxious Patriarchs: Gender, Race, and Power in Colonial Virginia* (Chapel Hill: University of North Carolina Press, 1996); Stephanie McCurry, *Masters of Small Worlds: Yeoman Households, Gender Relations, and the Political Culture of the Antebellum South Carolina Low Country* (New York: Oxford University Press, 1995); Bertram Wyatt-Brown, *Southern Honor: Ethics and Behavior in the Old South* (New York: Oxford University Press, 1982); Edmund S. Morgan, *American Slavery, American Freedom: The Ordeal of Colonial Virginia* (New York: W. W. Norton, 1975); Eugene D. Genovese, *The Political Economy of Slavery: Studies in the Economy and Society of the Slave South* (New York: Pantheon Books, 1965).

4. Works on southern nationalism include John McCardell, *The Idea of a Southern Nation: Southern Nationalists and Southern Nationalism, 1830–1860* (New York: W. W. Norton, 1979); Avery O. Craven, *The Growth of Southern Nationalism, 1848–1861* (Baton Rouge: Louisiana State University Press, 1953).

5. Michael F. Holt, *The Political Crisis of the 1850s* (New York: W. W. Norton, 1978), chapter 7; David M. Potter, *The Impending Crisis, 1848–1861* (New York: Harper Perennial, 1976), chapter 15.

6. Resolution as quoted in Jefferson Davis, *The Rise and Fall of the Confederate Government*, vol. 1 (New York: Thomas Yoseloff, 1958), 43; Percy Lee Rainwater, *Mississippi: Storm Center of Secession, 1856–1861* (Baton Rouge: Otto Claitor, 1938), 114–15; James McPherson, *Battle Cry of Freedom: The Civil War Era* (New York: Oxford University Press, 1988), 214.

7. *Mississippi Free Trader* (Natchez), May 21, 1860; Rainwater, *Mississippi*, 120–28; McPherson, *Battle Cry of Freedom*, 215–16.

8. *Mississippi Free Trader* (Natchez), June 28, 1860; *Semi-Weekly Mississippian* (Jackson), July 10, 1860.

9. *Daily Exchange* (Baltimore), May 11, 1860; John V. Mering, "The Slave-State Constitutional Unionists and the Politics of Consensus," *Journal of Southern History* 43 (August 1977): 395–410.

10. *Eastern Clarion* (Paulding), May 23, 1860.

11. Flavellus G. Nicholson, Diary-Journal, Mississippi Department of Archives and History, 15; *Mississippi Free Trader* (Natchez), November 8, 1860; *Semi-Weekly Mississippian* (Jackson), November 9, 1860; Edward Mayes, *Lucius Q. C. Lamar: His Life, Times, and Speeches, 1825–1893* (Nashville: Barbee and Smith, Agents, 1896), 625; *Oxford Intelligencer*, October 24, 1860.

12. *Oxford Intelligencer*, October 31, 1860.

13. *Mississippi Free Trader*, November 19, 1860.

14. *Semi-Weekly Mississippian* (Jackson), December 4, 1860; *Weekly Vicksburg Whig*, December 22, 1860.

15. *Semi-Weekly Mississippian* (Jackson), November 9, 1860.

16. *Oxford Intelligencer* (Oxford), December 19, 1860.

17. John W. Wood, *Union and Secession in Mississippi* (Memphis: Saunders, Parrish and Whitmore, 1863), 17.

18. *Weekly Vicksburg Whig*, November 21, 1860; *American Citizen* (Canton), November 24, 1860.

19. William C. Smedes, *Speech of William C. Smedes, Esq., Delivered at Apollo Hall, Vicksburg, Miss., on the 27th day of October, A.D. 1860, upon the Right of a State to Secede from the Union and other Political Topics* (Vicksburg: Job Office of M. Shannon, 1860), 8, 29, 31.

20. John H. Aughey, *The Iron Furnace: or, Slavery and Secession* (Philadelphia: William S. and Alfred Martien, 1863), 19–20.

21. Ibid., 39, 44, 47.

22. *Semi-Weekly Mississippian* (Jackson), November 9, 1860; Henry Craft, Diary, Department of Archives and Special Collections, J. D. Williams Library, The University of Mississippi, 47; Susan Sillers Darden, Diary, part one, Mississippi Department of Archives and History, 310.

23. Robert W. Dubay, *John Jones Pettus, Mississippi Fire-Eater: His Life and Times, 1813–1867* (Jackson: University Press of Mississippi, 1975), 32, 62, 67–68; *Semi-Weekly Mississippian* (Jackson), November 13, 1860.

24. *Mississippi Free Trader* (Natchez), December 10, 1860.

25. Rainwater, *Mississippi*, 170–72, 177, 196, 198–99; Dubay, *John Jones Pettus, Mississippi Fire-Eater*, 79. The percentages listed come from the compiled numbers in Rainwater's work. Some county returns are missing, and the percentages serve only as a barometer in gauging secessionist support in Mississippi.

26. Mississippi State Convention, *Journal of the State Convention and Ordinances and Resolutions Adopted in January, 1861* (Jackson: E. Barksdale, State Printer, 1861), 5; Rainwater, *Mississippi*, 203–5.

27. Mississippi State Convention, *Journal of the State Convention* , 92, 93, 94.

28. Charles B. Dew, *Apostles of Disunion: Southern Secession Commissioners and the Causes of the Civil War* (Charlottesville: University of Virginia Press, 2001), 84, 85, 85–86.

29. Fulton Anderson, Henry L. Benning, and John S. Preston, *Addresses Delivered before the Virginia State Convention* (Richmond): Wyatt M. Elliot, Printer, 1861), 6–7, 9, 11, 15.

30. Susan Sillers Darden, Diary, part one, 314; G. W. Bachman, *Sketches and Incidents of Life, Vol. 1: 1839–1885,* Special Collections, Mitchell Memorial Library, Mississippi State University, 10–11; Edward Fontaine, Journal, Special Collections, Mitchell Memorial Library, Mississippi State University, 189–90.

31. William J. Cooper, Jr., *Jefferson Davis, American* (New York: Vintage Books, 2000), 342–43.

32. Lynda Lasswell Crist, ed., *The Papers of Jefferson Davis,* vol. 7 (Baton Rouge: Louisiana State University Press, 1992), 21; Reuben Davis, *Recollections of Mississippi and Mississippians* (Jackson: University and College Press of Mississippi, 1972), 401.

33. Cooper, *Jefferson Davis, American,* 350–53; McPherson, *Battle Cry of Freedom,* 257–59; see also Emory M. Thomas, *The Confederacy as a Revolutionary Experience* (Englewood Cliffs, NJ: Prentice-Hall, 1971).

34. Crist *Papers of Jefferson Davis,* vol. 7, 46, 47, 49–50.

"Like Patriots of Old"

1. Harry Macarthy, "The Bonnie Blue Flag" (New Orleans: A. E. Blackmar and Bro., 1861).

2. Walter Chandler, ed., *Journal and Speeches of Greene Callier Chandler* (Memphis: Private printing, 1953), 56–57.

3. Macarthy, *Bonnie Blue Flag*; Ben Wynne, *Mississippi's Civil War: A Narrative History* (Macon: Mercer University Press, 2006), 32.

4. Historians have paid much attention to the formation of Confederate nationalism and whether or not it succeeded. An argument that underscores the concept of identity shows that a Confederate identity succeeded and remained pervasive at the same time that southerners deserted the military and evaded Confederate policies. Works on the failure of Confederate nationalism include Armstead L. Robinson, *Bitter Fruits of Bondage: The Demise of Slavery and the Collapse of the Confederacy, 1861–1865* (Charlottesville: University of Virginia Press, 2005); George C. Rable, *The Confederate Republic: A Revolution against Politics* (Chapel Hill: University of North Carolina Press, 1994); Richard E. Beringer, Herman Hattaway, Archer Jones, and William N. Still, Jr., *Why the South Lost the Civil War* (Athens: University of Georgia Press, 1986); Emory M. Thomas, *The Confederate Nation: 1861–1865* (New York: Harper and Row, 1979); Paul D. Escott, *After Secession: Jefferson Davis and the Failure of Confederate Nationalism* (Baton Rouge: Louisiana State University Press, 1978). Recent studies have focused on the successes of Confederate nationalism and the creation of a Confederate identity. Many have argued that despite war-weariness, attachment to a Confederate identity continued well past the war years. These studies tend to examine the creation of cultural symbols as a unifying force that white southerners rallied behind, such as Confederate leaders, the Rebel flag, and a shared history as Confederates. See Paul Quigley, *Shifting Grounds: Nationalism and the American South, 1848–1865* (New York: Oxford University Press, 2012); Anne Sarah Rubin, *A Shattered Nation: The Rise and Fall of the Confederacy, 1861–1868* (Chapel Hill: University of North Carolina Press, 2005); Gary W. Gallagher, *The Confederate War* (Cambridge: Harvard University Press, 1997); Drew Gilpin Faust, *The Creation of Confederate Nationalism: Ideology and Identity in the Civil War South* (Baton Rouge: Louisiana State University Press, 1988). The argument that interaction played a central role in the creation of a Confederate identity relies heavily on group identity theory and the concepts of social interactionism. For works on group identity theory, see Henri Tajfel and John Turner, "An Integrative Theory of Intergroup Conflict," in *The Social Psychology of*

Intergroup Relations, edited by William G. Austin and Stephen Worchel (Monterey: Brooks/Cole, 1979); James E. Cote and Charles G. Levine, *Identity Formation, Agency, and Culture: A Social Psychological Synthesis* (Mahwah, NJ: Lawrence Erlbaum Associates, 2002). The basic tenets of social interactionism come from Herbert Blumer, *Symbolic Interactionism: Perspective and Method* (Englewood Cliffs, NJ: Prentice-Hall, 1969). For a few works that incorporate social interaction and identity formation, see Marshall Sahlins, *Islands of History* (Chicago: University of Chicago Press, 1985); Richard C. Trexler, ed., *Persons in Groups: Social Behavior as Identity Formation in Medieval and Renaissance Europe* (Binghamton, NY: Medieval and Renaissance Texts and Studies, 1985); Clifford Geertz, *The Interpretations of Cultures: Selected Essays* (New York: Basic Books, 1973).

5. Ezekiel Armstrong, Diary, Mississippi Department of Archives and History, 2; Sophia Boyd Hays, Diary, box 4, Special Collections, Mitchell Memorial Library, Mississippi State University; M. A. Ryan, *Experience of a Confederate Soldier in Camp and Prison in the Civil War, 1861–1865*, Special Collections, Mitchell Memorial Library, Mississippi State University, 1; Betty B. Beaumont, *Twelve Years of My Life* (Philadelphia: T. B. Peterson and Brothers, 1887), 166–67; E. Grey Dimond and Herman Hattaway, eds., *Letters from Forest Place: A Plantation Family's Correspondence, 1846–1881* (Jackson: University Press of Mississippi, 1993), 233.

6. James W. Silver, ed., *A Life for the Confederacy: As Recorded in the Pocket Diaries of Pvt. Robert A. Moore, Co. G 17th Mississippi Regiment Confederate Guards, Holly Springs, Mississippi* (Jackson, TN: McCowat-Mercer Press, 1959), 39. For works concerning vilification of the enemy and the creation of an "other," see Jason Phillips, *Diehard Rebels: The Confederate Culture of Invincibility* (Athens: University Press of Georgia, 2007), 40–75; David R. Jansson, "Internal Orientalism in America: W. J. Cash's *Mind of the South* and the Spatial Construction of American National Identity," *Political Geography* 22 (2003): 293–316.

7. Edward Fontaine, Journal, June 3, 1861—February 1, 1864, Special Collections, Mitchell Memorial Library, Mississippi State University, 59–60; Flavellus G. Nicholson, Diary-Journal, Mississippi Department of Archives and History, 24; Jesse Roderick Sparkman, Civil War Diary, Special Collections, Mitchell Memorial Library, Mississippi State University, 10.

8. William M. Cash and Lucy Somerville Howorth, eds., *My Dear Nellie: The Civil War Letters of William L. Nugent to Eleanor Smith Nugent* (Jackson: University Press of Mississippi, 1977), 43; David A. Welker, ed., *A Keystone Rebel: The Civil War Diary of Joseph Garey, Hudson's Battery, Mississippi Volunteers* (Gettysburg: Thomas, 1996), 40; Jennifer W. Ford, ed., *The Hour of Our Nation's Agony: The Civil War Letters of Lt. William Cowper Nelson of Mississippi* (Knoxville: University of Tennessee Press, 2007), 102; G. W. Roberts, Diary, Mississippi Department of Archives and History, 117. For more information on soldiers' belief in God sustaining the Confederate cause, see Jason Phillips, *Diehard Rebels: The Confederate Culture of Invincibility* (Athens: University Press of Georgia, 2007), 9–39.

9. Edward Fontaine, Journal, November 3, 1866—December 10, 1866, Special Collections, Mitchell Memorial Library, Mississippi State University, 8–9; Silver, *Life for the Confederacy*, 137; Cash and Howorth, *My Dear Nellie*, 132; Richard A. Baumgartner, ed., *Blood and Sacrifice: The Civil War Journal of a Confederate Soldier* (Huntington: Blue Acorn Press, 1994), 32.

10. *Eastern Clarion* (Paulding), March 29, 1861; William Howard Russell, *My Diary North and South*, edited by Eugene H. Berwanger (Philadelphia: Temple University Press, 1988), 198; Joel Parker, *The Right of Secession: A Review of the Message of Jefferson Davis to the Congress of the Confederate States* (Cambridge, MA: Welch, Bigelow, 1861), 6.

11. William Peel, Diary, Mississippi Department of Archives and History, 28;; James W. Silver, ed., *A Life for the Confederacy*, 103; David A. Welker, ed., *A Keystone Rebel: The Civil War Diary of Joseph Garey, Hudson's Battery, Mississippi Volunteers* (Gettysburg: Thomas, 1996), 46. For information on American holiday celebration in the Confederacy, see Paul Quigley, "Independence Day Dilemmas in the American South, 1848–1865," *Journal of Southern History* 75 (May 2009): 235–66.

12. On gender and the Civil War, see Joyce L. Broussard, "Occupied Natchez, Elite Women, and the Feminization of the Civil War," *Journal of Mississippi History* 70 (Summer 2008): 179–207; LeeAnn White, *Gender Matters: Civil War, Reconstruction, and the Making of the New South* (New York: Palgrave Macmillan, 2005); Sheila R. Phipps, *Genteel Rebel: The Life of Mary Greenhow Lee* (Baton Rouge: Louisiana State University Press, 2004); Nancy Bercaw, *Gendered Freedoms: Race, Rights, and the Politics of Household in the Delta, 1861–1875* (Gainesville: University Press of Florida, 2003); Drew Gilpin Faust, *Mothers of Invention: Women of the Slaveholding South in the American Civil War* (Chapel Hill: University of North Carolina Press, 1996).

13. Dimond and Hattaway, *Letters from Forest Place*, 240, 252; Annie Harper, *Annie Harper's Journal: A Southern Mother's Legacy* (Denton: Flower Mound Writing Company, 1983), 11, 12. For organizing efforts during the Civil War and their impact, see Drew Gilpin Faust, *Mothers of Invention: Women of the Slaveholding South in the American Civil War* (Chapel Hill: University of North Carolina Press, 1996). For organizing efforts in Mississippi, see Wynne, *Mississippi's Civil War*, 44–45.

14. Cordelia Scales to Loulie, August 17, 1861, Mississippi Department of Archives and History; Sophia Boyd Hays, Diary, Box 4, June 14, 1862, Special Collections, Mitchell Memorial Library, Mississippi State University; Richard Barksdale Harwell, ed., *Kate: The Journal of a Confederate Nurse by Kate Cumming* (Baton Rouge: Louisiana State University Press, 1959), 38.

15. Baumgartner, *Blood and Sacrifice*, 13; Silver, *Life for the Confederacy*, 32; Cash and Howorth, eds., *My Dear Nellie*, 77.

16. Gordon A. Cotton, ed., *From the Pen of a She-Rebel: The Civil War Diary of Emilie Riley McKinley* (Columbia: University of South Carolina Press, 2001), 42.

17. Cordelia Scales to Loulie, January 27, 1863, Mississippi Department of Archives and History.

18. Cordelia Scales to Loulie, October 29 , 1862, Mississippi Department of Archives and History; Emma Balfour, Civil War Diary, Mississippi Department of Archives and History, 21; Anne Shannon Martin, Diary, 25 February 1864, Mississippi Department of Archives and History. For information of the "Battle of the Handkerchiefs," see Drew Gilpin Faust, *Mothers of Invention: Women of the Slaveholding South in the American Civil War* (Chapel Hill: University of North Carolina Press, 1996), 213.

19. Cotton, *From the Pen of a She-Rebel*, 45, 60–61.

20. Catherine (Kate) Foster, Diary, Mississippi Department of Archives and History, 3, 4; Elizabeth Christine Brown, Diary, Department of Archives and Special Collections, J. D. Williams Library, University of Mississippi, 32; Loretta and William Galbraith, eds., *A Lost Heroine of the Confederacy: The Diaries and Letters of Belle Edmondson* (Jackson: University Press of Mississippi, 1990), 19; Shepherd Spencer Neville Brown, Sr., ed., *War Years, C.S.A.: 12th Mississippi Regiment Major S. H. Giles, Q.M. Original Letters, 1860–1865* (Hillsboro: Hill College Press, 1998), 121.

21. Social scientist Herbert Blumer theorized that humans interact with others based on the meaning ascribed to "objects," whether individuals, social groups, institutions, etc. In the case of Confederate Mississippians, for example, they acted the part of a rebel in the presence of northerners because they expected that northerners would view them as such. Confederate Mississippians symbolized northerners as oppressive, power-hungry tyrants, which influenced their role and rhetoric as a "rebel" against a dictatorial regime and people. See Herbert Blumer, *Symbolic Interactionism: Perspective and Method* (Englewood Cliffs, NJ: Prentice Hall, 1969).

22. Sources for Confederate dissenters in Mississippi include Sally Jenkins and John Stauffer, *The State of Jones* (New York: Doubleday, 2009); M. Shannon Mallard, "'I Had No Comfort to Give the People': Opposition to the Confederacy in Civil War Mississippi," *North & South* 6 (May 2003): 78–86; Terry Whittington, "In the Shadow of Defeat: Tracking the Vicksburg Parolees," *Journal of Mississippi History* 64 (Winter 2002): 307–30; Victoria E. Bynum, *The Free State of Jones: Mississippi's Longest Civil War* (Chapel Hill: University of North Carolina Press, 2001); David B. Chesebrough, "Dissenting Clergy in Confederate Mississippi," *Journal of Mississippi History* 55 (May 1993): 115–31.

23. John H. Aughey, *The Iron Furnace; or, Slavery and Secession* (Philadelphia: William S. and Alfred Martien, 1863), 231, 228, 232.

24. John W. Wood, *Union and Secession in Mississippi* (Memphis: Saunders, Parrish, and Whitmore, Printers, 1863), 18, 47, 18, 55, 54.

25. William Howell to his mother, N. K. Howell, March 19, 1864, box 1, Department of Archives and Special Collections, J. D. Williams Library, University of Mississippi; Dimond and Hattaway, *Letters from Forest Place*, 268.

26. The 1860 census counted 436,631 slaves in the state of Mississippi; see U.S. Department of the Interior, *Population of the United States in 1860* (Washington, DC: Government Printing Office, 1864), 269; For a few works on the end of slavery during the Civil War, see Armstead L. Robinson, *Bitter Fruits of Bondage: The Demise of Slavery and the Collapse of the Confederacy, 1861–1865* (Charlottesville: University of Virginia Press, 2005); James McPherson, *The Negro's Civil War: How American Blacks Felt and Acted during the War for the Union* (New York: Vintage Books, 1965; 1993).

27. Winthrop D. Jordan, *Tumult and Silence at Second Creek: An Inquiry into a Civil War Slave Conspiracy*, rev. ed. (Baton Rouge: Louisiana State University Press, 1995), 310, 352.

28. George P. Rawick, Jan Hillegas, and Ken Lawrence, eds., *The American Slave: A Composite Autobiography, Supplement, Series I, Mississippi Narratives* (Westport, CT: Greenwood Press, 1977), 2280 (10:5); 1065 (8:3); 1119 (8:3); 1223 (8:3); 64 (6:1); 1650 (9:4).

29. Fonsylvania Plantation Diary, May–June 1863, Mississippi Department of Archives and History; Samuel Andrew Agnew, Journal, vol. 2, Special Collections, Mitchell Memorial Library, Mississippi State University, 123, 191, 192, 193; Rawick, Hillegas, and Lawrence, *American Slave*, vol. 7, 138.

30. McPherson, *Negro's Civil War*, 167, 190–91; Wynne, *Mississippi's Civil War*, 300.

31. Lynda Lasswell Crist, ed., *The Papers of Jefferson Davis*, vol. 9 (Baton Rouge: Louisiana University Press, 1997), 300.

32. Catherine (Kate) Olivia Foster, Diary, Mississippi Department of Archives and History, 11; Elizabeth Christine Brown, Diary, Department of Archives and Special Collections, J. D. Williams Library, University of Mississippi, 36.

33. Rawick, Hillegas, and Lawrence, *American Slave*, vol. 7, 1141 (8:3); 1601 (9:4).

"Dying Dixie"

1. Emmett Lloyd Ross, Supplementary Collection, "The Dying Soldier," Special Collections, Mitchell Memorial Library, Mississippi State University.

2. Walter Chandler, ed., *Journal and Speeches of Greene Callier Chandler* (Memphis: Private printing, 1953), 92, 95, 96, 97, 56.

3. Prominent psychologist Erik Erikson argued, "We are thus most aware of our identity when we are just about to gain it [and] when we are just about to enter a crisis." See Erik H. Erikson, *Identity and the Life Cycle* (New York: International Press, 1959), 118. Several books discuss the transitional period in the South from Civil War to Reconstruction, including Anne Sarah Rubin, *A Shattered Nation: The Rise and Fall of the Confederacy, 1861–1868* (Chapel Hill: University of North Carolina Press, 2005); LeeAnn White, *Gender Matters: Civil War, Reconstruction, and the Making of the New South* (New York: Palgrave Macmillan, 2005); Bradley G. Bond, *Political Culture in the Nineteenth-Century South: Mississippi, 1830–1900* (Baton Rouge: Louisiana State University Press, 1995); Eric Foner, *Reconstruction: America's Unfinished Revolution, 1863–1877* (New York: Perennial Classics, 1988); James L. Roark, *Masters without Slaves: Southern Planters in the Civil War and Reconstruction* (New York: W. W. Norton, 1977).

4. Charles Roberts to his wife, March 1, 1865, Department of Archives and Special Collections, J. D. Williams Library, University of Mississippi; Richard A. Baumgartner, ed., *Blood and Sacrifice: The Civil War Journal of a Confederate Soldier* (Huntington, WV: Blue Acorn Press, 1994), 194–95, 195; Edward Fontaine, Journal, November 3, 1864—December 10, 1866, Special Collections, Mitchell Memorial Library, Mississippi State University, 42.

5. James C. Neilson to Mary B. Barry, February 4, 1866, Special Collections, Mitchell Memorial Library, Mississippi State University; Catherine (Kate) Olivia Foster, Diary, Mississippi Department of Archives and History, 19–20; Edward Fontaine, Journal, November 3, 1864—December 10, 1866, Special Collections, Mitchell Memorial Library, Mississippi State University, 97–98.

6. Oscar F. Bledsoe, *"The Hopes and Duties of the Present Hour": Oration, before the Two Literary Societies of the University of Mississippi, June 27, 1866* (Memphis: Public Ledger Steam Book and Job Printing Office, 1866), 8, 9.

7. For works on presidential reconstruction in Mississippi, see William C. Harris, *Presidential Reconstruction in Mississippi* (Baton Rouge: Louisiana State University Press, 1967); James Wilford Garner, *Reconstruction in Mississippi* (New York: Macmillan, 1901; Gloucester: Peter Smith, 1964).

8. Samuel Andrew Agnew, Journal, vol. 4, Mitchell Memorial Library, Special Collections, Mississippi State University, 176; H.R. Brinkerhoff to Major General Howard, 8 July 1865, reel 10, *Records of the Assistant Commissioner for the State of Mississippi, Bureau of Refugees, Freedmen, and Abandoned Lands, 1865–1869* (Washington: National Archives Microfilm Publications, 1971).

9. *Journal of the Proceedings and Debates in the Constitutional Convention of the State of Mississippi, August, 1865* (Jackson: E. M. Yerger, State Printer, 1865), 3, 7, 6–7, 7.

10. Ibid., 44.

11. Ibid., 44, 45.

12. Ibid., 53, 54, 55.

13. Ibid., 56–70.

14. Ibid., 109, 70–164.

15. Ibid., 165. For further discussion on the topic, see Bradley G. Bond, *Political Culture in the Nineteenth-Century South: Mississippi, 1830–1900* (Baton Rouge: Louisiana State University Press, 1995), 156–61.

16. Nicholson (Flavellus G.) Diary-Journal, July 4, 1866, Mississippi Department of Archives and History, 36; "Northern Magnanimity and Southern Hatred," *American Citizen* (Canton), February 22, 1866.

17. Edward Fontaine, Journal, August 5, 1870 to January 29, 1873, Special Collections, Mitchell Memorial Library, Mississippi State University, 226, 267, 268.

18. *Journal of the Proceedings and Debates in the Constitutional Convention*, 203; "The Late Confederates and 'Treason,'" *American Citizen* (Canton), July 21, 1866.

19. Joseph C. Carter, ed., *Magnolia Journey: A Union Veteran Revisits the Former Confederate States. Arranged from Letters of Correspondent Russell H. Conwell to the Daily Evening Traveller* (Boston, 1869) (University: University of Alabama Press, 1974), 131, 132.

20. Whitelaw Reid, *After the War: A Tour of the Southern States, 1865–1866*, edited by C. Vann Woodward (New York: Harper and Row, 1965), 394, 395; Albert T. Morgan, *Yazoo; or, On the Picket Line of Freedom in the South: A Personal Narrative* (Columbia: University of South Carolina Press, 2000), 77; J. T. Trowbridge, *The South: A Tour of Its Battle-fields and Ruined Cities* (Hartford, CT: L. Stebbins, 1866), 294.

21. Henry W. Warren, *Reminiscences of a Mississippi Carpet-Bagger* (Worcester, Ma: Davis Press, 1914), 86, 87. The definitive work on Reconstruction in Mississippi remains William C. Harris, *The Day of the Carpetbagger: Republican Reconstruction in Mississippi* (Baton Rouge: Louisiana State University Press, 1979).

22. One of the best general overviews of Reconstruction is Eric Foner, *Reconstruction: America's Unfinished Revolution, 1863–1877* (New York: Perennial Classics, 1988).

23. Voting figures come from Harris, *Day of the Carpetbagger*, 76.

24. George P. Rawick, Jan Hillegas, and Ken Lawrence, eds., *The American Slave: A Composite Autobiography, Supplement, Series I, Mississippi Narratives* (Westport, CT: Greenwood Press, 1977), 2119 (10:5); Letter of Thomas Smith, Chaplain 53rd USA Infantry and Sub-Commissioner of Freedmen's Bureau to Captain J. H. Weber, November 3, 1865, in *Records of the Assistant Commissioner for the State of Mississippi, Bureau of Refugees, Freedmen, and Abandoned Lands, 1865–1869* (Washington, DC: National Archives Microfilm Publications, 1971), roll 12; Trowbridge, *The South*, 362; Robert C. Morris, *Freedmen's Schools and Textbooks, vol. 1. Semi-annual Reports on Schools for Freedmen by John W. Alvord, Numbers 1–10, January, 1866—July, 1870* (New York: AMS Press, 1980), 7.

25. Edward Fontaine, Journal, November 3, 1864—December 10, 1866, Special Collections, Mitchell Memorial Library, Mississippi State University, 57–59.

26. Ibid.

27. Flavellus G. Nicholson, Diary-Journal, Mississippi Department of Archives and History, 33; Trowbridge, *The South*, 369.

28. Trowbridge, *The South*, 362, 363; George P. Rawick, ed., *The American Slave: A Composite Autobiography, vol. 7: Oklahoma and Mississippi Narratives* (Westport, CT: Greenwood Press, 1972), 42.

29. For efforts at convincing blacks to register to vote, see *Records of the Assistant Commissioner for the State of Mississippi*, roll 30; Rawick, Hillegas, and Lawrence, *American Slave*, 588 (7:2); U.S. Congress, Senate, *Mississippi in 1875: Report of the Select Committee to Inquire into the Mississippi Election of 1875, with Testimony and Documentary Evidence*, vol. 1

(Washington, DC: Government Printing Office, 1876), 1292; Morris, *Freedmen's Schools and Textbooks, vol. 1.*, 7.

30. "The Election," *American Citizen* (Canton), November 16, 1867; figures come from *Journal of the Proceedings in the Constitutional Convention of the State of Mississippi* (Jackson: E. Stafford, 1871), 747.

31. Figures come from Harris, *Day of the Carpetbagger: Republican Reconstruction in Mississippi* (Baton Rouge: Louisiana State University Press, 1979), 115. On a personal note, three of the elected delegates did not serve in the convention. One of them, John Moody, elected to represent Greene, Perry, and Jackson Counties, was either my great-great-great-grandfather or great-great-great-great-grandfather. For some reason, he never showed up.

32. *Journal of the Proceedings in the Constitutional Convention of the State of Mississippi* (Jackson: E. Stafford, 1871), 4, 130.

33. Peter P. Bailey, *The Issues of 1868: An Address to the People of Mississippi* (Sataria: Published by author, 1868), 3, 7; James L. Alcorn, *Address of J. L. Alcorn*, (*Republican Candidate for Governor*,) *to the People of Mississippi* (Friar's Point: Published by author, 1869), 13.

34. One of the works dealing with black political participation and changes during Reconstruction is John R. Lynch, *The Facts of Reconstruction* (New York: Neale, 1913).

35. Jones-Smith Plantation Journal, January 11, 1872, Mississippi Department of Archives and History; Samuel Andrew Agnew, Diary, vol. 6, Special Collections, Mitchell Memorial Library, Mississippi State University, 165.

36. Albert T. Morgan, *Yazoo; or, On the Picket Line of Freedom in the South: A Personal Narrative* (Columbia: University of South Carolina Press, 2000), 49, 94, 96.

37. For works on Klan activity, see Allen W. Trelease, *White Terror: The Ku Klux Klan Conspiracy and Southern Reconstruction* (New York: Harper and Row, 1971); William Dudley Bell, "The Ku Klux Klan in Mississippi, 1866–1872" (master's thesis, Mississippi State University, 1963). Robert Somers, *The Southern States since the War, 1870–71* (University: University of Alabama Press, 1965), 153.

38. As quoted in *American Citizen*, March 21, 1868; Rawick, Hillegas, and Lawrence, *American Slave*, 746 (7:2); 1355–56 (9:4).

39. Jennie Shaw to Sister Anna, 30 March 1871, Special Collections, Mitchell Memorial Library, Mississippi State University; J. E. Robuck, *My Own Personal Experience and Observation as a Soldier in the Confederate Army during the Civil War, 1861–1865, also during the Period of Reconstruction*, reprint (Memphis: Burke's Book Store, 1978; 1911), 72; Maria Waterbury, *Seven Years among the Freedmen* (Chicago: T. B. Arnold, 1890), 22–24.

40. John Richard Dennett, *The South As It Is: 1865–1866*, edited by Henry M. Christman (New York: Viking Press, 1965), 354; John Moore to Merritt Barber, November 30, 1867, *Records of the Assistant Commissioner for the State of Mississippi, Bureau of Refugees, Freedmen, and Abandoned Lands, 1865–1869* (Washington: National Archives Microfilm Publications, 1971), roll 31; John Moore to S. Greene, July 31, 1868, *Records of the Assistant Commissioner for the State of Mississippi, Bureau of Refugees, Freedmen, and Abandoned Lands, 1865–1869* (Washington: National Archives Microfilm Publications, 1971), roll 33.

41. "State Monumental Association," *American Citizen* (Canton), June 14, 1866; Benjamin G. Humphreys, "Editorial and Miscellanies," *De Bow's Review* 1 (June 1866): 644, 665.

42. Emmett Lloyd Ross, Supplementary Collection, "Memorial Day, a Poem," Special Collections, Mitchell Memorial Library, Mississippi State University, 6–7.

43. "The Fourth of July," *American Citizen* (Canton), July 5, 1866.

44. "Memorial Day," *American Citizen* (Canton), April 17, 1869; Emmett Lloyd Ross, Supplementary Collection, "Memorial Day, a Poem," Special Collections, Mitchell Memorial Library, Mississippi State University, 9–10.

45. J. W. Clapp, Address Given at Franklin Female College at Holly Springs, folder 10, Department of Archives and Special Collections, J. D. Williams Library, University of Mississippi, 13, 14.

46. Edward Mayes, *Lucius Q.C. Lamar: His Life, Times, and Speeches, 1825–1893* (Nashville: Barbee and Smith, Agents, 1896), 657.

47. Ibid., 658.

"Thy Bright Sun Will Rise Again"

1. James D. Lynch, *Redpath: or The Ku-Klux Tribunal, a Poem* (Columbus: Excelsior Book and Job Printing Establishment, 1877), 16.

2. Walter Chandler, ed., *Journal and Speeches of Greene Callier Chandler* (Memphis: Private printing, 1953), 218, 222, 227.

3. Reverend A. C. McDonald, Sermon, Department of Archives and Special Collections, J. D. Williams Library, University of Mississippi, 3–4, 5, 12.

4. In their theory of intergroup conflict, Henri Tajfel and John Turner state that "when social identity is unsatisfactory, individuals will strive either to leave their existing group and join some more positively distinct group and/or to make their existing group more positively distinct." This process occurred in Mississippi during Reconstruction. Greene Chandler, for instance, decided to abandon his Confederate identity and his previous alliance with the Democrats and secessionists, and started championing the Republican cause. A majority of white Mississippians, however, refused to make such a leap, leaving them with the option to create a new, positive identity. The creation of this new national identity produced the Lost Cause legend. Scholars have shown how race helped the two sections reconcile by rejecting the emancipationist memory of the Civil War. They have also revealed the role memory played in southerners creating the Lost Cause legend. While memory played a major role in the process of reconciliation, white Mississippians actively sought to project a positive social identity that laid the groundwork on which they built the Lost Cause legend. Henri Tajfel and John Turner, "An Integrative Theory of Intergroup Conflict," in William G. Austin and Stephen Worchel, eds., *The Social Psychology of Intergroup Relations* (Monterey, CA: Brooks/Cole, 1979), 40. For works on the Lost Cause, memory, and reconciliation, see W. Fitzhugh Brundage, *The Southern Past: A Clash of Race and Memory* (Cambridge: Belknap Press of Harvard University Press, 2005); Sally Leigh McWhite, "Echoes of the Lost Cause: Civil War Reverberations in Mississippi from 1865 to 2001" (PhD diss., University of Mississippi, 2003); David W. Blight, *Race and Reunion: The Civil War in American Memory* (Cambridge: Belknap Press of Harvard University Press, 2001); W. Fitzhugh Brundage, ed., *Where These Memories Grow: History, Memory, and Southern Identity* (Chapel Hill: University of North Carolina Press, 2000); Gaines M. Foster, *Ghosts of the Confederacy: Defeat, the Lost Cause, and the Emergence of the New South* (New York: Oxford University Press, 1987); Patrick Gerster and Nicholas Cords, eds., *Myth and Southern History: The Old South* (Chicago: Rand McNally College Publishing, 1974).

5. William Henry Sparks, *The Memories of Fifty Years*, 3rd ed. (Philadelphia: Claxton, Remsen and Haffelfinger, 1872), 224, 225.

6. Edward Fontaine, Journal, April 15, 1874–May 17, 1875, Special Collections, Mitchell Memorial Library, Mississippi State University, 63, 64.

7. Ibid., 65, 66.

8. W. H. McRaven Papers, Mississippi Department of Archives and History, 7; Charles Nordhoff, *The Cotton States in the Spring and Summer of 1875* (New York: D. Appleton, 1876), 74. For more information about the inability to create a conservative biracial party, see William C. Harris, *The Day of the Carpetbagger: Republican Reconstruction in Mississippi* (Baton Rouge: Louisiana State University Press, 1979), chapters 2–9.

9. Governor Adelbert Ames Speech, Department of Archives and Special Collections, J. D. Williams Library, University of Mississippi, 5, 6.

10. Charles Nordhoff, *The Cotton States in the Spring and Summer of 1875* (New York: D. Appleton, 1876), 77. Examples abound of voter fraud in the testimonies collected by the U.S. Senate: United States Senate, *Mississippi in 1875: Report of the Select Committee to Inquire into the Mississippi Election of 1875, with the Testimony and Documentary Evidence*, 2 vols. (Washington: Government Printing Office, 1876). For more information about tactics during the campaign of 1875 see Warren A. Ellem, "The Overthrow of Reconstruction in Mississippi," *Journal of Mississippi History* 54 (May 1992): 175–201.

11. Henry W. Warren, *Reminiscences of a Mississippi Carpet-Bagger* (Worcester: Davis Press, 1914), 70, 71; U.S. Congress, Senate, *Mississippi in 1875: Report of the Select Committee to Inquire into the Mississippi Election of 1875, with the Testimony and Documentary Evidence* (Washington, DC: Government Printing Office, 1876), vol. 1, 106–7, 234, 236, 280; vol. 2, 1025.

12. U.S. Congress, *Mississippi in 1875*, vol. 2, 1025.

13. Ibid., vol. 2, Documentary Evidence. In 1873, total Republican votes for state treasurer equaled 70,462; in 1875, the Republican candidate received 67,171 votes. The Democratic candidate in 1873 received 47,486 votes and a whopping 98,715 in 1875. See also Harris, *Day of the Carpetbagger*, chapters 20–21.

14. *The Testimony in the Impeachment of Adelbert Ames, as Governor of Mississippi* (Jackson: Power and Barksdale, State Printers, 1877), 51.

15. The investigations span two volumes, in U.S. Congress, Senate, *Mississippi in 1875*.

16. Ibid., vol. 1, 119, 256, 463; vol. 2, 1052–53, 1054.

17. Ibid., vol. 2, 1064; vol. 1, 57.

18. Ibid., vol. 1, 805, 551, 270.

19. Ibid., vol. 2, 1076.

20. Ibid., vol. 1, 935–36.

21. U.S. Congress, Senate, *Mississippi. Testimony as to Denial of Elective Franchise in Mississippi at the Elections of 1875 and 1876* (Washington, DC: Government Printing Office, 1877), 1002.

22. John R. Lynch, *The Facts of Reconstruction* (New York: Neale, 1913), 153.

23. The best works dealing with politics in Mississippi following Reconstruction are Stephen Cresswell, *Rednecks, Redeemers, and Race: Mississippi after Reconstruction, 1877–1917* (Jackson: University Press of Mississippi, 2006); Stephen Cresswell, *Multi-party Politics in Mississippi, 1877–1902* (Jackson: University Press of Mississippi, 1995).

24. Mississippi Constitutional Convention, *Journal of the Proceedings of the Constitutional Convention of the State of Mississippi* (Jackson: E. L. Martin, 1890), 10. For further information on the Mississippi Constitutional Convention of 1890, see Cresswell, *Rednecks,*

Redeemers, and Race, and *Multi-party Politics in Mississippi, 1877–1902*; Neil R. McMillen, *Dark Journey: Black Mississippians in the Age of Jim Crow* (New York: Vintage Books, 1998).

25. Mississippi Constitutional Convention, *Journal of the Proceedings,* 22; J. P. Coleman, comp., *The Constitution of the State of Mississippi: Adopted by the People of Mississippi in a Constitutional Convention November 1, 1890 at Jackson and all Amendments Subsequently Adopted* (Jackson: Distributed by Heber Ladner, Secretary of State, 1954), 164, 179, 182, 183.

26. Isaiah T. Montgomery, *"What Answer?" Speech in Support of Franchise Committee Report, Mississippi Constitutional Convention,* 1890.

27. Booker T. Washington, *Up from Slavery: An Autobiography* (New York: Doubleday, Page, 1907), 220, 222; for more on Montgomery's accommodationism, see Janet Sharp Hermann, *The Pursuit of a Dream* (New York: Oxford University Press), 229–32.

28. For further information on Washington's accommodationism and the black community as a whole, see Mark Bauerlein, "Booker T. Washington and W.E.B. Du Bois: The Origins of a Bitter Intellectual Battle," *Journal of Blacks in Higher Education* 46 (Winter 2004–2005), 107.

29. The best source for Jim Crow's impact in Mississippi is McMillen, *Dark Journey.* For additional works, see Leon F. Litwack, *Trouble in Mind: Black Southerners in the Age of Jim Crow* (New York: Vintage Books, 1998); Grace Elizabeth Hale, *Making Whiteness: The Culture of Segregation in the South, 1890–1940* (New York: Vintage Books, 1998); James C. Cobb, *The Most Southern Place on Earth: The Mississippi Delta and the Roots of Regional Identity* (New York: Oxford University Press, 1992); C. Vann Woodward, *The Strange Career of Jim Crow* (New York: Oxford University Press, 1955).

"Long as Life Shall Last"

1. Emmett Lloyd Ross, Supplementary Collection, "Memorial Day, a Poem," Special Collections, Mitchell Memorial Library, Mississippi State University.

2. Walter Chandler, ed., *Journal and Speeches of Greene Callier Chandler* (Memphis: Private printing, 1953), 170, 171.

3. When dealing with the Lost Cause, historians have spent a lot of effort on memory, monument building, and memorial organizations. This chapter seeks to add to the scholarship already available by focusing on historical writing and the desire to sustain a positive social identity in the eyes of the rest of the nation and future posterity. Currently, there exist few works that discuss Mississippi's Lost Cause. The most comprehensive focuses on the interplay of memory, political power, and Confederate symbols during the twentieth century; see Sally Leigh McWhite, "Echoes of the Lost Cause: Reverberations in Mississippi from 1865 to 2001" (PhD diss., University of Mississippi, 2002). General studies on the Lost Cause, memory, and historical writing include W. Fitzhugh Brundage, *The Southern Past: A Clash of Race and Memory* (Cambridge: Belknap Press of Harvard University Press, 2005); James C. Cobb, *Away Down South: A History of Southern Identity* (New York: Oxford University Press, 2005); David Goldfield, *Still Fighting the Civil War: The American South and Southern History* (Baton Rouge: Louisiana State University Press, 2002); David W. Blight, *Race and Reunion: The Civil War in American Memory* (Cambridge: Belknap Press of Harvard University Press, 2001); W. Fitzhugh Brundage, ed., *Where These Memories Grow: History, Memory, and Southern Identity* (Chapel Hill: University of North Carolina Press, 2000); Gary W. Gallagher and Alan T. Nolan, eds., *The Myth of the Lost Cause and Civil War History* (Bloomington: Indiana University Press, 2000); William C. Davis, *The Cause Lost: Myths and Realities of the Confederacy* (Lawrence: University Press of Kansas, 1996);

Gaines M. Foster, *Ghosts of the Confederacy: Defeat, the Lost Cause, and the Emergence of the New South* (New York: Oxford University Press, 1987); C. Vann Woodward, *The Burden of Southern History*, updated 3rd ed. (Baton Rouge: Louisiana State University Press, 1960, 2008). For an excellent work on historical writing and identity construction, see Peter C. Messer, *Stories of Independence: Identity, Ideology, and History in Eighteenth-Century America* (DeKalb: Northern Illinois University Press, 2005).

4. Richard A. Baumgartner, ed., *Blood and Sacrifice: The Civil War Journal of a Confederate Soldier* (Huntington, WV: Blue Acorn Press, 1994), 119.

5. Dunbar Rowland, "Plantation Life in Mississippi before the War," *Publications of the Mississippi Historical Society*, vol. 3 (University: Printed for the Society, 1900), 87–88; Belle Kearney, *A Slaveholder's Daughter* (New York: Abbey Press, 1900), 1; Horace Fulkerson, *Random Recollections of Early Days in Mississippi* (Vicksburg: Vicksburg Printing and Publishing Company, 1885), 142–43.

6. Kearney, *Slaveholder's Daughter*, 2, 9; Rowland, "Plantation Life in Mississippi before the War," 93; Frank A. Montgomery, *Reminiscences of a Mississippian in Peace and War* (Cincinnati: Robert Clark, 1901), 20.

7. Reuben Davis, *Recollections of Mississippi and Mississippians* (Jackson: University and College Press of Mississippi, 1972; 1889), 297–98; Annie Harper, *Annie Harper's Journal: A Southern Mother's Legacy* (Denton, TX: Flower Mound Writing Company, 1983), 5.

8. Montgomery, *Reminiscences of a Mississippian in Peace and War*, 35–36; Thomas D. Cockrell and Michael B. Ballard, eds., *A Mississippi Rebel in the Army of Northern Virginia: The Civil War Memoirs of Private David Holt* (Baton Rouge: Louisiana State University Press, 1995), 62; Harper, *Annie Harper's Journal*, 6.

9. Davis, *Recollections of Mississippi and Mississippians*, 297; Thomas H. Woods, "A Sketch of the Mississippi Secession Convention of 1861,—Its Membership and Work," *Publications of the Mississippi Historical Society*, vol. 6 (University: Printed for the Society, 1902), 93; J. E. Robuck, *My Own Personal Experiences and Observation as a Soldier in the Confederate Army during the Civil War, 1861–1865, also during the Period of Reconstruction*, reprint (Memphis: Burkes' Book Store, 1978, 1911); 97.

10. Harper, *Annie Harper's Journal*, 10; Samuel W. Hankins, *Simple Story of a Soldier: Life and Service in the 2nd Mississippi Infantry* (Tuscaloosa: University of Alabama Press, 2004), 72; Fulkerson, *Random Recollections of Early Days in Mississippi*, 145–46, 149; James Dinkins, *1861 to 1865: Personal Recollections and Experiences in the Confederate Army by an "Old Johnnie"* (Dayton: Press of Morningside Bookshop, 1975), 261, 260.

11. One of the best, concise books on Jefferson Davis is William J. Cooper, Jr., *Jefferson Davis, American* (New York: Vintage Books, 2000).

12. Jefferson Davis, *The Rise and Fall of the Confederate Government*, vol. 1 (New York: Thomas Yoseloff, 1881), 6, 77, 78.

13. Ibid., 47, 49, 83.

14. Ibid., 762, 764, 763.

15. J. M. Gibson, *Memoirs of J. M. Gibson: Terrors of the Civil War and Reconstruction Days* (Houston: Private printing, 1929), 13; Rowland, "Plantation Life in Mississippi before the War," 89; Harper, *Annie Harper's Journal*, 36.

16. Dinkins, *1861 to 1865*, 277; Horace S. Fulkerson, *The Negro; As He Was; As He Is; As He Will Be* (Vicksburg: Commercial Herald, Printers, 1887), 30, 32–33.

17. Kearney, *Slaveholder's Daughter*, 12–13, 11; Montgomery, *Reminiscences of a Mississippian in Peace and War*, 21.

18. Dinkins, *1861 to 1865*, 270, 272; Fulkerson, *The Negro*, 43; Robuck, *My Own Personal Experience and Observation*, 96–97, 74–75; W. H. Hardy, "Recollections of Reconstruction in East and Southeast Mississippi," *Publications of the Mississippi Historical Society*, vol. 4 (University: Printed for the Society, 1901), 131.

19. Harper, *Annie Harper's Journal*, 41; Robuck, *My Own Personal Experience and Observation*, 96; Washington Lafayette Clayton, *Olden Times Revisited: W. L. Clayton's Pen Pictures*, edited by Minrose Gwin (Jackson: University of Mississippi Press, 1982), 151.

20. Gibson, *Memoirs of J.M. Gibson*, 70; Robuck, *My Own Personal Experience and Observation*, 75–81.

21. Clayton, *Olden Times Revisited*, 155; Kearney, *Slaveholder's Daughter*, 18, 19; Harper, *Annie Harper's Journal*, 44–45; Dinkins, *1861 to 1865*, 279–80.

22. Dunbar Rowland, *A Mississippi View of Race Relations in the South* (Jackson: Harmon, 1903), 8, 8–9, 9, 16, 17.

23. Fulkerson, *The Negro*, 68.

24. Brundage, *Southern Past*; James C. Cobb, *Away Down South: A History of Southern Identity* (New York: Oxford University Press, 2005); David Goldfield, *Still Fighting the Civil War: The American South and Southern History* (Baton Rouge: Louisiana State University Press, 2002); McWhite, "Echoes of the Lost Cause"; Blight, *Race and Reunion*; Brundage, *Where These Memories Grow*; Gallagher and Nolan, *Myth of the Lost Cause and Civil War History*; Davis, *Cause Lost*; Foster, *Ghosts of the Confederacy*; Woodward, *Burden of Southern History*.

25. Stephanie Cole and Natalie J. Ring, eds., *The Folly of Jim Crow: Rethinking the Segregated South* (College Station: Texas A&M University Press, 2012); Stephen Cresswell, *Rednecks, Redeemers, and Race: Mississippi after Reconstruction, 1877–1917* (Jackson: University Press of Mississippi, 2006); Neil R. McMillen, *Dark Journey: Black Mississippians in the Age of Jim Crow* (Urbana: University of Illinois Press, 1989).

26. W.E.B. Du Bois, *The Souls of Black Folk: Sketches and Essays* (Chicago: A. C. McClurg, 1903), 3; Howard W. Odum, "Social and Mental Traits of the Negro: Research into the Conditions of the Negro Race in Southern Towns," (PhD diss., Columbia University, 1910), 261.

27. George P. Rawick, Jan Hillegas, and Ken Lawrence, eds., *The American Slave: A Composite Autobiography, Supplement, Series I, Mississippi Narratives* (Westport, CT: Greenwood Press, 1977), 587 (7:2); 1011–12 (8:3); George P. Rawick, ed., *The American Slave: A Composite Autobiography*, vol. 7 (Westport, CT: Greenwood, 1972), 149; 83; 64.

28. Rawick, *American Slave*, 9; 59; 173; 122; Rawick, Hillegas, and Lawrence, *American Slave*, 1013 (8:3).

29. As quoted in Leon F. Litwack, *Trouble in Mind: Black Southerners in the Age of Jim Crow* (New York: Vintage Books, 1998), 24; Julius E. Thompson, *Lynchings in Mississippi: A History, 1865–1965* (Jefferson, NC: McFarland, 2007), 22, 35.

30. Emmett J. Scott, ed., "Letters of Negro Migrants of 1916–1918," *Journal of Negro History* 4 (July 1919), 318, 319, 323, 304; Emmett J. Scott, ed., "More Letters of Negro Migrants of 1916–1918," *Journal of Negro History* 4 (October 1919), 452.

31. U.S. Department of Commerce, *The Fifteenth Census of the United States: 1930. Population, vol. 3, part 1* (Washington, DC: Government Printing Office, 1932), 1265; U.S. Department of Commerce, *The Seventeenth Census of the United States: 1950. Census of Population, vol. 2, part 24* (Washington, DC: Government Printing Office, 1952), 22; U.S. Department of Commerce, *The Nineteenth Census of the United States: 1970. Advance Reports, vol. 2* (Washington, DC: Government Printing Office, 1972), 3. The best statistical analysis of Mississippi's

black diaspora comes from McMillen, *Dark Journey*, 257–81. For personal accounts of black migrants, see Isabel Wilkerson, *The Warmth of Other Suns: The Epic Story of America's Great Migration* (New York: Vintage Books, 2011).

32. Du Bois, *Souls of Black Folk*, 3, 4; W.E.B. Du Bois, *Black Reconstruction in America* (New York: Russell and Russell, 1935; 1962).

33. Levine, *Black Culture and Black Consciousness*.

34. For a strong assessment of the Delta blues and the creation of a regional identity, see James C. Cobb, *The Most Southern Place on Earth: The Mississippi Delta and the Roots of Regional Identity* (New York: Oxford University Press, 1992), chapter 12.

35. Ted Gioia, *Delta Blues: The Life and Times of the Mississippi Masters Who Revolutionized American Music* (New York: W. W. Norton, 2008); Charley Patton, "Down the Dirt Road Blues," *Complete Remastered Sessions*, Master Classic Records, 2009, compact disc; Robert Johnson, "Ramblin' on My Mind," "Walkin' Blues," "Stones in My Passway," *Robert Johnson: The Complete Recordings*, Sony BMG Music, 1990, compact disc; Son House, "Special Rider Blues," *The Delta Blues of Son House*, Grammercy Records, 1991, compact disc.

36. Robert Johnson, "Hellhound on My Trail," "Me and the Devil Blues," *Robert Johnson: The Complete Recordings*, Sony BMG Music, 1990, compact disc; Charley Patton, "A Spoonful Blues," "Lord I'm Discouraged," *Complete Remastered Sessions*, Master Classic Records, 2009, compact disc.

37. John W. Roberts, *From Trickster to Badman: The Black Folk Hero in Slavery and Freedom* (Philadelphia: University of Pennsylvania Press, 1989), 171–215.

38. McMillen, *Dark Journey*.

39. Harper, *Annie Harper's Journal*, 48; Rowland, "Plantation Life in Mississippi before the War," 97.

Conclusion: "Thou Art Not Dead"

1. "The Old South," in Horace S. Fulkerson, *The Negro; As He Was; As He Is; As He Will Be* (Vicksburg: Commercial Herald Printers, 1887), 2.

2. "KKK to Protest at LSU–Ole Miss," http://www.wwl.com/pages/5725358.php?, accessed December 29, 2009; "KKK Planning Rally in Miss.," *Daily Reveille* (Louisiana State University), November 19, 2009; "Students Rally to Oppose Klan's On Campus Protest," *Daily Mississippian* (University of Mississippi), November 30, 2009.

3. Stephen J. Whitfield, *A Death in the Delta: The Story of Emmett Till* (Baltimore: Johns Hopkins University Press, 1988).

4. Michael V. Williams, *Medgar Evers: Mississippi Martyr* (Fayetteville: University of Arkansas Press, 2011); James W. Silver, *Mississippi: The Closed Society*, new enl. ed. (New York: Harcourt, Brace and World, 1966).

5. Sally Leigh McWhite, "Echoes of the Lost Cause: Civil War Reverberations in Mississippi from 1865 to 2001" (PhD diss., University of Mississippi, 2003).

6. Annie Harper, *Annie Harper's Journal: A Southern Mother's Legacy* (Denton, TX: Flower Mound Writing Company, 1983), 48.

Bibliography

Primary Sources

Archival Sources

Mississippi Department of Archives and History,
Jackson, Mississippi

Armstrong (Ezekiel) Diary.
Balfour (Emma) Civil War Diary.
Cook (Mrs. Jared Reese) Diary.
Crawford (John Berryman) Civil War Letters.
Darden Family Papers.
Fonsylvania Plantation Diary.
Foster (Catherine [Kate] Olivia) Diary.
Garrett (Louisiana Dunlevy) Papers.
Harrington (Whitfield) Manuscript.
Jones-Smith Plantation Journal.
Martin (Anne Shannon) Diary.
McNamara (Timothy) Diary.
McRaven (W. H.) Papers.
Nicholson (Flavellus G.) Diary-Journal.
Peel (William) Diary.
Pepper (J. H.) Diary.
Power (John Logan) Diary.
Roberts (G. W.) Diary.
Scales (Cordelia Lewis) Letters.
Alfred H. Stone Collection.
Strickland (Belle F.) Diary.
Welles (Edward R.) Diary.

Mitchell Memorial Library, Special Collections,
Mississippi State University

Agnes (Samuel Andrew) Collection.
Bachman (G. W.) Collection.
Edwards (Edward D.) Family Papers.

Eldridge Papers.
Erwin (William) Diary and Account Book.
Fontaine (Edward) Papers.
Hancock Papers.
Hays-Ray-Webb Papers.
Lynch (James Daniel) Papers.
McRae (Sallie B.) Diary.
McRae (Thaddeus) Autobiography.
Neilson (Lillian) Collection.
Oswalt Family Collection.
Porter (Albert Quincy) Civil War Diary.
Posey (Alice Puckett) Life History.
Rollins (Berthie Shaw) Papers.
Ross (Emmett Lloyd) Papers.
Ryan (M. A.) Experience of a Confederate Soldier
Sparkman (Jesse Roderick) Civil War Diary.
Sykes (William E.) Papers.
Wallace (Thomas D.) Civil War Diary.
Wilson (John H.) Civil War Experience.
Young (William Humphreys) Letters.

*J. D. Williams Library, Department of Archives and Special Collections,
The University of Mississippi*

Governor Adelbert Ames Speech.
F.A.P. Barnard Collection.
Elizabeth Christine Brown Diary.
J. W. Clapp Collection.
Craft-Ford Papers.
Joseph E. Davis Collection.
John G. Deupree Collection.
Kate Walthall Freeman Collection.
William D. Howell Collection.
James T. Jones Collection.
Rev. A. C. McDonald Sermon.
William Terry Moore Reminiscence.
Charles Roberts Collection.

Newspapers

American Citizen (Canton).
Commonwealth (Canton).
Courier (Natchez).
Daily Exchange (Baltimore).
Eastern Clarion (Paulding).
Flag of the Union (Jackson).
Hinds County Gazette (Jackson).
Macon Beacon (Macon).

Mississippi Baptist (Jackson).
Mississippi Free Trader (Natchez).
Mississippi Free Trader and Natchez Gazette (Natchez).
Mississippi Palladium (Holly Springs).
Mississippian (Jackson).
Natchez Courier (Natchez).
Oxford Intelligencer (Oxford).
Port Gibson Herald, and Correspondent (Port Gibson).
Ripley Advertiser (Ripley).
Semi-Weekly Mississippian (Jackson).
Southern Standard (Columbus).
Southron (Jackson).
Vicksburg Sentinel (Vicksburg).
Vicksburg Weekly Whig (Vicksburg).
Weekly Mississippian (Jackson).
Weekly Vicksburg Whig (Vicksburg).
Woodville Republican (Woodville).
Yazoo Democrat (Yazoo).

Audiovisual Sources

House, Son. *The Delta Blues of Son House*. Grammercy Records, 1991. Compact Disc.
Johnson, Robert. *Robert Johnson: The Complete Recordings*. Sony BMG Music, 1990. Compact disc.
Patton, Charley. *Complete Remastered Sessions*. Master Classics Records, 2009. Compact disc.
Prom Night in Mississippi. Produced and directed by Paul Saltzman. 90 min. Return to Mississippi Productions, 2009. Digital video disc.

Published Sources

Alcorn, James L. *Address of J. L. Alcorn (Republican Candidate for Governor) to the People of Mississippi*. Friar's Point, MS: Published by author, 1869.
———. *Civil Rights: Speech of Hon. James L. Alcorn, of Mississippi, in the United States Senate, May 22, 1874*. Washington, DC: Government Printing Office, 1874.
Anderson, Fulton, Henry L. Benning, and John S. Preston. *Addresses Delivered before the Virginia State Convention*. Richmond: Wyatt M. Elliott, Printer, 1861.
Aughey, John H. *The Iron Furnace: or, Slavery and Secession*. Philadelphia: William S. and Alfred Martien, 1863.
Bailey, Peter P. *The Issues of 1868: An Address to the People of Mississippi*. Satartia, MS: Published by author, 1868.
Baumgartner, Richard A., ed. *Blood and Sacrifice: The Civil War Journal of a Confederate Soldier*. Huntington, WV: Blue Acorn Press, 1994.
Beaumont, Betty B. *Twelve Years of My Life*. Philadelphia: T. B. Peterson & Brothers, 1887.
Bestor, Arthur E., Jr., ed. "Letters from a Southern Opponent of Sectionalism, September, 1860, to June, 1861." *Journal of Southern History* 12 (February 1946):106–122.
Bledsoe, Oscar F. *"The Hopes and Duties of the Present Hour": Oration, before the Two Literary Societies of the University of Mississippi, June 27, 1866*. Memphis: Public Ledger Steam Book and Job Printing Office, 1866.

Boyd, Samuel S. *Speech of Hon. Samuel S. Boyd Delivered at the Great Union Festival, held at Jackson, Mississippi, on the 10th day of October, 1851.* Natchez, MS: Book and Job Office of the Natchez Courier, 1851.

Brown, Shepherd Spencer Neville, Sr., ed. *War Years, C.S.A.: 12th Mississippi Regiment Major S. H. Giles, Q.M.* Original Letters, 1860–1865. Hillsboro, TX: Hill College Press, 1998.

Brown, Stephen A. *Autobiography of Stephen A. Brown, 1823–1861.* Starkville, MS: Private Printing, 1955.

Bruce, H. C. *The New Man: Twenty-Nine Years a Slave, Twenty-Nine Years a Free Man.* New York: Negro University Press, 1969.

Carter, Joseph D., ed. *Magnolia Journey: A Union Veteran Revisits the Former Confederate States. Arranged from Letters of Correspondent Russell H. Conwell to the Daily Evening Traveller (Boston, 1869).* University: University of Alabama Press, 1974.

Cash, William M., and Lucy Somerville Howorth, eds. *My Dear Nellie: The Civil War Letters of William L. Nugent to Eleanor Smith Nugent.* Jackson: University Press of Mississippi, 1977.

Chandler, Walter, ed. *Journal and Speeches of Greene Callier Chandler.* Memphis: Private Printing, 1953.

Chronicles of the Fire-Eaters of the Tribe of Mississippi by Seraiah the Scribe. Brandon: Republican Office, 1853.

Clayton, Washington Lafayette. *Olden Times Revisited: W. L. Clayton's Pen Pictures.* Edited by Minrose Gwin. Jackson: University Press of Mississippi, 1982.

Cluskey, M. W., ed. *Speeches, Messages, and Other Writings of the Hon. Albert G. Brown, A Senator in Congress from the State of Mississippi.* Philadelphia: Jas. B. Smith, 1859.

Cockrell, Thomas D., and Michael B. Ballard, eds. *A Mississippi Rebel in the Army of Northern Virginia: The Civil War Memoirs of Private David Holt.* Baton Rouge: Louisiana State University Press, 1995.

Coleman, J. P., comp. *The Constitution of the State of Mississippi: Adopted by the People of Mississippi in a Constitutional Convention November 1, 1890 at Jackson and all Amendments Subsequently Adopted.* Jackson: Distributed by Heber Ladner, Secretary of State, 1954.

Congress of the Confederate States of America. *Journal of the Congress of the Confederate States of America, 1861–1865.* 7 vols. Washington, DC: Government Printing Office, 1904–5.

Cotton, Gordon A., ed. *From the Pen of a She-Rebel: The Civil War Diary of Emilie Riley McKinley.* Columbia: University of South Carolina Press, 2001.

Crist, Lynda Lasswell, ed. *The Papers of Jefferson Davis.* 12 vols. Baton Rouge: Louisiana State University Press, 1971–2008.

Dance, Daryl Cumber, ed. *From My People: 400 Years of African American Folklore.* New York: W. W. Norton, 2002.

Davis, Jefferson. *The Rise and Fall of the Confederate Government.* 2 vols. New York: Thomas Yoseloff, 1881; 1958.

Davis, Reuben. *Recollections of Mississippi and Mississippians.* Jackson: University and College Press of Mississippi, 1972.

Davis, Sidney Fant. *Mississippi Negro Lore.* Jackson, TN: McCowat-Mercer, 1914.

J.D.B. De Bow, ed. *De Bow's Review.* 1846–1869. Nashville, New Orleans, New York.

Dennett, John Richard. *The South as It Is: 1865–1866.* Edited by Henry M. Christman. New York: Viking Press, 1965.

Dennis, Frank Allen, ed. *Kemper County Rebel: The Civil War Diary of Robert Masten Holmes, C.S.A.* Jackson: University and College Press of Mississippi, 1973.

The Devil in America: A Dramatic Satire. Mobile, AL: J. K. Randall, 1867.

Dimond, E. Grey, and Herman Hattaway, eds. *Letters from Forest Place: A Plantation Family's Correspondence, 1846–1881.* Jackson: University Press of Mississippi, 1993.

Dinkins, James. *1861 to 1865: Personal Recollections and Experiences in the Confederate Army by an "Old Johnnie."* Dayton: Press of Morningside Bookshop, 1975.

Du Bois, W.E.B. *The Souls of Black Folk: Essays and Sketches.* Chicago: A. C. McClurg, 1903.

Elliott, Ebenezer Newton, ed. *Cotton Is King, and Pro-Slavery Arguments: Comprising the Writings of Hammond, Harper, Christy, Stringfellow, Hodge, Bledsoe, and Cartwright, on This Important Subject.* Augusta: Pritchard, Abbott and Loomis, 1860.

Foote, Henry S. *War of the Rebellion; or, Scylla and Charybdis: Consisting of Observations upon the Causes, Course, and Consequences of the Late Civil War in the United States.* New York: Harper and Brothers, 1866.

Ford, Jennifer W., ed. *The Hour of Our Nation's Agony: The Civil War Letters of Lt. William Cowper Nelson of Mississippi.* Knoxville: University of Tennessee Press, 2007.

Fulkerson, Horace S. *The Negro; As He Was; As He Is; As He Will Be.* Vicksburg: Commercial Herald, 1887.

———. *Random Recollections of Early Days in Mississippi.* Vicksburg: Vicksburg Printing and Publishing, 1885.

Furlong, Chas. E. *Origin of the Outrages at Vicksburg: Speech of Hon. Chas. E. Furlong, Senator from Warren County, in the Senate of Mississippi, December 18, 1874.* Vicksburg: Vicksburg Herald Print, 1874.

Galbraith, Loretta and William, eds. *A Lost Heroine of the Confederacy: The Diaries and Letters of Belle Edmondson.* Jackson: University Press of Mississippi, 1990.

Gerow, R. O., ed. *Civil War Diary (1862–1865) of Bishop William Henry Elder, Bishop of Natchez.* Natchez: Diocese of Natchez-Jackson, 1961.

Gibson, J. M. *Memoirs of J. M. Gibson: Terrors of the Civil War and Reconstruction Days.* Houston: Private Printing, 1929.

Hankins, Samuel W. *Simple Story of a Soldier: Life and Service in the 2nd Mississippi Infantry.* Tuscaloosa: University of Alabama Press, 2004.

Hardy, Toney A., ed. *No Compromise with Principle: Autobiography and Biography of William Harris Hardy.* New York: American Book-Stratford Press, 1946.

Harper, Annie. *Annie Harper's Journal: A Southern Mother's Legacy.* Denton, TX: Flower Mound Writing Company, 1983.

Harwell, Richard Barksdale, ed. *Kate: The Journal of a Confederate Nurse by Kate Cumming.* Baton Rouge: Louisiana State University Press, 1959.

Hogan, William Ransom, and Edwin Adams Davis, eds. *William Johnson's Natchez: The Ante-Bellum Diary of a Free Negro.* Baton Rouge: Louisiana State University Press, 1951; 1993.

Hudson, Weldon I., ed. *The Civil War Diary of William Spencer Hudson.* St. Louis: Micro-Records, 1973.

Ingraham, J. H., ed. *The Sunny South; or, the Southerner at Home.* Philadelphia: G. G. Evans, 1860.

Jones, Laurence C. *The Bottom Rail: Addresses and Papers on the Negro in the Lowlands of Mississippi and on Inter-Racial Relations in the South during Twenty-Five Years.* New York: Fleming H. Revell, 1935.

Jones, Mary Miles and Leslie Jones Martin, eds. *The Gentle Rebel: The Civil War Letters of William Harvey Berryhill First Lieutenant, Co. D, 43rd Regiment, Mississippi Volunteers.* Yazoo City: Sassafras Press, 1982.

Journal of the Convention of the State of Mississippi, and the Act Calling the Same; with the Constitution of the United States, and Washington's Farewell Address. Jackson: Thomas Palmer, 1851.

Journal of the Proceedings in the Constitutional Convention of the State of Mississippi. Jackson: E. Stafford, Printer, 1871.

Journal of the State Convention, and Ordinances and Resolutions, Adopted in March, 1861. Jackson: E. Barksdale, State Printer, 1861.

Kearney, Belle. *A Slaveholder's Daughter.* New York: Abbey Press, 1900.

King, Edward. *The Great South.* Edited by W. Magruder Drake and Robert R. Jones. Baton Rouge: Louisiana State University Press, 1972.

Lamar, Lucius Q. C. *Letter of Lucius Q. C. Lamar, in reply to Hon. P.F. Liddell, of Carrollton, Mississippi.* Carrollton, MS: Private printing, 1860.

Lynch, James D. *Redpath: Or The Ku-Klux Tribunal, a Poem.* Columbus: Excelsior Book and Job Printing Establishment, 1877.

Lynch, John R. *The Facts of Reconstruction.* New York: Neale, 1913.

———. *Reminiscences of an Active Life: The Autobiography of John Roy Lynch.* Edited by John Hope Franklin. Chicago: University of Chicago Press, 1970.

Macarthy, Harry. "The Bonnie Blue Flag." New Orleans: A. E. Blackmar and Bro., 1861.

Mayes, Edward. *Lucius Q. C. Lamar: His Life, Times, and Speeches, 1825–1893.* Nashville: Barbee and Smith, Agents, 1896.

McCollum, J. K., Sr., and J. K. McCollum, Jr., eds. *The Diary of Captain Duncan McCollum, Co. A, 4th Mississippi Cavalry, 1865.* San Bernardino: Private printing, 1964.

Mississippi Constitutional Convention. *Journal of the Proceedings of the Constitutional Convention of the State of Mississippi.* Jackson: E. L. Martin, 1890.

Mississippi State Convention. *Journal of the State Convention and Ordinances and Resolutions Adopted in January, 1861.* Jackson: E. Barksdale, State Printer, 1861.

Montgomery, Frank A. *Reminiscences of a Mississippian in Peace and War.* Cincinnati: Robert Clark, 1901.

Montgomery, Isaiah T. *"What Answer?" Speech in Support of Franchise Committee Report, Mississippi Constitutional Convention, 1890.* Edited by Matthew Holden, Jr. Isaiah T. Montgomery Studies Project, 2004.

Morgan, Albert T. *Yazoo; or, On the Picket Line of Freedom in the South: A Personal Narrative.* Columbia: University of South Carolina Press, 2000.

Morris, Robert C. *Freedmen's Schools and Textbooks, vol. 1. Semi-Annual Report on Schools for Freedmen by John W. Alvord, Numbers 1–10, January, 1866–July, 1870.* New York: AMS Press, 1980.

Nordhoff, Charles. *The Cotton States in the Spring and Summer of 1875.* New York: D. Appleton, 1876.

Osofsky, Gilbert, ed. *Puttin' On Ole Massa.* New York: Harper and Row, 1969.

Parker, Joel. *The Right of Secession. A Review of the Message of Jefferson Davis to the Congress of the Confederate States.* Cambridge: Welch, Bigelow, 1861.

Rawick, George P., ed. *The American Slave: A Composite Autobiography.* 19 vols. Westport, CT: Greenwood, 1972.

Rawick, George P., Jan Hillegas, and Ken Lawrence, eds. *The American Slave: A Composite Autobiography, Supplement, Series I. Volumes 6–10: Mississippi Narratives.* Westport, CT: Greenwood Press, 1977.

Records of the Assistant Commissioner for the State of Mississippi, Bureau of Refugees, Freedmen, and Abandoned Lands, 1865–1869. 50 reels. Washington, DC: National Archives Microfilm Publications, 1971.

Reid, Whitelaw. *After the War: A Tour of the Southern States, 1865–1866.* Edited by C. Vann Woodward. New York: Harper and Row, 1965.

Riley, Franklin L., ed. *Publications of the Mississippi Historical Society.* 14 vols. University, MS: Printed for the Society, 1898–1914.

Robuck, J. E. *My Own Personal Experience and Observation as a Soldier in the Confederate Army during the Civil War, 1861–1865, also during the Period of Reconstruction.* Reprint. Memphis: Burke's Book Store, 1978.

Rowland, Dunbar. *A Mississippi View of Race Relations in the South.* Jackson: Harmon Publisher Company Printers, 1903.

Russell, William Howard. *My Diary North and South.* Edited by Eugene H. Berwanger. Philadelphia: Temple University Press, 1988.

Schlesinger, Arthur M., ed. *The Cotton Kingdom: A Traveller's Observations on Cotton and Slavery in the American Slave States by Frederick Law Olmsted.* New York: Alfred A. Knopf, 1953.

Silver, James W., ed. *A Life for the Confederacy: As Recorded in the Pocket Diaries of Pvt. Robert A. Moore, Co. G 17th Mississippi Regiment Confederate Guards, Holly Springs, Mississippi.* Jackson, TN: McCowat-Mercer Press, 1959.

Singleton, Otho R. *Speech of Hon. Otho R. Singleton, of Mississippi on Resistance to Black Republican Domination; Delivered in the House of Representatives, December 19, 1859.* Washington, DC: Congressional Globe Office, 1859.

Smedes, Susan Dabney. *Memorials of a Southern Planter.* Edited by Fletcher M. Green. Jackson: University Press of Mississippi, 1981.

Smedes, William C. *Speech of William C. Smedes, Esq., Delivered at Apollo Hall, Vicksburg, Miss., on the 27th day of October, A.D. 1860, upon the Right of a State to Secede from the Union and Other Political Topics.* Vicksburg: Job Office of M. Shannon, 1860.

Somers, Robert. *The Southern States since the War, 1870–71.* Introduction by Malcolm C. McMillan. University: University of Alabama Press, 1965.

Sparks, William Henry. *The Memories of Fifty Years.* 3rd ed. Philadelphia: Claxton, Remsen and Haffelfinger, 1872.

The Testimony in the Impeachment of Adelbert Ames, as Governor of Mississippi. Jackson: Power & Barksdale, State Printers, 1877.

Trowbridge, J. T. *The South: A Tour of Its Battle-Fields and Ruined Cities.* Hartford: L. Stebbins, 1866.

U.S. Congress. Senate. *Mississippi. Testimony as to Denial of Elective Franchise in Mississippi at the Elections of 1875 and 1876.* Washington, DC: Government Printing Office, 1877.

———. *Mississippi in 1875: Report of the Select Committee to Inquire into the Mississippi Election of 1875, with the Testimony and Documentary Evidence.* 2 vols. Washington, DC: Government Printing Office, 1876.

U.S. Department of Commerce. *The Fifteenth Census of the United States: 1930.* Washington, DC: Government Printing Office, 1932.

———. *The Seventeenth Census of the United States: 1950.* Washington, DC: Government Printing Office, 1952.

———. *The Nineteenth Census of the United States: 1970.* Washington, DC: Government Printing Office, 1972.

U.S. Department of the Interior. *The Seventh Census of the United States: 1850.* Washington, DC: Robert Armstrong, Public Printer, 1853.

———. *The Eighth Census of the United States: 1860.* Washington, DC: Government Printing Office, 1864.

———. *The Ninth Census of the United States: 1870.* Washington, DC: Government Printing Office, 1872.

———. *The Tenth Census of the United States: 1880.* Washington, DC: Government Printing Office, 1883.

U.S. War Records Office. *The War of the Rebellion: A Compilation of the Official Records of the Union and Confederate Armies.* 70 vols. Washington, DC: Government Printing Office, 1880–1901.

Wade, Walter. *Dr. Walter Ross Wade's Rosswood Plantation Diary, 1834–1862.* 3 vols. Compiled by Walter R. Hylander. [CD-ROM] Lorman, MS: Rosswood Plantation, 2003.

Warren, Henry W. *Reminiscences of a Mississippi Carpet-Bagger.* Worcester, MA: Davis Press, 1914.

Washington, Booker T. *Up from Slavery: An Autobiography.* New York: Doubleday, Page, 1907.

Waterbury, Maria. *Seven Years among the Freedmen.* Chicago: T. B. Arnold, 1890.

Welker, David A., ed. *A Keystone Rebel: The Civil War Diary of Joseph Garey, Hudson's Battery, Mississippi Volunteers.* Gettysburg: Thomas, 1996.

Wilds, Ellen Sheffield, ed. *Far from Home: The Diary of Lt. William H. Peel, 1863–1865.* Carrollton, MS: Pioneer, 2005.

Wilkes, Abner James. *A Short History of My Life in the Late War between the North and the South.* Prentiss, MS: Private printing, 1957.

Wood, John W. *Union and Secession in Mississippi.* Memphis: Saunders, Parrish and Whitmore, 1863.

Wrenn, Lynette Boney, ed. *A Bachelor's Life in Antebellum Mississippi: The Diary of Dr. Elijah Millington Walker, 1849–1852.* Knoxville: University of Tennessee Press, 2004.

Wright, Richard. *Black Boy (American Hunger): A Record of Childhood and Youth.* New York: HarperPerennial, 1993.

Yelverton, Thérèse. *Teresina in America.* 2 vols. London: Richard Bentley and Son, 1875.

Secondary Sources

Articles

Bauerlein, Mark. "Booker T. Washington and W.E.B. Du Bois: The Origins of a Bitter Intellectual Battle." *Journal of Blacks in Higher Education* 46 (Winter 2004–2005): 106–114.

Broussard, Joyce L. "Occupied Natchez, Elite Women, and the Feminization of the Civil War." *Journal of Mississippi History* 70 (Summer 2008): 179–207.

Chesebrough, David B. "Dissenting Clergy in Confederate Mississippi." *Journal of Mississippi History* 55 (May 1993): 115–31.

Crane, J. Michael. "Controlling the Night: Perceptions of the Slave Patrol System in Missis-sippi." *Journal of Mississippi History* 61 (Summer 1999): 119–36.

Degler, Carl N. "Thesis, Antithesis, Synthesis: The South, the North, and the Nation." *Journal of Southern History* 53 (February 1987): 3–18.

Dresser, Rebecca M. "Kate and John Minor: Confederate Unionists of Natchez." *Journal of Mississippi History* 64 (Fall 2002): 188–216.

Ellem, Warren A. "The Overthrow of Reconstruction in Mississippi." *Journal of Mississippi History* 54 (May 1992): 175–201.

Gleason, Philip. "Identifying Identity: A Semantic History." *Journal of American History* 69 (March 1983): 910–31.

Jansson, David R. "Internal Orientalism in America: W. J. Cash's *The Mind of the South* and the Spatial Construction of American National Identity." *Political Geography* 22 (2003): 293–316.

Kelley, Donald Brooks. "Harper's Ferry: Prelude to Crisis in Mississippi." *Journal of Missis-sippi History* 27 (Winter 1965): 351–72.

Koeniger, A. Cash. "Climate and Southern Distinctiveness." *Journal of Southern History* 54 (February 1988): 21–44.

Mallard, M. Shannon. "'I Had No Comfort to Give the People': Opposition to the Confed-eracy in Civil War Mississippi." *North & South* 6 (May 2003): 78–86.

Mering, John V. "The Slave-State Constitutional Unionists and the Politics of Consensus." *Journal of Southern History* 43 (August 1977): 395–410.

Peabody, Charles. "Notes on Negro Music." *Journal of American Folklore* 16 (July to Septem-ber 1903): 148–52.

Phillips, Adrienne Cole. "The Mississippi Press's Response to John Brown's Raid." *Journal of Mississippi History* 48 (Summer 1986): 119–34.

Phillips, Jason. "The Grape Vine Telegraph: Rumors and Confederate Persistence." *Journal of Southern History* 72 (November 2006): 753–88.

Phillips, Ulrich Bonnell. "The Central Theme of Southern History." *American Historical Review* 34 (October 1928): 30–43.

Quigley, Paul. "Independence Day Dilemmas in the American South, 1848–1865." *Journal of Southern History* 75 (May 2009): 235–66.

Scott, Emmett J., ed. "Letters of Negro Migrants of 1916–1918." *Journal of Negro History* 4 (July 1919): 290–340.

———. "More Letters of Negro Migrants of 1916–1918." *Journal of Negro History* 4 (October 1919): 412–65.

Sioussat, St. George L. "Tennessee, the Compromise of 1850, and the Nashville Convention." *Mississippi Valley Historical Review* 2 (December 1915): 313–347.

Smith, Timothy. "'A Siege from the Start': The Spring 1862 Campaign against Corinth, Missis-sippi." *Journal of Mississippi History* 66 (Winter 2004): 403–24.

Stryker, Sheldon, and Peter J. Burke. "The Past, Present, and Future of an Identity Theory." *Social Psychology Quarterly* 63:4 (2000): 284–97.

Upchurch, Thomas Adams. "Speaking on Behalf of the Vagabond Rebels: The Mississippi Press on Race and Reconstruction in 1865." *Journal of Mississippi History* 61 (Winter 1999): 351–70.

Waldrip, C. B. "Sex, Social Equality, and Yankee Values: White Men's Attitudes toward Misce-genation during Mississippi's Reconstruction." *Journal of Mississippi History* 64 (Summer 2002): 125–45.

Whittington, Terry. "In the Shadow of Defeat: Tracking the Vicksburg Parolees." *Journal of Mississippi History* 64 (Winter 2002): 307–30.

Williams, Clay. "Lost Chance to Save Vicksburg." *Journal of Mississippi History* 60 (Spring 1998): 5–19.

Williams, Frank J. "Lincoln, Secession, and Mississippi: Constitutional Acts?" *Journal of Mississippi History* 70 (Spring 2008): 3–25.

Winter, William F. "Mississippi's Civil War Governors." *Journal of Mississippi History* 51 (May 1989): 77–88.

Theses and Dissertations

Bell, William Dudley. "The Ku Klux Klan in Mississippi, 1866–1872." Master's thesis, Mississippi State University, 1963.

McWhite, Sally Leigh. "Echoes of the Lost Cause: Civil War Reverberations in Mississippi from 1865 to 2001." PhD diss., University of Mississippi, 2003.

Odum, Howard W. "Social and Mental Traits of the Negro: Research into the Conditions of the Negro Race in Southern Towns." PhD diss., Columbia University, 1910.

Monographs

Anderson, Benedict. *Imagined Communities: Reflections on the Origin and Spread of Nationalism*. Rev. ed. New York: Verso, 1983; 1991.

Appleby, Joyce. *Inheriting the Revolution: The First Generation of Americans*. Cambridge: Belknap Press of Harvard University Press, 2000.

Ashdown, Paul, and Edward Caudill. *The Myth of Nathan Bedford Forrest*. Lanham, MD: Rowman and Littlefield, 2005.

Austin, William G., and Stephen Worchel, eds. *The Social Psychology of Intergroup Relations*. Monterey, CA: Brooks/Cole, 1979.

Ayers, Edward L. *In the Presence of Mine Enemies: The Civil War in the Heart of America, 1859–1863*. New York: W. W. Norton, 2003.

Ballard, Michael B. *The Civil War in Mississippi: Major Campaigns and Battles*. Jackson: University Press of Mississippi, 2012.

———. *Vicksburg: The Campaign That Opened the Mississippi*. Chapel Hill: University of North Carolina Press, 2004.

Barney, William L. *The Secessionist Impulse: Alabama and Mississippi in 1860*. Princeton: Princeton University Press, 1974.

Becker, Howard S., and Michal M. McCall, eds. *Symbolic Interactionism and Cultural Studies*. Chicago: University of Chicago Press, 1990.

Bercaw, Nancy. *Gendered Freedoms: Race, Rights, and Politics of Household in the Delta, 1861–1875*. Gainesville: University Press of Florida, 2003.

Beringer, Richard E., Herman Hattaway, Archer Jones, and William N. Still, Jr. *Why the South Lost the Civil War*. Athens: University of Georgia Press, 1986.

Bettersworth, John K. *Confederate Mississippi: The People and Policies of a Cotton State in Wartime*. Baton Rouge: Louisiana State University Press, 1943; Philadelphia: Porcupine Press, 1978.

Blassingame, John W. *The Slave Community: Plantation Life in the Antebellum South*. New York: Oxford University Press, 1972.

Blight, David W. *Race and Reunion: The Civil War in American Memory.* Cambridge: Belknap Press of Harvard University Press, 2001.

Blumer, Herbert. *Symbolic Interactionism: Perspective and Method.* Englewood Cliffs, NJ: Prentice-Hall, 1969.

Boles, John B. *Black Southerners, 1619–1869.* Lexington: University Press of Kentucky, 1984.

Bond, Bradley, G. *Political Culture in the Nineteenth-Century South: Mississippi, 1830–1900.* Baton Rouge: Louisiana State University Press, 1995.

Bonner, Robert E. *Colors and Blood: Flag Passions of the Confederate South.* Princeton: Princeton University Press, 2002.

Brown, Kathleen M. *Good Wives, Nasty Wenches, and Anxious Patriarchs: Gender, Race, and Power in Colonial Virginia.* Chapel Hill: University of North Carolina Press, 1996.

Brundage, W. Fitzhugh. *Lynching in the New South: Georgia and Virginia, 1880–1930.* Urbana: University of Illinois Press, 1993.

———. *The Southern Past: A Clash of Race and Memory.* Cambridge: Belknap Press of Harvard University Press, 2005.

———, ed. *Where These Memories Grow: History, Memory, and Southern Identity.* Chapel Hill: University of North Carolina Press, 2000.

Bynum, Victoria E. *The Free State of Jones: Mississippi's Longest Civil War.* Chapel Hill: University of North Carolina Press, 2001.

———. *Unruly Women: The Politics of Social and Sexual Control in the Old South.* Chapel Hill: University of North Carolina Press, 1992.

Calt, Stephen, and Gayle Wardlow. *King of the Delta Blues: The Life and Music of Charlie Patton.* Newton, NJ: Rock Chapel Press, 1988.

Camp, Stephanie M. H. *Closer to Freedom: Enslaved Women and Everyday Resistance in the Plantation South.* Chapel Hill: University of North Carolina Press, 2004.

Carter, Samuel. *The Final Fortress: The Campaign for Vicksburg, 1862–1863.* New York: St. Martin's Press, 1980.

Cash, W. J. *The Mind of the South.* New York: Alfred A. Knopf, 1941.

Chaplin, Joyce E. *An Anxious Pursuit: Agricultural Innovation and Modernity in the Lower South, 1730–1815.* Chapel Hill: University of North Carolina Press, 1993.

Clark, Thomas D., ed. *Travels in the New South, a Bibliography. Volume One: The Postwar South, 1865–1900.* Norman: University of Oklahoma Press, 1962.

Cobb, James C. *Away Down South: A History of Southern Identity.* New York: Oxford University Press, 2005.

———. *The Most Southern Place on Earth: The Mississippi Delta and the Roots of Regional Identity.* New York: Oxford University Press, 1992.

Cole, Stephanie, and Natalie J. Ring, eds. *The Folly of Jim Crow: Rethinking the Segregated South.* College Station: Texas A&M University Press, 2012.

Cooper, William J., Jr. *Jefferson Davis, American.* New York: Vintage Books, 2000.

———. *The South and the Politics of Slavery, 1828–1856.* Baton Rouge: Louisiana State University Press, 1978.

Cote, James E., and Charles G. Levine. *Identity Formation, Agency, and Culture: A Social Psychological Synthesis.* Mahwah, NJ: Lawrence Erlbaum Associates, 2002.

Cowdrey, Albert E. *This Land, This South: An Environmental History.* Lexington: University Press of Kentucky, 1983.

Cozzens, Peter. *The Darkest Days of the War: The Battles of Iuka and Corinth.* Chapel Hill: University of North Carolina Press, 1997.

Craven, Avery O. *The Growth of Southern Nationalism, 1848–1861*. Baton Rouge: Louisiana State University Press, 1953.

Cresswell, Stephen. *Multi-party Politics in Mississippi, 1877–1902*. Jackson: University Press of Mississippi, 1995.

———. *Rednecks, Redeemers, and Race: Mississippi after Reconstruction, 1877–1917*. Jackson: University Press of Mississippi, 2006.

Daniel, Pete. *Lost Revolutions: The South in the 1950s*. Chapel Hill: University of North Carolina Press, 2000.

Davis, William C. *The Cause Lost: Myths and Realities of the Confederacy*. Lawrence: University Press of Kansas, 1996.

Dew, Charles B. *Apostles of Disunion: Southern Secession Commissioners and the Causes of the Civil War*. Charlottesville: University of Virginia Press, 2001.

Dubay, Robert W. *John Jones Pettus, Mississippi Fire-Eater: His Life and Times, 1813–1867*. Jackson: University Press of Mississippi, 1975.

Du Bois, W.E.B. *Black Reconstruction in America*. New York: Russell and Russell, 1935; 1962.

Eagles, Charles W., ed. *The Mind of the South: Fifty Years Later*. Jackson: University Press of Mississippi, 1992.

Elkins, Stanley M. *Slavery: A Problem in American Institutional and Intellectual Life*. Chicago: University of Chicago Press, 1959.

Erikson, Erik H. *Identity and the Life Cycle*. New York: International Universities Press, 1959.

Escott, Paul D. *After Secession: Jefferson Davis and the Failure of Confederate Nationalism*. Baton Rouge: Louisiana State University Press, 1978.

Faust, Drew Gilpin. *The Creation of Confederate Nationalism: Ideology and Identity in the Civil War South*. Baton Rouge: Louisiana State University Press, 1988.

———. *Mothers of Invention: Women of the Slaveholding South in the American Civil War*. Chapel Hill: University of North Carolina Press, 1996.

———. *A Sacred Circle: The Dilemma of the Intellectual in the Old South, 1840–1860*. Baltimore: Johns Hopkins University Press, 1977.

Ferris, William. *Blues from the Delta*. New York: Anchor Press, 1978.

Fischer, David Hackett. *Albion's Seed: Four British Folkways in America*. New York: Oxford University Press, 1989.

Fite, Gilbert C. *Cotton Fields No More: Southern Agriculture, 1865–1980*. Lexington: University Press of Kentucky, 1984.

Fogel, Robert William, and Stanley L. Engerman. *Time on the Cross: The Economics of American Negro Slavery*. New York: W. W. Norton, 1974.

Foner, Eric. *Free Soil, Free Labor, Free Men: The Ideology of the Republican Party before the Civil War*. New York: Oxford University Press, 1995.

———. *Reconstruction: America's Unfinished Revolution, 1863–1877*. New York: Perennial Classics, 1988.

Foote, Shelby. *The Civil War: A Narrative*. 3 vols. New York: Random House, 1959, 1963, 1974.

Foster, Gaines M. *Ghosts of the Confederacy: Defeat, the Lost Cause, and the Emergence of the New South*. New York: Oxford University Press, 1987.

Fox-Genovese, Elizabeth. *Within the Plantation Household: Black and White Women of the Old South*. Chapel Hill: University of North Carolina Press, 1988.

Fox-Genovese, Elizabeth, and Eugene D. Genovese. *The Mind of the Master Class: History and Faith in the Southern Slaveholders' Worldview*. New York: Cambridge University Press, 2005.

Frankel, Noralee. *Freedom's Women: Black Women and Families in Civil War Era Mississippi.* Bloomington: Indiana University Press, 1999.

Franklin, John Hope. *The Militant South, 1800–1861.* Cambridge: Belknap Press of Harvard University Press, 1956.

Freehling, William W. *Prelude to Civil War: The Nullification Controversy in South Carolina, 1816–1836.* New York: Harper and Row, 1965.

———. *The South vs. the South: How Anti-Confederate Southerners Shaped the Course of the Civil War.* New York: Oxford University Press, 2001.

Gallagher, Gary W. *The Confederate War.* Cambridge: Harvard University Press, 1997.

Gallagher, Gary W., and Alan T. Nolan, eds. *The Myth of the Lost Cause and Civil War History.* Bloomington: Indiana University Press, 2000.

Garner, James Wilford. *Reconstruction in Mississippi.* New York: Macmillan, 1901; Gloucester, MA: Peter Smith, 1964.

Geertz, Clifford. *The Interpretation of Cultures: Selected Essays.* New York: Basic Books, 1973.

Gellner, Ernest. *Nations and Nationalism.* Ithaca: Cornell University Press, 1983.

Genovese, Eugene D. *The Political Economy of Slavery: Studies in the Economy and Society of the Slave South.* New York: Pantheon Books, 1965.

———. *Roll, Jordan, Roll: The World the Slaves Made.* New York: Vintage Books, 1972.

Gerster, Patrick, and Nicholas Cords, eds. *Myth and Southern History: The Old South.* Chicago: Rand McNally College Publishing, 1974.

Gioia, Ted. *Delta Blues: The Life and Times of the Mississippi Masters Who Revolutionized American Music.* New York: W. W. Norton, 2008.

Goldfield, David R. *Black, White, and Southern: Race Relations and Southern Culture, 1940 to the Present.* Baton Rouge: Louisiana State University Press, 1990.

———. *Still Fighting the Civil War: The American South and Southern History.* Baton Rouge: Louisiana State University Press, 2002.

Gomez, Michael A. *Exchanging Our Country Marks: The Transformation of African Identities in the Colonial and Antebellum South.* Chapel Hill: University of North Carolina Press, 1998.

Grant, Susan-Mary. *North over South: Northern Nationalism and American Identity in the Antebellum Era.* Lawrence: University Press of Kansas, 2000.

Greenberg, Kenneth. *Honor and Slavery.* Princeton: Princeton University Press, 1996.

Hadden, Sally E. *Slave Patrols: Law and Violence in Virginia and the Carolinas.* Cambridge: Harvard University Press, 2001.

Hahn, Steven. *A Nation under Our Feet: Black Political Struggles in the Rural South from Slavery to the Great Migration.* Cambridge: Belknap Press of Harvard University Press, 2003.

Hale, Grace Elizabeth. *Making Whiteness: The Culture of Segregation in the South, 1890–1940.* New York: Vintage Books, 1998.

Hamilton, Marybeth. *In Search of the Blues.* New York: Basic Books, 2008.

Harris, William C. *The Day of the Carpetbagger: Republican Reconstruction in Mississippi.* Baton Rouge: Louisiana State University Press, 1979.

———. *Presidential Reconstruction in Mississippi.* Baton Rouge: Louisiana State University Press, 1967.

Hayes, Carlton J. H. *Nationalism: A Religion.* New York: Macmillan, 1960.

Hearon, Cleo. *Mississippi and the Compromise of 1850.* New York: AMS Press, 1913; 1972.

Hermann, Janet Sharp. *The Pursuit of a Dream.* New York: Oxford University Press, 1981.

Heyrman, Christine Leigh. *Southern Cross: The Beginnings of the Bible Belt*. Chapel Hill: University of North Carolina Press, 1997.

Holt, Michael F. *The Political Crisis of the 1850s*. New York: W. W. Norton, 1978.

Howe, Daniel Walker. *What Hath God Wrought: The Transformation of America, 1815–1848*. New York: Oxford University Press, 2009.

Jackson, Broadus B. *Civil War and Reconstruction in Mississippi: Mirror of Democracy in America*. Jackson: Town Square Books, 1998.

Jenkins, Sally, and John Stauffer. *The State of Jones*. New York: Doubleday, 2009.

Johnson, Michael P. *Toward a Patriarchal Republic: The Secession of Georgia*. Baton Rouge: Louisiana State University Press, 1977.

Jordan, Winthrop D. *Tumult and Silence at Second Creek: An Inquiry into a Civil War Slave Conspiracy*. Rev. ed. Baton Rouge: Louisiana State University Press, 1995.

———. *White over Black: American Attitudes toward the Negro, 1550–1812*. 2nd ed. Chapel Hill: University of North Carolina Press, 2012.

Joyner, Charles. *Shared Traditions: Southern History and Folk Culture*. Urbana: University of Illinois Press, 1999.

Kierner, Cynthia A. *Beyond the Household: Women's Place in the Early South, 1700–1835*. Ithaca: Cornell University Press, 1998.

Knouff, Gregory T. *The Soldiers' Revolution: Pennsylvanians in Arms and the Forging of Early American Identity*. University Park: Pennsylvania State University Press, 2004.

Kolchin, Peter. *American Slavery, 1619–1877*. New York: Hill and Wang, 1993.

Lepore, Jill. *The Name of War: King Philip's War and the Origins of American Identity*. New York: Vintage Books, 1998.

Levine, Lawrence W. *Black Culture and Black Consciousness: Afro-American Folk Thought from Slavery to Freedom*. New York: Oxford University Press, 1977.

Libby, David J. *Slavery and Frontier Mississippi, 1720–1835*. Jackson: University Press of Mississippi, 2004.

Litwack, Leon F. *Been in the Storm So Long: The Aftermath of Slavery*. New York: Alfred A. Knopf, 1979.

———. *Trouble in Mind: Black Southerners in the Age of Jim Crow*. New York: Vintage Books, 1998.

May, Robert E. *John A. Quitman: Old South Crusader*. Baton Rouge: Louisiana State University Press, 1985.

McCardell, John. *The Idea of a Southern Nation: Southern Nationalists and Southern Nationalism, 1830–1860*. New York: W. W. Norton, 1979.

McCurry, Stephanie. *Masters of Small Worlds: Yeoman Households, Gender Relations, and the Political Culture of the Antebellum South Carolina Low Country*. New York: Oxford University Press, 1995.

McMillen, Neil R. *Dark Journey: Black Mississippians in the Age of Jim Crow*. Urbana: University of Illinois Press, 1989.

McPherson, James. *Battle Cry of Freedom: The Civil War Era*. New York: Oxford University Press, 1988.

———. *For Cause and Comrades: Why Men Fought in the Civil War*. New York: Oxford University Press, 1997.

———. *The Negro's Civil War: How American Blacks Felt and Acted during the War for the Union*. New York: Vintage Books, 1965; 1993.

Messer, Peter C. *Stories of Independence: Identity, Ideology, and History in Eighteenth-Century America.* DeKalb: Northern Illinois University Press, 2005.

Miller, David. *On Nationality.* New York: Oxford University Press, 1995.

Morgan, Edmund S. *American Slavery, American Freedom: The Ordeal of Colonial Virginia.* New York: W. W. Norton, 1975.

Morgan, Philip D. *Slave Counterpoint: Black Culture in the Eighteenth-Century Chesapeake and Lowcountry.* Chapel Hill: University of North Carolina Press, 1998.

Mullin, Michael. *Africa in America: Slave Acculturation and Resistance in the American South and the British Caribbean, 1736–1831.* Urbana: University of Illinois Press, 1992.

Norton, Mary Beth. *Founding Mothers and Fathers: Gendered Power and the Forming of American Society.* New York: Vintage Books, 1996.

Olsen, Christopher J. *Political Culture and Secession in Mississippi: Masculinity, Honor, and the Antiparty Tradition, 1830–1860.* New York: Oxford University Press, 2000.

Owens, Harry P., and James J. Cooke, eds. *The Old South in the Crucible of War.* Jackson: University Press of Mississippi, 1983.

Owsley, Frank L. *Plain Folk of the Old South.* Baton Rouge: Louisiana State University Press, 1949.

Parent, Anthony S. *Foul Means: The Formation of a Slave Society in Virginia, 1660–1740.* Chapel Hill: University of North Carolina Press, 2003.

Phillips, Jason. *Diehard Rebels: The Confederate Culture of Invincibility.* Athens: University of Georgia Press, 2007.

Phillips, Ulrich Bonnell. *Life and Labor in the Old South.* Boston: Little, Brown, 1929.

Polisensky, J. V. *The Thirty Years War.* Translated by Robert Evans. Berkeley: University of California Press, 1971.

Potter, David M. *The Impending Crisis, 1848–1861.* New York: Harper Perennial, 1976.

———. *The South and the Sectional Conflict.* Baton Rouge: Louisiana State University Press, 1968.

Quigley, Paul. *Shifting Grounds: Nationalism and the American South, 1848–1865.* New York: Oxford University Press, 2012.

Rable, George C. *The Confederate Republic: A Revolution against Politics.* Chapel Hill: University of North Carolina Press, 1994.

Raboteau, Albert J. *Slave Religion: The "Invisible Institution" in the Antebellum South.* New York: Oxford University Press, 1978.

Rainwater, Percy Lee. *Mississippi, Storm Center of Secession, 1856–1861.* Baton Rouge: Otto Claitor, 1938.

Roark, James L. *Masters without Slaves: Southern Planters in the Civil War and Reconstruction.* New York: W. W. Norton, 1977.

Roberts, John W. *From Trickster to Badman: The Black Folk Hero in Slavery and Freedom.* Philadelphia: University of Pennsylvania Press, 1989.

Robinson, Armstead L. *Bitter Fruits of Bondage: The Demise of Slavery and the Collapse of the Confederacy, 1861–1865.* Charlottesville: University of Virginia Press, 2005.

Royster, Charles. *The Destructive War: William Tecumseh Sherman, Stonewall Jackson, and the Americans.* New York: Vintage Books, 1991.

Rubin, Anne Sarah. *A Shattered Nation: The Rise and Fall of the Confederacy, 1861–1868.* Chapel Hill: University of North Carolina Press, 2005.

Sahlins, Marshall. *Islands of History.* Chicago: University of Chicago Press, 1985.

Sewell, George Alexander, and Margaret L. Dwight. *Mississippi Black History Makers.* Rev. and enl. ed. Jackson: University Press of Mississippi, 1984.

Sheehan-Dean, Aaron. *Why Confederates Fought: Family and Nation in Civil War Virginia.* Chapel Hill: University of North Carolina Press, 2007.

Silver, James W. *Mississippi: The Closed Society.* New enl. ed. New York: Harcourt, Brace and World, 1966.

Smith, Anthony D. *The Nation in History: Historiographical Debates about Ethnicity and Nationalism.* Hanover: University Press of New England, 2000.

Smith, Timothy B. *Mississippi in the Civil War: The Home Front.* Jackson: University Press of Mississippi, 2010.

Stampp, Kenneth M. *The Peculiar Institution: Slavery in the Ante-Bellum South.* New York: Vintage Books, 1956.

Sydnor, Charles Sackett. *Slavery in Mississippi.* Gloucester: Peter Smith, 1933; 1965.

Taylor, William R. *Cavalier and Yankee: The Old South and American National Character.* New York: Oxford University Press, 1961; 1993.

Thomas, Emory M. *The Confederacy as a Revolutionary Experience.* Englewood Cliffs, NJ: Prentice-Hall, 1971.

———. *The Confederate Nation: 1861–1865.* New York: Harper and Row, 1979.

Thompson, Julius E. *Lynchings in Mississippi: A History, 1865–1965.* Jefferson, NC: McFarland, 2007.

Thornton III, J. Mills. *Politics and Power in a Slave Society: Alabama, 1800–1860.* Baton Rouge: Louisiana State University Press, 1978.

Trelease, Allen W. *White Terror: The Ku Klux Klan Conspiracy and Southern Reconstruction.* New York: Harper and Row, 1971.

Trexler, Richard C., ed. *Persons in Groups: Social Behavior as Identity Formation in Medieval and Renaissance Europe.* Binghamton, NY: Medieval and Renaissance Texts and Studies, 1985.

Wald, Elijah. *Escaping the Delta: Robert Johnson and the Invention of the Blues.* New York: HarperCollins, 2004.

Waldstreicher, David. *In the Midst of Perpetual Fetes: The Making of American Nationalism, 1776–1820.* Chapel Hill: University of North Carolina Press, 1997.

Waldrep, Christopher. *Vicksburg's Long Shadow: The Civil War Legacy of Race and Remembrance.* Lanham, MD: Rowman and Littlefield, 2005.

Walther, Eric H. *The Fire-Eaters.* Baton Rouge: Louisiana State University Press, 1992.

Weaver, Herbert. *Mississippi Farmers, 1850–1860.* Nashville: Vanderbilt University Press, 1945.

Wharton, Vernon Lane. *The Negro in Mississippi, 1865–1890.* New York: Harper and Row, 1947; 1965.

White, Deborah Gray. *Ar'n't I a Woman? Female Slaves in the Plantation South.* New York: W. W. Norton, 1985.

Whitfield, Stephen J. *A Death in the Delta: The Story of Emmett Till.* Baltimore: Johns Hopkins University Press, 1988.

Wilkerson, Isabel. *The Warmth of Other Suns: The Epic Story of America's Great Migration.* New York: Vintage Books, 2011.

Williams, Michael Vinson. *Medgar Evers: Mississippi Martyr.* Fayetteville: University of Arkansas Press, 2011.

Willis, John C. *Forgotten Times: The Yazoo-Mississippi Delta after the Civil War.* Charlottesville: University Press of Virginia, 2000.

Wilson, Charles Reagan. *Baptized in Blood: The Religion of the Lost Cause, 1865–1920*. Athens: University of Georgia Press, 1980.

Woodward, C. Vann. *The Burden of Southern History*. Updated 3rd ed. Baton Rouge: Louisiana State University Press, 1960; 2008.

——. *Origins of the New South, 1877–1913*. Baton Rouge: Louisiana State University Press, 1951.

——. *The Strange Career of Jim Crow*. New York: Oxford University Press, 1955.

Wyatt-Brown, Bertram. *Southern Honor: Ethics and Behavior in the Old South*. New York: Oxford University Press, 1982.

——. *Yankee Saints and Southern Sinners*. Baton Rouge: Louisiana State University Press, 1985.

Wynne, Ben. *A Hard Trip: A History of the 15th Mississippi Infantry, CSA*. Macon, GA: Mercer University Press, 2003.

——. *Mississippi's Civil War: A Narrative History*. Macon, GA: Mercer University Press, 2006.

Zelinsky, Wilbur. *Nation into State: The Shifting Symbolic Foundations of American Nationalism*. Chapel Hill: University of North Carolina Press, 1988.

Index

CPSIA information can be obtained
at www.ICGtesting.com
Printed in the USA
BVHW071726231220
596247BV00002B/11